"I had given up believing I would ever read an intelligent and useful book on entrepreneurship—until I read *Building on Bedrock*. No tiresome Silicon Valley narcissism. No hagiography. Refreshingly, Derek Lidow provides cogent analysis and insights on the bedrock entrepreneurs that make our economy prosper. It is, flat out, the best book on entrepreneurship I have ever read."
     —ROGER MARTIN, Thinkers 50 legend, Institute Director of the
          Michael Lee-Chin Family Institute for Corporate Citizenship,
               former Dean of the Rotman School of Management,
                    and author including *Creating Great Choices*

"How have extraordinary entrepreneurs achieved greatness? Lidow's *Building on Bedrock* sheds new light on the practical keys to success. He thoughtfully examines the lives, mindsets, strategies, and actual practices of eight founders. You'll see their secrets and thought processes as they choose partners, build teams, scale, and obtain and deploy precious capital. The book delivers an insider's perspective rarely shared anywhere else—partly because Lidow not only teaches entrepreneurship, he is a serial entrepreneur himself. His book is a must read for anyone seeking success as a Bedrock Entrepreneur."
     —STEPHEN CHRISTENSEN, Dean of Concordia University's
          School of Business, Entrepreneur Catalyst, and Start-Up Coach

"While hot startups get the headlines, 'bedrock' entrepreneurs like Sam Walton and Estée Lauder build lasting businesses. Lidow charts a path for entrepreneurs to create sustainable value for themselves and the communities they serve. *Building on Bedrock* is essential reading for every entrepreneur and policy maker."
     —BRIAN O'KELLEY, Founder and CEO of AppNexus
          and serial entrepreneur

"*Building on Bedrock* is a refreshing reality check—a much-needed intervention to remedy the misalignments in today's startup arena. Revealing many truths about entrepreneurship, it is a simple read that belongs in every entrepreneur's tool kit. This powerful book unlocks the latent potential in all entrepreneurs. It also inspires readers to self-define life's core values like purpose, success, and happiness. *Building on Bedrock* is a 'must read' for every founder—and for anyone with vision and gumption."
     —SHIKHA UBEROI BAJPAI, Founder and CEO

of Impact Media360, Executive Producer of *The Real Deal*, and Co-founder of India at Indi.com

"*Building on Bedrock* is bedrock reading for anyone interested in understanding the myths and mysteries of entrepreneurship. Beyond challenging the status quo, the book tackles what it really takes to create a successful, lasting business from scratch. Lidow, a serial entrepreneur himself, provides valuable insights as he shares fresh, real-life stories about several founders (some famous, some not). His book will be your essential companion if you want to get below the 'puff' surrounding Silicon Valley-style entrepreneurship and see the 'stuff' of everyday entrepreneurs who drive economies the world over."
—JOHN DANNER, Teacher at UC Berkeley and Princeton, consultant, and author including *Built for Growth*

"Finally, the truth about entrepreneurship. Lidow methodically and entertainingly debunks the popular myths and magical thinking around successful entrepreneurs. Think they need to take big risks, raise large amounts of money, and disrupt industries? Think again. Blending honest startup stories and current research, Lidow exposes a vital but perhaps un-sexy reality: the vast majority of successful entrepreneurs 'start small and grow as they gain confidence.' Lidow's rare access to Sam Walton's earliest hunches about Walmart is a fascinating tale of that iterative process. *Building on Bedrock* challenges how entrepreneurs are taught, supported, and mythologized. We need this more than ever, because our future depends on them."
—MARTIN JOHNSON, Professor of social entrepreneurship and pioneering social entrepreneur

"Enough about the celebrity founder, working magic! *Building on Bedrock* provides the right tools and role models for the other 99% of intrepid people who are launching enterprises. This is one of the few books where I can recognize my own real-life experiences. A great toolkit for entrepreneurs."
—LARRY GILSON, Founder and Chairman of Focusing Philanthropy and serial entrepreneur in transportation, finance, and consulting

"If you're serious about entrepreneurship, this book is the key to unlocking what you don't yet know—but must learn. Lidow introduces little-known secrets behind famous and little-known entrepreneurs, then ingeniously

refocuses the conversation on entrepreneurship's myths and truths. Each story will make you see entrepreneurship from an entirely different perspective. In fact, *Building on Bedrock* will change the way you think."
—DANIELLE COHEN-SHOHET, CEO and co-founder of GlossGenius

"I found myself nodding in agreement as I read *Building on Bedrock*. It is a no-nonsense, well-written book by a proven entrepreneur who shares personal experiences and life lessons learned—his own, plus those of eight other founders. A must-read for budding and current entrepreneurs."
—GREG OLSEN, *Inc. Magazine* Entrepreneur of the Year, serial entrepreneur, and Founder and Chairman of GHO Ventures

"High profile entrepreneurs are often seen as gods of the marketplace with exceptional foresight, wisdom, and energy; this can intimidate and confuse potential and nascent entrepreneurs. *Building on Bedrock* reflects the practical realities of routine business creation, and should help many ordinary people join the millions of founders who are finding satisfaction and success working for themselves."
—PAUL D. REYNOLDS, Author of *Entrepreneurship in the United States: The Future Is Now*

"Derek Lidow is the best chronicler of entrepreneurship of our age. This book is filled with breathtaking insights on what it takes to succeed as any type of entrepreneur—whether your enterprise is 'bedrock' or high-risk. Every entrepreneur, or soon-to-be-founder, must have this book!"
—BRUCE HACK, Chairman of the Board of Technicolor, former CEO of Vivendi Games (*World of Warcraft* and *Starcraft*), and angel investor

"Thoroughly researched and loaded with beautifully-told stories about fascinating entrepreneurs, both known and unknown, *Building on Bedrock* showcases people who built their enterprises the right way—based on bedrock principles and values. The book is instructive and inspirational for readers considering an entrepreneurial life path. It is also for those who are well along that journey who are seeking better ideas, greater understanding, and new meaning in their work."
—ED ZSCHAU, Professor, Silicon Valley entrepreneur, venture capitalist, and Congressman

"Derek Lidow has effectively stripped the sheen away from the entrepreneurial myth and demonstrates how enduring value is created, illuminating his points with incredible stories of famous and lesser-known entrepreneurs. Lidow reveals the largely-misunderstood differences between 'bedrock' and 'high risk' entrepreneurship. He also isolates the drivers of enduring value creation—and highlights the troubling shift in the mix of today's entrepreneurs moving from bedrock to high risk. This work has significant implications for all of us who study, teach, and work within the entrepreneurial ecosystem."

> —CHRIS KUENNE, Author of *Built for Growth* and teacher of
> "High Tech Entrepreneurship" at Princeton

"*Building on Bedrock* exposes fundamental, under-recognized, and seldom acknowledged truths about entrepreneurship—and the dangerous gulf between 'bedrock' and high-risk ventures. Lidow's carefully articulated distinctions can help entrepreneurs avoid the missteps that will trip them up and drop their enterprise off the cliff. As a disruptor and entrepreneur, I applaud his encouragement that almost anyone can be a successful entrepreneur if they understand what that means and what it takes—hard work and perseverance more often than lightning strikes of genius and luck."

> —WHITNEY JOHNSON, Investor, speaker, and author including
> *Disrupt Yourself: Putting the Power of Disruption to Work*

BUILDING
ON
BEDROCK

What Sam Walton, Walt Disney, and Other Great Self-Made Entrepreneurs Can Teach Us About Building Valuable Companies

DEREK LIDOW

DIVERSIONBOOKS

Diversion Books
A Division of Diversion Publishing Corp.
443 Park Avenue South, Suite 1008
New York, New York 10016
www.DiversionBooks.com

For more information, email info@diversionbooks.com

First Diversion Books edition January 2018.
Hardcover ISBN: 978-1-63576-176-4
eBook ISBN: 978-1-63576-175-7

Printed in the U.S.A.
SDB/1711
1 3 5 7 9 10 8 6 4 2

In memory of my parents,
Eric and Leza Lidow.

"High expectations are the key to everything."

—Sam Walton

CONTENTS

CHAPTER 1

TRUTH MATTERS

There is a tide in the affairs of men,
Which, taken at the flood, leads on to fortune;
Omitted, all the voyage of their life
Is bound in shallows and in miseries.
On such a full sea are we now afloat,
And we must take the current when it serves
Or lose our ventures.

—William Shakespeare,
Julius Caesar, Act 4, Scene 3, Brutus: Lines 224–230

By opening day for store number two, the team felt fried. For the two weeks leading up to the grand opening, they had been working for as many hours as they could stand to get the store ready. Rebuilding and installing old fixtures salvaged from another store that had recently gone bankrupt had been a huge struggle. The team had unloaded truckloads of merchandise late into the night and had barely finished moving in and placing the merchandise on the shelves, on tables, and in front of the store. On top of that, the July heat had been punishing, the building wasn't air-conditioned, the restrooms hadn't been working, and the parking lot wasn't fully paved.

A great deal was at stake. Store number one had struggled to make money and was not as successful as hoped. Sam Walton had borrowed as much money as the bank would loan him, using everything he and his wife owned as collateral. He needed Wal-Mart store number two to prove that a discount retail chain focused on small towns could be highly profitable. If store two performed like store one, Sam and his team would have to put their growth plans on hold.

To get as much attention for the opening as possible, Sam advertised great deals on brand-name staples like toilet paper and detergent. To give the opening a family feel, Sam arranged free donkey rides for kids in the parking lot right in front of the main entrance. He also bought every ripe watermelon that any farmer within a day's drive could deliver. The team had piled them four feet high along the front of the store (and along the edge of the unpaved areas of the parking lot to keep the customers away from tripping over the old wooden forms still lying around).

Opening day was the hottest day of the summer, with temperatures in the upper 90s. But the heat didn't keep the crowds away. To buy at the advertised low prices, they began lining up even before the store opened at nine in the morning. The team worked with hardly a break all day manning the cash registers and keeping the shelves, tables, and floors stocked with the items that were being snapped up. The customers were clearly excited.

With all the crowds and all the business, nobody noticed or really cared that some of the watermelons were breaking open in the heat, their juices flowing onto the sidewalk and into the parking lot—nor did anyone notice or care that the man running the donkey rides didn't have time to pick up all the donkey droppings as soon as they hit the ground. Over the course of the day, the watermelon juices and the donkey dung covered growing portions of the sidewalk. The acrid donkey-watermelon mix was soon tracked inside and permeated the store.

A top financial officer of a well-established Midwestern drug store chain was perhaps the only person that *did* care. His company had heard that Sam Walton had some interesting ideas about how to get customers excited, and he had driven from Missouri to check out the opening. He was appalled by the smells and broken watermelons, and by the merchandise piled high on tables instead of laid out neatly on the shelves. He reported back that the opening was the worst he had ever seen; anyone in his company who ran an opening like the one he witnessed would have been fired on the spot.

But the top financial officer had ignored the store full of customers and the long lines at the cash registers. He had judged the opening by conventional big-city store aesthetics, missing the real story. Sam and his team understood that in the rural heartland, everyone was used to animal smells. He understood how to make his customers happy by making their dollars go much farther, and that his customers would feel better served in a humble-looking (and smelling) store.

That Midwestern drug store chain long ago went out of business. But its top financial officer eventually began to understand what was pleasing Sam's customers and that Sam was willing to change things in ways his company would never consider. David Glass later joined Wal-Mart and became an exemplary student of Sam's, excelling at leading rapid changes aimed at pleasing evermore customers. He eventually became Walmart's CEO.*

Sam, like the other entrepreneurs you will meet in these pages, provides a useful corrective to what we think we know about starting a business. Yes, Walmart is now one of the most valuable companies in the world, but it didn't get that way overnight, and its success didn't depend on "network effects" or venture capital. It depended on some hard and humble truths about entrepreneurship that have gotten lost amid all the publicity about a few young Silicon Valley billionaires—truths that would-be entrepreneurs and their loved ones ignore at their peril.

---

* Sam originally called his store "Wal-Mart" but over the years the name was simplified to Walmart. I will use the style of the name that was in use at the time referred to in the text.

Essential Understanding

No matter what you do in life, you need to understand entrepreneurship. The facts are: Over 60 percent of working men and women in the US want to start their own business, and if you're male, the chances are about fifty-fifty that you will actually attempt to be an entrepreneur sometime during your working life; if you're female, the chances are about one in three.* More than 30 percent of the population in the United States at any point in time is either engaged in entrepreneurship or directly related to someone that is. Since funding from friends and family constitutes an important source of revenue for many startups, you stand a great chance of being asked to invest in a startup sometime in your life, regardless of how much money you have in the bank.

But entrepreneurship is not what most people think it is. And if you act on what you think, you will likely make a big mistake, lose money, destroy relationships, and waste precious years of your life. Conversely, what you think you know could make you too afraid to seize the lucrative entrepreneurial opportunities around you.

A simple remedy for your lack of knowledge may be to do nothing—nothing risked, nothing lost. That's what most people do. But that won't work, because confronting entrepreneurship is not a choice. Modern life forces you to make decisions that are, at their core, about entrepreneurialism. The company you work for, your boss, co-workers, relatives, and friends all have as much say as you do about whether entrepreneurship will impact your life! You could lose your job, or someone you can't stand might replace your wonderful boss, forcing you to decide whether being your own boss is the right thing for you. You are also likely to be asked to support a friend or relative in starting a company, whether through a loan, an

---

* To make the book more readable, I will not cite references in the text nor will I use footnotes unless it adds directly to the text. You can find a complete set of supporting notes in the back of the book, including references for all the facts cited.

investment, or part-time work. To make the right decision—whether it's about being your own boss or investing in your favorite cousin's startup—you must understand entrepreneurship.

We all dream to some extent about achieving a combination of the fortune, fame, and control over our lives that we associate with successful entrepreneurs. Those are admirable aspirations in a society that counts on entrepreneurs to innovate, create new jobs, and grow our economy. Society encourages us to take the entrepreneurial bait, but how can you know if being an entrepreneur will end as a dream come true or a nightmare from which you cannot awake?

This book will help you answer that question by focusing on whether or not you should take the entrepreneurial bait, and if entrepreneurship is the right thing for you—as a founder, co-founder, or investor. Based on research, and told through the stories of real entrepreneurs, it will help you answer all of the critical questions about entrepreneurship: the who, what, when, where, how, how much, and why. The answers probably aren't what you think.

Unfortunately, almost everything we read about entrepreneurs is highly filtered, glorifying entrepreneurs whether they ultimately succeeded or not. Most highly successful entrepreneurs retain PR people to get the media to tell the positive elements of their story. There is nothing wrong with that. When I was a CEO, I had PR people on my staff; they were good for business. But the stories that were written about me, or that are written about the super-successful entrepreneurs featured on magazine covers, are not the stories we should be telling people we care about—people who want to follow in our footsteps.

A few unsuccessful entrepreneurs have blogged about their mistakes or misfortunes, purporting to offer guidance to would-be entrepreneurs. You should take their guidance with a grain of a salt—they cannot be counted on to be objective. How often do we misdiagnose or ignore our own ailments, or dismiss our own incompetency and quirks? I failed on my first try at entrepreneurship, and I didn't understand why my effort to start a tabletop retail concept was doomed from the beginning. It took years of working with mentors and coaches and reading avidly on the subject of leadership and performance to figure out where I went wrong. Most entrepreneurs have neither the background nor the time to accurately unravel what went wrong with their enterprises.

Learning from Role Models

Throughout history, people have learned how to conduct their lives by adopting role models. Having *realistic* role models helps people achieve their objectives, entrepreneurial or otherwise, at home or in the world at large. When someone succeeds, they give us the confidence to go after our own dreams; when someone fails, they teach us to beware of making the same mistakes.

Most successful entrepreneurs differ dramatically from the ones we read about. It is these unheralded and not-recently-heralded successes that we need to study. They can be great role models—and there are millions of them. They have succeeded as entrepreneurs and achieved impressive levels of fortune, respect (as opposed to great fame), and control over their own lives. These are the entrepreneurs we can aspire to be like, whose accomplishments we can hope to match by following their examples. Their stories reflect the real truth about entrepreneurship. And it is their stories that this book will tell, warts and all.

You will meet some remarkable people here—realistic and broadly applicable role models who can help you understand the critical elements of embarking on your own startup or investing in a friend's. What you will learn may surprise you. These lessons include:

- *What types of ideas lead to successful companies and how innovative do your ideas need to be?* Entrepreneurship is not usually about tech and dazzling breakthroughs—all types of ideas can create great companies. Innovation is not about doing something completely new, but rather doing something that succeeds in getting people to change for the better.

- *What abilities do you need to succeed?* You need very few.
- *What essential knowledge is needed?* Most of what you need to know you will learn on the job.
- *Whom do you need to know and when should you ask for help?* Most entrepreneurs either fail to ask for help or accept it naively, thereby making expensive mistakes they could have avoided.
- *How do you find and pick your partners and smoothly part company with them when they start to slow you down?* Deciding to work closely with strangers, friends, family, and lovers all have their upsides and downsides.
- *How much money do you need to start your company and to be able to afford to make a few mistakes?* It doesn't take much.
- *Where and how do you raise funds to grow fast?* Beware of strangers bearing money.
- *How do you deal with the "fog of war" that is an everyday challenge in knowing what to do?* When it comes to dealing with unknowns and risky situations, self-confidence is overrated.
- *When and how can you stay in control as you grow your company?* Though this is rarely discussed, it's extremely challenging; even great entrepreneurs sometimes lose control.
- *What are the mistakes you need to avoid at all costs versus the mistakes you expect to learn from?* Some mistakes will bring you down, while other types of mistakes provide valuable education at a cheaper cost than any entrepreneurship classes you could take.

Role models illustrate what it is really like to be an entrepreneur. They can help you decide if entrepreneurship is the right thing for you—or for your cousin that's asking you for an investment. Their stories are interesting, easy to read, and hard to forget. And I tell their stories with plenty of detail so you can fully understand what went right and what went wrong. Was it luck, talent, passion, charm, a rich uncle, or other things that were the keys to this person's success? That might be the keys to *your* success?

Many of the stories we hear or read about concern entrepreneurs who succeeded under very specific circumstances or at particularly opportune times. Luck and serendipity can certainly play a role in entrepreneurial achievement, but you gain nothing by emulating actions that led to a few random successes. The stories I have chosen to tell are relevant to everyone, not to the lucky few.

I call most of the people you will meet in these pages *bedrock entrepreneurs*. That term describes the 99.5 percent of all entrepreneurs who create more than 90 percent of all the new wealth generated by entrepreneurs in developed economies. Bedrock entrepreneurs are normal people. They are not the smartest, best-educated, most aggressive, tech-savvy people on the planet. And they grow their businesses in less risky ways than the "it's OK to crash-and-burn," "shoot-for-the-moon," "use-other-people's-money" *high-risk entrepreneurs* we read so much about.

Being a bedrock entrepreneur does not mean slow growth, low aspirations, or small enterprises. It means control, low risk, and patience. Sam Walton (Wal-Mart) was a bedrock entrepreneur, as were Ray Kroc (McDonald's), Walt Disney, and Estée Lauder. So are Bill Gates and Michael Dell. It seems safe to say that all these great entrepreneurs would understand and empathize with the role models in this book as people very much like themselves.

Take Jordan Monkarsh, founder of Jody Maroni's Sausage Kingdom. Jordan was the son of a butcher. A religion major in college, he never took a business course, yet he quickly created the country's largest maker and seller of specialty sausages, all from his small savings. His story applies to anyone who aspires to create a large business selling products to consumers. It illustrates what's important to know and what's not. It's also a story that will help you visualize the many answers to the question, "What does it mean to be a successful entrepreneur?"

Stephanie DiMarco created a large and successful software company. She's not a computer programmer, engineer, or scientist (she's an accountant); and she didn't need venture capital until it was entirely in her best interests to seek it. Initially, Stephanie had a computer engineer as a partner. How that became both a blessing and a curse is an important story in itself. Choosing partners and making early hires is one of the trickiest aspects of starting a company, something many entrepreneurs fumble, killing their chance of success. Stephanie serves as an excellent role model in many different entrepreneurial dimensions. Her company sold its software to other companies, the company had a successful IPO, and it grew to be global and immensely valuable. I doubt you've ever heard of her or of Advent Software, but her story illustrates the contrast between how most successful entrepreneurs grow their companies and how the high-risk entrepreneurs we read so much about grow theirs.

You will also meet Vidal Herrera, a disabled entrepreneur who had no choice but to start his own business or see his family starve. The world is filled with people who, like him, became entrepreneurs out of necessity. Almost all of them learn on the job how to succeed as business people. They go on to build valuable companies, often with the goal of creating a lifestyle that rewards them for having survived onerous hardships. Vidal, who grew up very poor and barely made it through high school, created a company based on the only skill he possessed that anyone cared about: performing autopsies. When he founded 1-800-AUTOPSY he had no idea what entrepreneurship was about, yet he succeeded without earning a fancy degree or plowing through complicated books on the topic.

Ken Marlin is a college dropout who joined the marines and eventually founded one of the most profitable, valuable, and influential boutique investment banks on Wall Street. Wall Street seems impenetrable and scary to virtually all entrepreneurs (particularly since we've seen so many large, old investment banks go down in flames in the past few years). Ken's story shows us that prevailing establishment wisdom about what's possible and what's not doesn't apply to entrepreneurs that are diligent and genuinely open to learning new skills.

Getting to know legendary entrepreneurs poses challenges, whether they're dead or alive. Their companies, families, financial trusts, and others have vested interests in maintaining their image. And their autobiographies are often exercises in making myths. If we are to understand such people, we need to get below the surface of the myth to a level that illuminates how things really happen.

Consider Sam Walton. On many measures he is the most successful entrepreneur of all time—Walmart has greater revenues than any company in the world, and it has created more jobs, both directly and indirectly, than any company in history by far. And Sam's family still owns a large percentage of the company, which is another amazing feat. How did he do it? Was he just lucky? Was he a pre-digital-era phenomenon? Who is the man behind the myth?

As someone who studies and teaches entrepreneurship, I needed to know the answers to these questions about Sam. I have been very fortunate to have been granted access to the archives of the Walmart Museum in Bentonville, Arkansas, where I have immersed myself in his personal papers and notes. A diligent team of archivists, aided by the Walton family and many of Sam's closest associates over the years, have collected a warehouse full of Sam's notes, reports, artifacts, and memorabilia. All this documentation and all these artifacts mean that there is plenty to learn from Sam, beyond the legend.

Having been an entrepreneur, as well as a CEO of a global public company, I can directly relate to the context and tone of his notes, letters, and memos. Reading them, you can see where his thinking started and how it evolved relative to key aspects of entrepreneurship that are just as relevant today—his experiments in making money, scaling up, finding people who would dedicate their lives to his vision, staying in control, and out-foxing even the most well-funded and experienced competitors.

He was clearly a bedrock entrepreneur. He grew his company based on coaxing ever-increasing profits from the small retail stores he initially franchised. He was supported in his efforts with money he borrowed from family and then from banks. He relentlessly learned through experimentation and from emulating others. He took on risk but he never "bet the company." He knew what the people he put in key positions had achieved for others and he was confident that he could provide them with the support, and surround them with a culture, that would enable them to do even better working for him. The lessons we can learn from Sam are relevant to every entrepreneur that's ever lived, including today's digital age high-risk entrepreneurs.

Sam wasn't perfect and he would be the first one to say so. While you may aspire to be better than Sam in certain areas after reading this book, you will nonetheless come to understand that being a great entrepreneur has nothing to do with perfection. But every aspiring or practicing entrepreneur today, bedrock or high-risk, needs to understand Sam.

You will also get to know Estée Lauder, Ray Kroc, and Walt Disney, all of whom embody important truths about entrepreneurship. Walt Disney serves as a particularly relevant juxtaposition to Sam Walton. Sam was focused on relentlessly improving the performance of his stores, and he borrowed good ideas from wherever he found them. Walt Disney was driven by his desires to do things that had not been done before. He was open to incorporating the ideas of others into his visions, but he wanted to entertain people in completely new ways. Walt Disney innovated more businesses that directly impacted the lives of more people around the world than even Steve Jobs. Walt worked in the entertainment industry when it was the hotbed of innovations, investment, and aspiring startups, completely analogous to the period of development of the personal computer and digital electronics that served as the fertile bed of possibilities for Steve Jobs.

Walt and Steve share many personality traits, quite a few of which made them difficult to deal with but which led them to develop products they considered beautiful and perfect, often to the consternation of their colleagues. Similar to Jobs, Disney suffered setbacks too; he went bankrupt, had his second business taken away from him by his distributor, and was sidelined by his board (at the insistence of his bankers).

Estée Lauder serves as a particularly relevant role model for young aspiring entrepreneurs who want to turn their natural interests into vast enterprises. Estée aspired to rise above her very humble beginnings. Starting as a teenager, she relentlessly experimented with how to sell beauty products. It took her decades of making small profits to find out how to make the large profits that would allow her to live the life she wanted.

By contrast, Ray Kroc was fifty-two years old when he decided to dedicate the rest of his life to licensing McDonald's franchises. His story is particularly relevant to entrepreneurs seeking a career change. Ray had spent his career up until then perfecting his selling skills, which he relied upon to create a large business, when he finally spotted the major entrepreneurial opportunity he was hoping to find: selling McDonald's franchises on a national scale.

You need to understand high-risk entrepreneurs as well. With the support of venture capital they create companies that grow faster than the companies of bedrock entrepreneurs, especially when economies of scale or network effects provide a competitive advantage over everyone else. Although high-risk entrepreneurs represent less than 1 percent of all successful entrepreneurs in the United States, they do generate about 10 percent of all new entrepreneurial wealth. Not surprisingly, however, aspiring high-risk entrepreneurs fail at a much higher rate than bedrock entrepreneurs. Mark Zuckerberg, Larry Page, and Travis Kalanick (of Uber) are high-risk entrepreneurs. Their stories are well known, and won't be retold here, but you will learn why they made the right decisions in taking higher-risk paths to success. But their paths are for the very few, and I will make clear why almost all successful entrepreneurs, including many tech entrepreneurs, correctly choose not to emulate them.

Occasionally, we are fascinated with entrepreneurs who found companies that they sell quickly for large amounts of money. These "fast-flip" entrepreneurs often have interesting personalities and lifestyles, but they make terrible role models for aspiring entrepreneurs. And fast-flipping can only occur during the short windows of time associated with the hyper-adoption of major new tools and technologies. How fast-flip entrepreneurs achieve high-risk/short-term pay-offs has virtually no relationship with what entrepreneurs need to do to achieve long-term growth and profitability, and so in this book I will ignore them.

The conclusions I reach in the book are at every point consistent with the research in the field. Since the goal of this book is to describe real, potent, and relevant role models for aspiring entrepreneurs, I often rely on storytelling to convey what is important. I pay particular attention to the critical emotional components that drive entrepreneurs to do what they do. Because emotions drive actions, they ultimately drive entrepreneurial success or failure.

Unfortunately, much of what is written about entrepreneurship is misleading or wrong. Worse, our fascination with high-risk entrepreneurs can lead us to make faulty decisions that result either in failure or missed opportunity. Our fascination has encouraged more entrepreneurs to undertake risks not commensurate with the economic or social value delivered—risks taken for the purpose of setting valuation records rather than bettering the lives of others. These risks can lead to behaviors that are unethical or asocial—their sole purpose can be to increase valuations at the expense of the public. Only by becoming better educated about entrepreneurship can our fascination be refocused on the bedrock entrepreneurs that are essential to our happiness and well-being.

Entrepreneurship is a hot topic. It encourages people to claim expertise on the basis of limited personal experience. Experience can give context to the How and some of the What, When, and Where that describe entrepreneurship. But experience doesn't provide a complete picture because, as we'll see in the next chapter, entrepreneurship differs for everyone. Even among so-called experts, significant confusion has always existed about who qualifies as an entrepreneur. This confusion is so fundamental to deciding whether entrepreneurship is a good thing for you that we must start by resolving it. Fortunately, by untangling "the who," we can make the subject all the more relevant to just about everyone.

CHAPTER 2

WHO

"I deliver joy!"

—Jordan Monkarsh

It's embarrassing: We, the people who claim to be experts on entrepreneurship, cannot agree on the definition of who is really an entrepreneur. "Entrepreneur" is a loaded term used in almost countless ways, each expression conveying a distinct message.

Most of those messages distract potential and existing entrepreneurs from their real task. For example, some economists think all of us are entrepreneurs as long as we are capable of making decisions for ourselves. Why? Because in deciding where to work, what to buy, and how we spend our time, we all weigh what we perceive as risk. Collectively known as the *Austrian School,* these economists argue that we are always reaping the gains and losses of the economic decisions we make. They see no difference between deciding to start a company and deciding what job to take. In their view, everyone who is cognizant enough to make decisions about how to lead their lives is an entrepreneur.

The simplest definition of entrepreneurship, and one that I will use throughout the book, is this: *An entrepreneur is someone who founds a business or runs a business he or she owns, whether that business is officially incorporated or not.* This definition focuses on the founding of companies and the continuing role of the entrepreneur as the boss of the enterprise. It sets the bar for being able to claim "entrepreneur" as a title to people who are in business for themselves. This definition also closely resembles the one found in many dictionaries.

I have encountered close to a hundred other definitions that various groups of people use for "entrepreneur," each with its own implied criterion of success. The requirements to be considered an entrepreneur that these common definitions state or imply, alone or in various combinations, include: achieving minimum levels of revenues, profits, growth rates, value creation, jobs creation, ability to utilize resources, personal self-satisfaction (short-term and/or long-term), aspirations, lasting impact on the world, self-sustainability, personal control, risk tolerance, and independence.

Each definition implies or states a minimum threshold a person must meet in order to be counted and acknowledged as an entrepreneur. Many definitions of entrepreneur exclude people who work for themselves or who have not formally incorporated their businesses. Some entrepreneurship research uses a definition that requires an entrepreneur aspire to grow a large incorporated business, otherwise they're just a "small business owner" or "self-employed." The funny thing is that all the ultra-successful entrepreneurs profiled in this book started out as small business owners. Sam Walton began by running a variety store in a small town. Like Sam, most successful founders of large companies started out running small operations.

The most extreme definition is used among some venture capitalists, extremely rich former entrepreneurs, a few writers, and some media pundits who define entrepreneurs (often denoted with the qualifier "real" or "born" to denote specialness) as people who are driven to risk their well-being in order to have a lasting impact on some major market. You can often spot this definition in stories about Henry Ford, Steve Jobs, Bill Gates, Mark Zuckerberg, and the like. It implies that entrepreneurs like these—young when they succeeded, untrained, and inexperienced—are simply born with special traits.

This "real entrepreneurs are born genius-heroes" definition is often unintentionally self-serving. If you are a major venture capitalist who needs to invest a billion dollars a year in startups, then you want to deal only with people who aspire to disrupt major markets; you don't want to waste your time with anyone aiming lower or patiently growing. Media pundits like this heroic definition because it ties directly to stories about very uncommon situations—stories that will attract many readers. But this definition applies to just a few thousand individuals in the world. And it discourages potential entrepreneurs in communities where such role models may be lacking. Describing entrepreneurs as people with extraordinary innate traits is particularly harmful to aspiring women and minority entrepreneurs and is an insidious form of discrimination. And no research shows that you must possess special genetic material to be an entrepreneur.

Anyone who starts a company or is self-employed can choose his or her own definition of "entrepreneur" and its criterion of success. As we'll discuss, since entrepreneurs take full responsibility for supporting themselves they can also decide what it will take to feel satisfied that they have succeeded.

Unfortunately, most entrepreneurs do not think about what they really want, which causes real problems. The definition of entrepreneur you choose influences the decisions you make and affects the outcomes you achieve. Entrepreneurs who lack a clear definition of what they're doing make inconsistent decisions, ultimately wasting time and money and causing unnecessary anxiety—a subject treated in greater depth in the Why chapter.

Someone To Care About

Meet Jordan Monkarsh, aka Jody Maroni, who fits virtually all definitions of "entrepreneur." I met Jordan over thirty years ago and I still savor the encounter. He leaned out of the window of his Venice Beach sausage stand and motioned to me and my wife. "Hey you,

Handsome, you want to impress your girlfriend? Come over here and try a free sample. Show her you've got taste."

I couldn't resist, nor could many other passers-by; the sausages he was offering smelled and looked great. I ordered a mild Italian sausage that came tightly packed inside a warm roll surrounded by freshly grilled caramelized onions and red peppers. It was delicious.

When Jordan founded Jody Maroni's Sausage Kingdom he did not fit today's stereotype of the brilliant tech-savvy revolutionary. He still doesn't. He does typify the bedrock entrepreneurs you don't hear much about but who actually drive our economy.

Jordan grew up in one of LA's sprawling suburbs in a middle-class household. His dad was a butcher and his mom stayed home and took care of their three children. Jordan was the oldest. He liked being on his own, he read a lot, and he asked lots of questions at the dinner table. His parents sometimes wondered why their twelve-year-old son was asking so many questions about various religions and other perplexing things. They thought he should be talking about the Dodgers' chances in the World Series. But he was more interested in reading each issue of the family's *National Geographic* cover to cover as soon as it arrived. He found other cultures and landscapes fascinating. He dreamed of visiting new places and watching people perform exotic rituals. He cared nothing about business or entrepreneurship.

All the Monkarsh kids did chores to help their father Max, who worked long hours at his butcher shop. Besides presiding at the counter during business hours, Max had to make sure the shop was spotless each night before returning home for dinner with the family. In the morning, before the shop opened, he had to decide what meats and cuts he would feature that day, what prices to adjust, and what orders to place with his meat suppliers.

After Jordan turned thirteen, Max assigned him the job of making the sausages that would be offered for sale in his shop. After school Jordan took the bus to his dad's shop to do his assigned work. In the basement he diligently ground and mixed the meats, added salts and preservatives, and then operated a machine that tightly packed the ground meat into the cow intestines used to hold the sausages together. This was Jordan's chore for four years, for which he received three dollars an hour, money he saved to buy a car when he turned sixteen. He hated his assigned job in the basement, but there was no chance of negotiating something else with his dad. So Jordan worked away, meanwhile daydreaming of someday being free and visiting foreign lands.

Jordan graduated from college with a degree in religion and a love for reading and writing poetry. He wasn't sure what he wanted to do, but he knew what he didn't want to do: go work for his dad and become a butcher. Jordan loved his father, but he did not fantasize about a life of working together, even if his father did.

After several months of wandering the world following his graduation from college, Jordan returned to LA and began his first entrepreneurial venture. In his travels he had developed a passion for eating interesting foods from street vendors. Since there were no street vendors in LA, he hit on the idea of building food carts to get into the street food business. It seemed like a good way to make enough money to live on.

He knew nothing about business plans, so he didn't create one, but he did make a sketch of the cart he arranged to be built by someone he knew. A few weeks later, on the day after receiving the cart that looked like a backyard barbeque on wheels, he loaded it up with 500 sausages he had made the day before. He put the cart in the back of his old beat-up van, stopped by his favorite bakery to pick up 500 rolls fresh out of the oven, and then drove to his favorite spot in Los Angeles—Venice Beach. Within ten hours he had sold everything he had on the cart. Jordan made enough profit that day to pay for the cart he had built. He soon hired an assistant to handle the money so that he could concentrate on grilling and serving more sausages in a day, ultimately selling close to $2,500 on his busiest day. He loved grilling sausages wherever he wanted and offering his wares to strangers; he did so for four years before the health authorities even noticed. It turned out that the lack of street food in LA was not due to the unavailability of carts. It was due to the Department of Public Health: their rules prohibited street food. Within a year of Jordan's being noticed by the health department, they cited him a dozen times for his unlicensed food cart, ultimately threatening him with jail if he stayed in the street food business.

Jordan had sold his street food for much more than it cost to make. He pocketed over a dollar for every $1.75 sausage he sold. By the time his business was shut down, he had saved over $25,000. After making his own money, Jordan knew he would never be satisfied working nine to five for anyone else. And he had enough money to start another business.

Having developed some confidence that, with the right permits, he could still make and sell food people would want, Jordan now dreamed of creating a business that would put him in the center of the place he loved most: Venice Beach. It was there that Jordan, within weeks of leaving the cart business, used much of the profits he had saved to rent a fast food stand. He knew in his bones that he could make delicious sausages with new tastes that would bring in even more customers. And making sausages for *his* business felt much more satisfying than making them for his dad's.

After renting the food stand, he installed the appliances needed to make, cook, and refrigerate his sausages. Unfortunately, the process of applying for permits and passing the inspections required to serve food on Venice Beach took almost two years to complete. By then, Jordan was in debt to his family and friends for the extra money he had not projected he would need in order to get to opening day. But Jody Maroni's Sausage Kingdom (Jordan's intuition told him that "Jordan Monkarsh's Sausage Kingdom" didn't sound as appetizing) was an instant success. Everyone involved felt that all the hard work, time, and accumulated debts had been worthwhile.

Jordan is not a big guy, but because the interior of his Venice Beach food stand was designed to be two steps higher than the boardwalk, his persona, "Jody," looked larger than life when he leaned out over the counter shouting at passers-by. He had a great smile and was hard to ignore, so plenty of people stopped to sample his sausages. The dozen or so different sausages Jordan offered were are all savory and high quality. People loved them, and on a sunny day at the beach, with the help of three others, he could sell $6,000 worth of sausages, French fries, and soda. With such a profitable business, Jordan was debt free within eighteen months.

Serving a great product day in and day out to the thousands of people on Venice Beach gets you noticed. "Jody" loved the attention and accolades. "I deliver joy," he would tell his customers. Trying to make them happy never felt like work to Jordan. The icing on the cake came when his efforts resulted in multiple mentions by a famous *Los Angeles Times* food critic— "Jody" became a local celebrity.

Jody and Jordan have very different personalities. Jordan was an introvert who read poetry and liked to stay at home with his family. Jody shouted at strangers, flashed a huge smile, and was quick with the quips—an alter ego created by the passion and anxiety that go with having your future on the line.

Jordan spent long hours running his Sausage Kingdom, as his dad had done with the butcher shop. Within five years he supervised more employees than his dad, the additional help required as the Sausage Kingdom served far more customers daily. It was open seven days a week, and Jordan oversaw the making of every sausage he served. He hired some people he knew from his food cart days, and they introduced him to their friends, some of whom he also hired. To make sure everything was done the way he wanted, Jordan was at the stand from the time he opened the doors in the early morning until he locked up a couple of hours after sundown.

He was a demanding yet patient coach for his team, and the vibe at Sausage Kingdom was a good one. Even though Jordan paid only the going rate for food service workers, about 20 percent above minimum wage, employee turnover was low. He shared his recipes with his staff and taught them to emulate what he did. He even persuaded some of his staff to shout at passers-by in broken English. They didn't make exactly the same impression "Jody" did, but they got attention and sold more sausages than they otherwise would have. Because Jordan cared about training his low-paid team and sharing his skills with them, they respected him, and he didn't suffer from the employee theft that caused many other food stands on Venice Beach to struggle or to close.

Soon after opening the stand, Jordan got married. In the next three years, Jordan and his wife had two children. Having paid off his debts to relatives and friends and created a business that was thriving, he savored his success and his independence—he felt he had it all.

Big Numbers

Jordan is just one of the fifteen million full-time entrepreneurs in the United States today, people who are in business for themselves or run the almost six million businesses that they started. Nearly eighteen million people are actively trying to start about 9.5 million businesses, and millions more are thinking about it. As previously noted, when you take into account spouses, parents, and siblings, you find that more than 30 percent of the adult population is engaged in starting a company or directly related to someone who is. For all the attention that entrepreneurship does get, it probably doesn't get enough.

No specific mental, emotional, or physical qualities distinguish Jordan, or any other entrepreneur, from someone who works for others. On average, an entrepreneur is no smarter, stronger, more extroverted, or insomniac than the rest of us. Given the large numbers of people in the entrepreneurial and the employee worlds, this is not surprising. If such a vast array of entrepreneurs had any distinguishing physiological or psychological characteristic or characteristics, we would have learned long ago how to spot them in a crowd.

When we think about entrepreneurs, most of us think about the less than 10 percent of all entrepreneurs who are far richer than the rest of the working population. The wealth represented in the *Forbes* magazine's list of 400 wealthiest Americans has been almost entirely created by entrepreneurial endeavors. Because the overall number of entrepreneurs, working and retired, is so large, the number of rich entrepreneurs is in the millions, though that represents just a small minority of entrepreneurs across all tax brackets. And because the very rich attract a disproportionate amount of attention, most of us have a distorted perception of entrepreneurs and their wealth. We think, "If an entrepreneur can stay in business for a while, he or she must likely be wealthy." The opposite is true. Ninety percent of entrepreneurs, no matter how long they've been in business, make *less* than they could by offering their same sets of skills and experiences to an established employer. At the point in Jordan's story where we left off, he had less in his bank account than if he had worked for his dad or been the manager of a nice restaurant, even though Jordan's sausage stand was doing well.

Are there characteristics that differentiate very wealthy entrepreneurs from everyone else? That's a loaded question. Surely, some people become much wealthier than the rest of us for a reason. But our inherent biases lead us to believe that we see patterns in what we read about famous entrepreneurs—they're tech savvy, they have unique talents, they don't have feelings, whatever. Those distorted perceptions arise, however, because we don't know the truth about most successful entrepreneurs.

Stephanie DiMarco is a classic example. She recently sold the software company she founded for $2.7 billion. Stephanie is not a programmer—she has a great personality, she's shy, and relatively few people have ever heard of her. An exceedingly practical person, she majored in accounting in college. Though Stephanie feels more comfortable measuring risks rather than taking them, she never considered being an entrepreneur as unreasonably risky. Her father ran a small public relations agency, the guy she fell in love with in college and married after graduation started his own art gallery, and her father-in-law to-be was a freelance photographer with his own studio.

Nevertheless, when she graduated from college she took the road most traveled, going to work as an accountant for one of the biggest banks in the world. She hated it. After less than two years she left to work for a small boutique investment advisor with ten employees instead of twenty thousand, but that wasn't much better. Neither job gave her the career opportunities she craved or the chance to develop her full potential. As she puts it, "It was really unattractive to work to the beat of someone else's drum, and I could see there weren't a lot of women on the top floors."

Stephanie, understanding that her fiancé had entrepreneurial ambitions that she might be called on to support, took one more stab at finding a satisfying job. Another small boutique investment advisor was willing to hire her and also let her work on a project to automate the tedium that went into preparing the monthly statements sent to their clients—once she finished with her normal accounting tasks.

Stephanie had worked with computers in college and become somewhat familiar with them at the large bank, but had never had responsibility for one herself. This was back in the mid-1980s, when computers were expensive and nobody other than computer engineers could get enough time on a computer to really learn how to program them. So she submitted a project idea with a budget that included buying the latest model mini-computer (a $30,000 DEC PDP-11 with a 5MB hard drive) and hiring a talented part-time programmer, Steve, whom she knew from college. As promised, the boss of the investment boutique approved her proposal, and Stephanie was able to launch a challenging project that made her feel she had picked the right place to work.

Because she did much of the firm's tedious manual bookkeeping herself, she knew exactly how a new program should work. Business accounting programs for the more affordable mini-computers were available at that time, but Stephanie could not find anyone interested in creating a program that did the arcane bookkeeping involved with investing other people's money—the field was far too specialized to interest existing software companies. Stephanie and Steve focused on automating the simple but tedious task of listing the transactions made on behalf of each client, which had previously required a full-time bookkeeper to record hand-written entries in a large ledger book and then a full-time typist to prepare all the monthly statements to be sent to clients.

Working well as a team, Stephanie and Steve began commuting to work together to have more time to talk about the project. Steve asked lots of questions about the *hows* and *whys* of keeping track of the stocks and bonds being bought and sold on behalf of clients. Stephanie asked lots of questions about what could be automated with a computer and how data could be collected more accurately. They both became knowledgeable about the possibilities of automating transaction ledgers and other boutique investment business arcana that nobody else cared about. They completed the project to automate the job of the full-time typist on time and under budget. The boss of the boutique investment firm was delighted. She encouraged Stephanie and Steve to build additional functionality into their program.

Less than a year after Stephanie bought the PDP-11 mini-computer, IBM introduced its XT personal computer. The machine captivated her. It cost just $5,000 and its hard drive had twice the capacity to store accounting records. Steve, however, was not impressed. During their commutes she heard in great detail how PCs were ill-suited for the task of business automation—they couldn't multitask and they didn't have robust operating systems. Unintimidated by Steve or his technical jargon, Stephanie kept asking, "Why?" Determined to make Steve admit accounting could be done on a PC, she spent her weekends researching companies that were starting to offer more robust operating systems and programming languages for the XT. After more than a month of debate, Steve finally admitted that it should be possible to write the equivalent of their mini-computer programs for the new IBM XT—but it would take some pioneering work. That's when Stephanie dropped the bombshell on Steve: "We should start our own company and sell this software to others."

Steve was not so sure. He was married and had a mortgage and a child to support. He felt starting a company would limit his ability to write the programs he found interesting. Stephanie, however, was—and still is—a very determined person. She offered solutions or mitigations to each of Steve's objections. After a week of discussion and de facto negotiation, Stephanie got Steve to agree to co-found an asset management accounting software company. She offered to pay him a salary while she lived off of her personal savings and accepted nothing until the company became profitable.

Stephanie quickly created a business plan for the proposed

business and showed it to her friends and other people she knew personally. One family friend, "out of friendship," says Stephanie, offered to invest $50,000 for a fifth of the company, with Stephanie and her programming buddy each owning 40 percent. Having secured the funds to start the company, she then went to give her notice of resignation to her boss at the investment boutique, but also offered her a chance to invest. "I have no interest in investing," she said. "Just leave." She did, and Advent Software was born.

It took Steve almost a year to write the computer programs to work on an IBM PC. Unfortunately, potential customers, in spite of the IBM name on the computer, felt uncomfortable running critical bookkeeping functions on a PC. It was a much harder sell than expected, and it took another year to persuade asset management businesses to take PC-based software seriously. But within two years of the founding of Advent, IBM had introduced a more powerful generation of PC, Novell had introduced computer-networking software, and the amount of data that could be stored on a hard drive had more than doubled. That extra year enabled Advent's software to mature, become networked and easier to use, and have a more professional feel. That extra year of development also required more money, so Stephanie had to ask the family friend to give her another $50,000 to keep the company going.

Virtually all trained computer programmers and virtually all computer software companies at the time shared Steve's disdain for using PCs as a platform for business software development. So when asset managers finally did feel comfortable using PCs, Advent was alone in offering an affordable package of the specialized accounting software. Almost exactly two years after founding, orders to buy their software started to roll in, and Advent was immediately profitable and cash-flow positive.

Plenty of researchers have attempted to find characteristics that correlate with entrepreneurial success. Their research to date shows that the correlation between success and any characteristic or even any group of characteristics is so small as to be irrelevant to anyone's decision to become an entrepreneur.

We can say that wealthy entrepreneurs have invested more hours at work than the average person, but that is more effect than cause. Wealthy entrepreneur-CEOs work about as hard or harder than CEOs of other similarly sized companies growing at the same rate. Managing the complexities of a business that produces lots of value *always* requires putting in long hours. Young and growing companies require constant management attention to avoid pitfalls that can kill a fragile enterprise, and handling ever larger numbers of customers requires constant change and increasing complexity, making managing a startup very time-intensive.

We can also say of wealthy entrepreneurs that virtually none of them succeeded by themselves. Whether or not they had a partner or more co-founders, they had key employees and teammates who helped them build their enterprises (perhaps hired as contractors rather than employees). These entrepreneurs may have been introverted or extroverted, they may have been open or secretive, generous or miserly in how they worked with the people that helped them create and run their businesses, but a great deal of productive work must have been accomplished by others to create the significant value required to make an enterprise profitable and its owner wealthy. Working alone, as you could choose to do as a bookkeeper, gardener, or Uber driver, virtually disqualifies you from becoming a wealthy entrepreneur.

Differences Matter

To ask about the characteristics of wealthy entrepreneurs, or any other category of entrepreneur, is to focus on what's unimportant about entrepreneurs. Understanding entrepreneurship is *not* about understanding numbers or averages—an average entrepreneur does not exist. Individual entrepreneurs differ from each other more than they resemble each other. Resembling everyone else creates very little value for an individual offering services for hire or for the company he or she may create. To be average or the same is to be a commodity. *Entrepreneurs exploit their differences to make a living and to con-*

trol their own lives. The pressure of asking for money from strangers in return for doing something good for them exerts a pressure on entrepreneurs to differentiate themselves and their business from everyone else around them. In essence, successful entrepreneurs have to be distinct and special (and this differentness may trick us into thinking that the differentness was the cause—the special something entrepreneurs are born with—rather than the effect—what they do to be special). This differentiation may be on a very local scale, such as running a neighborhood bakery that serves the best croissants within a mile, but *some* differentiation must exist for a business to find any traction. And the differentiation starts with the entrepreneur accentuating personal differences, in business *and* in life.

What set Jordan Monkarsh up for success as a sausage stand entrepreneur cannot be captured in any discussion about an average entrepreneur's IQ, EQ, years of schooling, or age upon founding. Jordan chose to exploit a combination of abilities to make sausages that tasted different—and better, in the opinion of many—than anything else people could eat on Venice Beach. He possessed several different-than-average traits and abilities that drove him to consider starting such a business. Specifically, Jordan had sensitive taste buds that were essential in creating sausages with new combinations of flavors. His taste buds had been cultivated in his travels around the world after he graduated from college. Although an introvert, Jordan knew how to act the part of a fast-quipping salesman. And he had masterful sausage-making skills that he learned from his experienced father.

Jordan serves as an excellent role model because there is much to learn from him in order to survive and prosper as an entrepreneur. As is true for many entrepreneurs, he tends to live in the moment; he's not a planner or a strategist. He never wrote a business plan. Jordan acquired the additional skills necessary to run his business the way the vast majority of entrepreneurs do—by learning what they don't know, by making mistakes, and by looking at their checking accounts to see how much is left over at the end of the month. Then they decide what to do next.

Stephanie is almost the exact opposite. She likes to make plans, surround herself with experienced advisors, and forecast her bank balances months in advance. Either type of person—a Jordan or a Stephanie—can succeed as an entrepreneur.

Jordan chose well what he wanted to do with his life and accordingly did well—at least in the eyes of most people. (More on that later.) He did not choose to do something at which he was mediocre or that he found boring. The same can be said of Stephanie and virtually everyone else who has created an enterprise that generated a great deal of value.

Ultimately, who you are is not what matters in entrepreneurship. What matters is what you want to do with who you are.

When "Who" Means "We"

Contrary to a commonly held perception, the majority of enterprises are founded by a single person, not by a team. Over half of the entrepreneurs in the United States work on their own and want to keep it that way. Most see no reason to pay good money to incorporate. Beauticians that rent chairs in a beauty parlor are a classic example, as are most gardeners who own their own truck and lawn mower, as well as full-time Uber drivers.

Founding a company with a spouse or other direct relative as a partner is also common, occurring in over a quarter of the cases. Rarely, however, do people found companies with non-relatives as full partners. Most entrepreneurs inherently understand that giving significant ownership to partners or co-founders increases risk, especially if they're strangers. Stephanie is an exception. But her partner Steve was not a stranger—rather, someone that she knew from college. She felt that working with him minimized the risk of Advent failing; minimizing the risk of failure or loss of control is consistent with being a bedrock entrepreneur.

Among high-risk entrepreneurs, however, founding companies with relative strangers is common. High-risk entrepreneurs often justifiably feel the need to grow fast or perish. The risks associated with breaking up with a co-founder whom you didn't have the time to get to know well can seem reasonable when survival appears otherwise impossible. To attract investments and capital that may be critical to establishing a competitive advantage, high-risk entrepreneurs often must attract co-founders who have complementary experience and expertise. Still, making strangers partners is a huge risk, and many high-risk entrepreneurial ventures fail at least in part because of a break-up among key members of the founding team.

Finally, whether acknowledged with ownership shares in the company or not, spouses and family are always de facto partners in startups. Creating an enterprise, growing an enterprise, fixing the constant problems that arise, and all the other high-stress activities entrepreneurs must endure to succeed take time, attention, and resources away from family and intimate friends. While no evidence shows that entrepreneurship leads to higher rates of divorce, research shows that it *does* increase familial stress, no matter how supportive the spouse and kids. Regardless of how the business is founded, entrepreneurship is always a family affair.

Who Fails

Entrepreneurs who don't know what they want from entrepreneurship and don't have the energy or time to figure it out are likely to fail. So are entrepreneurs who partner with people they don't actually want to work with. And, perhaps most important of all, people who are afraid of being different have little hope of finding ways to get strangers to voluntarily give them, or their companies, enough money to survive.

Apart from these caveats, entrepreneurship may be a good career path for you or someone you care about and therefore worth it to you to read on.

CHAPTER 3

WHAT

"The deceased must be protected and given a voice, without a witness they will be forgotten."

—Vidal Herrera

Entrepreneurial opportunities are everywhere.*

Consider: The United States collects a great deal of data about its businesses and has a well-established system for organizing them into over 1,000 different industries. Most people are shocked by how many different industries there are, particularly considering that each of these general categories can include many different types of businesses. For example, the US Census Bureau lists thirty-one kinds of construction-oriented industries that include 1,270,691 distinct businesses (as of the end of 2012). They range from "Highway, Street, and Bridge Construction" (24,315 of them) to "Tile and Terrazzo Contractors" (19,925 of them). Within retailing there are nine different types of retail industries listed just for the things we wear

---

* This statement is not intended to imply that all entrepreneurial opportunities are easy to exploit.

31

every day. *And in every single industry classification startup activity is occurring.*

In every one of these industries, there is room for improvement and innovation. Because almost all established businesses do things that frustrate some or all of their customers, they are ripe to be preyed upon by a startup. And many businesses are owned by burnt-out or older entrepreneurs who are happy to sell to an entrepreneur intent on growing the business anew.

It can be hard to appreciate how varied the opportunities are, partly because there are so many, and partly because the media focuses on high-risk entrepreneurs. Currently, high-risk entrepreneurial activity *is* concentrated in software-related businesses, yet of the 1,000 industry categories tracked, only five encompass software ("Software Publishing," "Custom Computer Programming Services," "Computer Systems Design Services," "Other Computer Related Services," and "Data Processing, Hosting, and Related Services"). Stephanie's company, Advent, is included under Custom Computer Programming Services. Today, software plays an important role in most businesses, but unless software is something a company sells directly to its customers, then software is merely a tool to support the sales and delivery of the product. Tools differ greatly from products, and products are the essential "what" that entrepreneurs must create in order to create value.

To understand what entrepreneurs do, consider two entrepreneurs who found what they wanted to do in vastly different yet very typical ways: Vidal Herrera and Sam Walton.

Desperate to be Needed

Vidal Herrera's entrepreneurial journey was precipitated by his despondency. Having risen from an impoverished upbringing to a middle class lifestyle, he was, at the age of thirty-two, once again destitute after suffering a spinal injury on his job as a coroner's investigator. Unable to stand for any length of time without being overcome with pain, he was put on permanent disability by the County of Los

Angeles. Unfortunately, his workman's compensation payouts were not enough to feed, clothe, and shelter his family. Herrera had applied for more than 2,000 jobs, but nobody wanted to hire someone who couldn't stand for long periods of time or handle heavy objects.

Vidal had grown up in the barrio of East LA. When he was three years old, his mother was evicted from her home so developers could make way for Dodger Stadium. With nowhere to live and no longer able to feed Vidal and his six siblings, she was forced to give them up to foster care. Five years later she managed to retrieve them, but she made it clear that they would all have to work to support the family. So at the age of eight, Vidal began redeeming discarded soda bottles for pennies and selling newspapers on the street corners of downtown Los Angeles. Every day when he turned over to his mother the fifteen to twenty cents he had made, he felt proud. Work took on a special meaning for him: being respected. From that early age, Vidal did whatever it took to be respected for his work—to be respected as a man.

School was a low priority because the jobs he held, from newspaper boy to shoeshine boy to busboy, didn't require schooling, *and* they were exhausting. When he graduated from high school with a D average, he was two years older than his peers. After high school, Vidal hitchhiked around the country for two years, trying to find out what freedom from constant work felt like. But traveling was lonely, and so he returned to LA to take a job making pizzas.

Vidal was always on the lookout for ways to make more money. A few months after he returned, a bartender told him he could make "real money" working in the morgue—if he could stomach the work. At that time, more money meant more parties, booze, and drugs, and Vidal started looking the next day. He quickly found a job as a Mortuary Attendant at a big LA hospital. Most orderlies try to avoid working with dead people and don't look happy and motivated when cleaning up after the deceased. The work is grisly and the stench is nauseating. But Vidal liked the work, and it showed. His supervisors took note, and pathologists soon took time to explain the causes of death and the anatomy of corpses to him. When his friends started calling him "El Muerto," The Dead One, Vidal was delighted—he knew he was onto something.

Vidal worked as many hours as possible, earning as much he could in order to live large. He and his barrio friends, some of them infamous drug dealers, were notorious for their Saturday night parties with plenty of booze, drugs, and fun-loving women. Vidal lived from paycheck to paycheck—until he met Vicki. She was a bohemian girl from LA's San Fernando Valley. During an especially raucous party, Vicki caught Vidal's attention when she screamed at him over the pulsing music that he would never amount to anything. He had never had a girlfriend—"why get tied down?" But now a girl smarter and prettier than he ever imagined was interested in him enough to berate him for the way he was living his life. This girl was clearly special. He wanted her and he resolved to make something of himself to win her love.

During the time Vidal and Vicki were falling in love, three years after Vidal had started working at the hospital, a coroner's assistant assigned to pick up bodies tipped Vidal about a job: "We're looking for a Latino to work at our place to fill a quota; you have a good work ethic; you should apply." Two weeks later, Vidal started at the bottom of the pecking order on the staff of the Los Angeles County Coroner.

As a civil servant, he would now have to win promotions not only through hard work but also by acing exams. Vidal hated taking tests. Determined to show Vicki that he could amount to something and in spite of his poor grades in school, Vidal hit the books. Five years and several exams later he advanced to coroner's assistant, serving as the right-hand man for the county's coroners during autopsies. Among the coroners, including with the infamous "coroner to the stars" Dr. Thomas Noguchi, he developed a reputation for knowing as much as they did about organs and types of tissue, the signs for various causes of death, and the kinds of incisions needed to get to any part of the body without destroying evidence. Vidal found medical texts and medical terms easy to understand and remember because they were directly associated with work he loved to do. When he received the top grade on the Investigator's exam, he was promoted yet again to Deputy Medical Investigator, and sent to crime scenes to perform medical investigations, just like on the television series *CSI*.

One holiday, working alone because nobody else wanted to give up their time off, Vidal arrived at a possible crime scene where he was confronted with a dead woman who weighed almost 300 pounds. The EMTs from the fire department, who were locked in a contract dispute with the county, refused to help Vidal handle the body. Exerting all of his strength, he rolled the dead woman onto her back by himself. As he did so, three of his vertebrae collapsed.

After three weeks of treatment, Vidal was released from the hospital. His doctors told him he was lucky he hadn't been permanently paralyzed—and that he would never be able to stand for long periods or be able to lift anything weighing more than a few pounds. The Coroner's office put him on permanent disability, which entitled him to a monthly check totaling only a third of his pay as a medical investigator.

With a wife, a young child, and a mortgage, Herrera was terrified that he wasn't going to be able to make ends meet. For two years he searched in vain for a job, receiving over 2,000 rejections. With no money left in the bank and thousands of dollars of bills to pay, he felt like a deadbeat, a failure. Sinking ever deeper into self-hatred, he contemplated suicide.

Then, unexpectedly, he received a letter offering him a job assisting with autopsies for the Veterans Administration (VA). But when he interviewed for the position, he found that the salary was less than the disability payments he received. If he took the job, the disability payments would cease and he would be in even worse shape!

Feeling this was his only remaining chance to survive, he pleaded with the VA administrator to help him make the opportunity work. As they talked, he learned that the VA had a large and delinquent backlog of autopsies. So he made a counteroffer: instead of accepting the salaried position, he would work as an independent contractor. The VA said yes, provided he would accept $150 per autopsy and take responsibility for his own benefits and taxes. Herrera calculated that if he could perform at least two autopsies a day, working five days a week, he could make about $6,500 a month. That was more than enough to live on. It was decided—he was going to be an independent businessperson.

It wasn't easy. To get across town to the VA, he had to take three different buses, consuming two hours each way. And because he still couldn't stand for long periods, he had to improvise, using stools to prop himself up in the right position for each incision he performed. At times he passed out from the pain. Vidal didn't care. Nor did he care about the hassle of being a contractor to the Veterans Administration—he was ecstatic about having an income and a first customer. And as the VA's backlog of autopsies gradually fell, that customer was increasingly happy.

Wanting more than just to perform contract autopsies for the VA, he worked to expand his business. He saved his money so he could buy a car and then his own saws and autopsy tools. He organized the VA's autopsy procedures so they could be performed more efficiently, freeing up more of his time. Vidal also read business magazines; one day while reading about how 800-numbers worked, inspiration hit. He called AT&T and asked if 1-800-AUTOPSY was available. He bought the rights to the number—over the strong objections of Vicki, who thought it was pure vanity. Undaunted, he printed up 1-800-AUTOPSY flyers and began visiting local funeral homes, hundreds of them, telling them that he could perform autopsies at the funeral home for any family that asked. He arranged to pay a retired coroner to preside over the autopsies when work showed up. Even though private autopsies had never been offered before, Vidal's phone started to ring within days. Some families wanted to find out why their loved ones had died, even if nothing nefarious had happened. As more families learned about the service, the business grew and money finally became something Vidal didn't have to worry about.

What's In Front of You

While Vidal grew up with not enough, Sam Walton grew up with just enough. There was food on the table when he was hungry and clothes to keep him warm in the winter (it gets cold in Missouri), but his father did not have stable employment throughout much of Sam's childhood. Sam's parents were frugal to make sure they'd have enough saved up for the proverbial rainy day, which was fortunate the time or two the savings were needed to tide over the family. Every family member took responsibility for their own needs money-wise, but everyone more or less got to choose how they did it. Sam's mother raised a few cows and sold their milk, and Sam delivered newspapers and sold magazine subscriptions. Every dollar went toward basic necessities like food, clothing, and fixing things that broke.

Sam never felt the need to reward or distinguish himself with objects; he cared far more about people. He liked being with his friends and playing sports, activities where having fun and feeling good didn't cost anything. Sam was an extrovert supreme, and he felt good being around people and being respected by people. He was such an extrovert that he would sometimes introduce himself to everyone he'd cross paths with to make sure they knew who he was. Sam loved his childhood and aspired to live a similar life; he did not dream about making lots of money, nor did he dream about moving far away.

But Sam was driven to excel at whatever he did. He especially enjoyed tasks and activities that were tied to some ultimate goal. He loved being part of a team, and being respected for helping his teams succeed. He felt especially good when he was elected captain of a sports team, and he felt even better when his sports team won a league championship (both his football and basketball high school teams won state championships). But football and basketball were not enough. Sam also loved being a member and leader of church youth organizations, and running for elected positions in the organizations he was a member of. He had more energy than any one group could handle.

To Sam, money had nothing to do with fun, happiness, or success. Money was an enabler of things that he felt he needed to do. Sam needed to pay for his own tuition, books, and clothes, and he wanted to buy a car so he could feel good about taking girls out on dates. To pay for college and the things he needed for college, Sam kept his newspaper delivery routes going till he graduated, routinely hiring young local kids to actually make his deliveries on his behalf.

As he neared graduation from University of Missouri, Sam had no special role model or mentor, nor were his parents expecting him to do anything specific. In looking for a job, Sam, along with many of his fellow seniors, applied for positions with the companies that interviewed students on campus. Even though Sam hadn't been a top student—not a shock considering all his extra-curricular activities— he went on just two interviews and got two offers to be a management trainee from the most successful and prestigious retailing companies of the era: J. C. Penney and Sears Roebuck. He accepted the position at J. C. Penney, and that's how Sam Walton chose retailing, or per- haps, how retailing chose Sam Walton.

Sam was trained and tutored at the Des Moines, Iowa J. C. Penney store by one of the retail chain's best managers. Unsurprisingly, Sam was quickly molded into an excellent department store salesman. But Sam couldn't help himself from wanting to be in front of the custom- ers—he felt the recordkeeping piece of his job should come second to a customer's needs. That attitude made him terrible at paperwork, so bad that a personnel supervisor from headquarters recommended he be fired. While the job gave Sam great confidence about his sales abilities, it also made him question whether he wanted to deal with corporate hierarchies. Within eighteen months, Sam resigned from J. C. Penney to try and sign up for World War II.

But World War II didn't turn out for Sam Walton the way he wanted—he soon found that a heart irregularity would keep him from active duty. After leaving J. C. Penney, Sam worked at a gunpowder factory in Tulsa so that he could feel good about his contributions to the war effort. But he had plenty of time for himself when he wasn't working, which translated into time to make friends and meet people—he wasn't into being alone. On an outing to a bowling alley, Sam tried to pick up a pretty girl. "Haven't I met you somewhere before?" It wasn't original, but it got the conversation going. And he didn't care one bit that she was on a date with another guy. Helen

Robson was the daughter of a prominent rancher and lawyer in a small town outside of Tulsa. Sam couldn't believe his luck in meeting such a smart, attractive, and ambitious young lady. (She had been valedictorian and a varsity athlete at her high school.) They quickly started discussing their future plans, and soon started planning their futures together. Helen and her entire family fell in love with Sam's energy and ambition; Sam was ecstatic about being part of a family that could help him succeed.

Sam treated Helen as a full partner from the start. He admired her different and thoughtful perspectives on people, plans, and family. It's hard to tell the exact moment when Sam decided he wanted to be his own boss. I suspect the idea was already percolating when he was working at J. C. Penney and bristling at the rebukes he received for spending too much time with customers and not enough time on paperwork. Sam likely had dreamt out loud about the possibility with Helen and probably even Helen's dad. We know he was focused on starting his own retail business by the time the war ended, because immediately upon his discharge from the army (he had been finally called up for the last two years of the war to organize and supervise efforts to guard government facilities), Sam drove to St. Louis to see his childhood friend, whose dad had owned the local department store in the small town where they grew up. They met and concocted a plan to go 50/50 in buying a franchise to open a department store in St. Louis. Sam didn't have the money, but planned to borrow it from his new father-in-law.

Sam likely had been aligned with Helen, and even her family, about owning a retail business, but the specifics of Sam planning to go into partnership with his friend was clearly news to Helen, who quickly vetoed the idea. Her family had suffered setbacks from frayed partnerships, and Helen didn't want her and Sam to endure any similar setbacks. Furthermore, Helen hated the idea of starting a business in St. Louis—she liked small town life, and a small town is where the business would be. Sam immediately dropped his St. Louis plan and focused instead on buying a small-town Ben Franklin–franchised variety store.* Within a couple of months, backed by a $20,000 loan from Helen's dad, the couple found and purchased a franchise in Newport, Arkansas.

Retailing is the most common of all entrepreneurial businesses. And opening a franchised retail outlet is a popular way to this day for nascent entrepreneurs with little relevant experience to break into retailing. Borrowing money from family to open the business is also extremely common. There was nothing exotic or unique about what Sam decided to do. He went into a business where the only competitive advantage would be him.

Ideas Are Not a "What"

Vidal may have been the first to offer private autopsies, but being a pioneer had nothing to do with why Vidal started 1-800-AUTOPSY. He just wanted more customers once his contract with the VA was under control and spinning off extra cash. Entrepreneurship is often fantasized as an ability to think up entirely new businesses or come up with ideas that disrupt existing industries. This is never the case. Ford did not think up the combustion engine or automobiles, Edison did not think up incandescent light bulbs, Larry Page did not think up search engines. Disney didn't think up animated films, or even amusement parks. These great entrepreneurs succeeded by working tirelessly to tune existing ideas and inventions in ways that excited vast numbers of new consumers.

Ideas are not the keys to entrepreneurial success. Even a once in a lifetime, an unprecedented, world-changing, patent-protected new

---

* A "variety" store was also referred to as a five and dime. These stores sold general merchandise that was not perishable, and they were the most common type of store until they were replaced by discount stores from the 1960s to 1980s. Many retail store chains in the US are still operated as franchises. ACE Hardware is an example of a franchised chain of stores today. Ben Franklin went bankrupt and ceased operating in 1996.

idea won't guarantee success. The true story of what was arguably the most brilliant idea of the twentieth century, the transistor, illustrates this perfectly.

The invention of the transistor made the *New York Times*. People knew it would be world-changing, and they were right. Transistors have given rise to computers, modern communications, the Internet, smartphones, and all the ubiquitous electronics that we have come to rely upon. The transistor was co-invented by William Shockley, a man universally recognized as a great scientist (and, along with his co-inventors, later rewarded with a Nobel Prize in Physics). Wanting the transistor to be his legacy, he formed a startup to commercialize the device and easily found a wealthy businessperson eager to underwrite the company with as much money as might be needed. Shockley then recruited the smartest people he could find with the skills he thought were necessary to produce these revolutionary devices.

Despite all this brainpower, a deep understanding of this new technology, and a world waiting with bated breath to buy transistors, nothing happened. Shockley routinely belittled his recruits in front of their peers. He instructed lab technicians to ignore their bosses and secretly report to him. He took credit for everyone else's ideas and he changed his mind constantly. Within a year, the smart people started to flee. They went on to create pioneering companies like Fairchild Semiconductor, Intel, and venture capital firms like Kleiner Perkins. The Shockley Semiconductor Laboratory never produced a single product. Shockley was a leadership disaster, and as a result the electronics revolution was set back by years. *Poor leadership and poor execution can sink even the greatest ideas.*

No new idea comes formed ready for delivery to the market. The more unique the idea, the less any human is able to predict or assess all the complexities of how supply and demand will evolve. Nobody has ever shown they have infallible, let alone reliable, instincts for anticipating how customers and markets receive new ideas. Sure, you can do a ton of research to forecast how customers and suppliers will react to an incremental change to an existing product or service. Established companies attempt to do that with their new product introduction (they call it NPI) processes. All ideas change significantly as PhD marketing experts at large companies, or entrepreneurs, come to understand the reaction of real customers, suppliers, partners, and investors. Steve Jobs and Steve Wozniak initially tried to sell PC boards to hobbyists, which almost nobody wanted; then they sold Apple 1 computers that only a couple of hundred people wanted, before Steve Jobs knew enough to convince Wozniak to design what became the wildly successful and profitable Apple 2. *No idea is a good entrepreneurial idea until it has been prototyped, sold to real users, modified extensively, and iterated to the point that it appeals to significant numbers of customers.*

Ideas are not the "what." The real "what" is doing something different that makes customers so happy they gladly give you money. But that difference that customers look for to choose who they'll do business with is rarely ever patent protected—it's more often the case that improved service, convenience, or some variation on an existing product or service convinces initial customers to buy from a new company.

The Unifying Principle of Entrepreneurship

The substance of Stephanie, Vidal, Jordan, and Sam's businesses could not be more different. But despite all the differences in these entrepreneurs' paths, they are all ultimately doing the same thing.

Stephanie's business requires getting other businesses to license her software and to stake their business success on using her programs. Beyond buying rights to use Advent's software, customers invest many thousands of dollars to install the software and to train their staff to use it properly. To succeed, Stephanie has to ensure that her customers use her software for a long time.

Vidal's business gives comfort and closure to families that have questions about the sudden death of a loved one. Other than the VA, Vidal's initial customers were all one-time users of his services. Jordan Monkarsh sells fun food that tastes really good in a fun place. He initially sold his sausages to people on Venice Beach who happened to be passing by, and quickly got customers who loved his sausages enough to make repeated trips to his stand.

But all these entrepreneurs, like all successful entrepreneurs, ultimately operate under the same guiding principle: *They make their customers so happy that they gladly give them money in return.*

This statement embodies three essential truths. First, it describes the earliest and most basic form of all entrepreneurship—trade. "I will give you the fur from the antelope I killed (my product) in return for you giving me a basket full of grain (your currency)." The antelope fur will make one person happy, while the other person will be happier with the basket of grain. Trade is at its core *the* entrepreneurial transaction, whether you're trading real estate, products, or services.

Entrepreneurship has not changed. Often today's more complex entrepreneurship terminology—phrases like "value proposition" and "product market fit"—can obscure what it has always been about. Students and other aspiring entrepreneurs I counsel get distracted by such terms, particularly when these terms are introduced before the aspiring entrepreneur knows what they want to do. But aspiring entrepreneurs know intuitively how to answer when I ask, "What can you do to make some group of people so happy that they'll give you lots of money?"

Second, this unifying principle of entrepreneurship conveys an essential insight: emotions drive all actions, including the actions required to complete a transaction. Clearly, then, the positive emotions associated with delivering a product or service must be big enough to swamp the negative emotions associated with handing over money. Entrepreneurs who overlook or forget this principle become frustrated and distracted when somebody doesn't buy their product or service even though they said they liked it. A person who likes something that you do or make may not like it *enough* to actually want to part with their money to buy it. Building a product or service to be more positively emotive will increase the chances people will want to pay real money for it.

Third, understanding the emotional state of your potential customer pre- and post-sale is critical. Stephanie succeeded because she knew exactly what would excite someone who ran an asset management business, which was not having to train, supervise, and pay so many bookkeepers. The jargon of value propositions causes many businesses and entrepreneurs to neglect monitoring or measuring the emotive responses of customers once they have received the product or service. Our prehistoric entrepreneur could see that antelope fur kept his customer warm in the winter and therefore knew he could barter away the furs of all the antelope he could kill. A modern developer of Android apps has a much harder time knowing whether his or her app actually made the person who downloaded it happy enough to recommend it to others so that her business can grow and prosper. Most don't even care to find out—and most app developers fail. Further, to sell a product or service to a business, you usually have to make many people simultaneously happy. And because business people may feel pressured in different ways at work and at home, making businesses happy enough to buy can be enormously challenging.

Entrepreneurs who cease to control or care about how they deliver happiness will ultimately fail. And when you cease to control or care about being rewarded for delivering ever more happiness to ever more customers, it's time to sell or retire.

Making a business customer happy to hand over hundreds of thousands of dollars to rent software is typically more complex than making a passer-by happy to hand over $6 for a spicy sausage, which may or may not be as tricky as dealing with a bereaved family contemplating spending $1,500 to feel more settled with the unexpected loss of a loved one. We'll discuss more about how you can make customers happy later, but first we need to understand the psychology of being in business serving others.

"What" You Do is About Social Status

Almost every industry is undergoing change, every industry has weak players, every industry has disgruntled or unsatisfied customers, and every neighborhood needs its hangouts.

But many aspiring entrepreneurs decline to take advantage of the lucrative opportunities that surround them. That's because most aspiring entrepreneurs, consciously and subconsciously, attach a social status to the entrepreneurial opportunities they decide to pursue or reject. We're all social beasts who can't help ourselves: we want to know where we rank socially among those whom we consider peers and those whom we think are essential to our well-being. We want to know where we rank among the people our parents care about, where we rank with our boss, and where we rank in the social order at work or among our friends. While it's often difficult to know for sure where we rank, we mostly gauge our ranking based on the feelings and opinions of the people we spend time with and read about.

When we consider entrepreneurship we can't help asking ourselves, "What will my friends think? My parents? My neighbors?" And we have our perceptions of which types of entrepreneurial endeavors will raise our status and which will diminish it. You may privately barbeque the best ribs anyone has ever tasted, but people with degrees from expensive colleges may feel humiliated opening a BBQ restaurant because their parents and sorority sisters would not approve. Our social rank precludes many of us from delivering the greatest happiness we're able to generate.

The lower someone's perceived social status, the more willing they are to consider more diverse entrepreneurial opportunities. Vidal wanted to do something that utilized his skills and could make him a decent living. Stephanie, of higher economic status than Vidal, did not consider the unglamorous idea of starting a temp agency for bookkeepers, though that can be a lucrative, low-risk venture.

We all have our perceptions of what conveys social status and what diminishes it. Media coverage is a big shaper of those social perceptions. Nobody is writing cover stories about how cool it is to own a franchise, despite top franchises like McDonald's contributing to the success of thousands of entrepreneurs. Sam considered being a small-town operator of a retail franchise a socially acceptable occupation, and used the experience to increase his chances of success while simultaneously learning how to run his own store.

The media's concept of entrepreneurial social status relates directly to the instantaneous valuation of a startup. Unfortunately, this ideal leads many entrepreneurs to focus on starting businesses that will generate buzz in the press and be perceived as growing fast. In fact, much media attention gets lavished on entrepreneurs just because they raise lots of money. That attention encourages entrepreneurs to raise more than required, spend more than necessary, and to prioritize making investors happy by increasing their share price, rather than making customers so happy they buy and pay more. The perception that high-risk entrepreneurship increases social status is predicated on our society's insistence on gauging social status according to size and wealth.

This view also encourages many aspiring entrepreneurs to attempt an endeavor they consider attention-grabbing but do not have the skills to accomplish. Not surprisingly, they fail. Ironically, almost all these failed entrepreneurs had low-risk entrepreneurial opportunities to compete in the same industry they were interested in breaking into through much less risky but less "cool" pathways, which we'll discuss further in the chapter on How Good.

When I first began to teach, I would help any student or aspiring entrepreneur who came to me seeking advice. I made it a point to aid them in finding three or more solid ideas for creating rapidly growing, profitable businesses using the skills they had or thought they could easily acquire. But those meetings usually resulted in the student or would-be entrepreneur feeling frustrated. When asked "why," the common refrain was, "The ideas aren't cool enough—they're too mundane." "But what's mundane about feeling fulfilled, being financially independent, and making scores of customers happy?" I would ask. It turns out that's a hard question to answer accurately and sincerely, and it requires we understand "why" people really want to be an entrepreneur—the subject of the next chapter.

CHAPTER 4

WHY

In spite of almost limitless entrepreneurial possibilities, there are relatively few reasons why you would want to dedicate yourself to becoming an entrepreneur. After all, entrepreneurship is risky, stressful, and all-consuming; it leaves little room for family and friends and usually sucks up all of your available cash. Nobody just wakes up one day effortlessly transformed into an entrepreneur. Without great sacrifice there will be no business of your own! So why do so many people try it? Do we so lust after fortune, fame, and independence that we're willing to risk almost everything? You need a reason—and it must be a really good reason—to chase the dream.

Do you understand why you want to be an entrepreneur?

Over one million aspiring entrepreneurs every year in the United States do succeed in starting profitable enterprises. Their dreams were powerful enough to make them want to overcome the many obstacles they encountered. But about 70 percent of the people who actually become full-time entrepreneurs in a typical year abandon their efforts or do not make any money back whatsoever, wasting time and likely damaging close relationships. They claim a multitude of reasons and excuses for giving up on their dream, including it being more risky, stressful, expensive, and all-consuming than they thought. Some allege that something better came up. Some of these disappointments result from uncontrollable external forces all entrepreneurs are prey to: the economy, competitors, changing tastes, and much else. But often these misgivings and regrets result from not understanding the original dream itself.

To become a happy and successful entrepreneur you must understand the nature of your entrepreneurial dream. Jordan Monkarsh was so driven to see his Sausage Kingdom succeed that he created a whole new persona, Jody Maroni, to encourage the world to embrace his products. He worked long hours. He burned himself countless times grilling his sausages and making his condiments. He didn't make excuses; he was doing something too important to him, proving to himself that he could be as successful as his father.

Picking up where we left off with Jordan's story . . . After four years on Venice Beach, Jordan felt secure about his checking account balance. He was able to buy new awnings for the store every other year, and he was in a good position to afford college for his kids someday. So almost exactly four years after opening day, feeling great, with customers lined up to sample and to buy, Jordan thought to himself, "This is running smoothly, so what next?"

Jordan couldn't pin down the exact sequence of the thoughts that were running through his mind, but he was not thinking about making more money—he was already making more than he had ever dreamed. Rather, he felt a combination of boredom and pride. He had fans who were asking for more, and they would adore him more if he gave them more. Why not be in constant contact with his ardent fans by making sausages he could sell in supermarkets? He fell in love with the idea.

Some entrepreneurs consider new opportunities by investigating them. But most entrepreneurs start by seeing how far they can go before hitting the proverbial brick wall. Jordan, when he decides what he wants, goes at it with all his heart and might, brick walls be damned.

He began looking for a food factory that was for sale, affordable, and appropriate for making sausages. Because many entrepreneurs attempt food manufacturing, it's not difficult to find gleaming stainless steel kitchens that a failed entrepreneur needs to unload. Jordan bought a small, former catering kitchen, but he needed a quarter million dollars' worth of equipment to turn it into a sausage factory. Though his month-end bank balances continued to grow, they fell well short of a quarter million dollars. But because the Sausage Kingdom had been profitable from the day it opened, Jordan's bank manager introduced him to someone who was willing to buy the required manufacturing equipment and lease it back to Jordan for an affordable monthly fee.

Profitable entrepreneurs like Jordan can use de facto loans—that is, leases. They do not need venture capital (which I will treat more fully later), an uncommon form of financing that is unnecessarily expensive unless you need it to survive. Jordan didn't need it and he was well advised by his bank manager to lease the equipment rather than selling an ownership stake to strangers and bringing them into the business.

A quarter million dollars' worth of equipment transformed the catering kitchen into a plant that could produce two tons of frozen sausages a week. Jordan recruited a friend with little factory management experience to help supervise the project. Yet again, permits and inspections caused months of delays. Before the factory could start to sell its output, Jordan had to spend much of the money in his bank account to pay for these unanticipated expenses.

As he had suspected, the glorious reviews his sausages received from famous food critics, combined with the excitement his customers felt when he shared with them his aspiration of selling sausages in supermarkets, made it relatively easy to convince Trader Joe's, then just a regional specialty food market, to offer his sausages along with their other frozen foods. So when the FDA finally permitted Jordan to ship his sausages, he had a big customer to ship to. And once again, almost immediately in fact, the month-end bank balances grew.

On a Sunday afternoon, about the time Trader Joe's started selling Jody Maroni sausages, a man paying for a spicy Italian sausage combo handed Jordan a business card with a Los Angeles Dodgers baseball team logo on it. The man asked if he could come by sometime the following week and talk to Jordan about an opportunity. When the gentleman visited again, he asked Jordan if he'd be interested in operating a sausage concession at Dodger Stadium—the equivalent to being offered a chance at playing in the big leagues. If Jordan could do well at Dodger Stadium, he'd be able to market his brand nationally and open many more stands.

But concessions at sports venues are expensive to run and not very profitable. Worse, after yet another run-in with health inspectors, Jordan learned that at Dodger Stadium he would not have a kitchen, which meant he would have to serve pre-cooked sausages. Getting warmed-up sausages to taste great long after they've been cooked is an entirely different ball game, so to speak, than making them to order. Jordan's factory required some completely new types of expensive equipment, and he had to quickly learn the art and science of smoking meats in order to reformulate all the sausage flavors his fans expected. This turned out to be a great skill to master—over the next five years virtually every sport venue in Southern California contracted to offer Jody Maroni sausages.

While Jordan was launching his brand at Dodger Stadium, another gentleman stopped by his Venice Beach stand and handed him a card with a Universal Studios logo on it. Universal planned to build a sprawling new theme mall at the entrance to its popular Universal Studio Tours, not far from the LA suburb where Jordan grew up. The Studio was trying to populate its mall with interesting and fun shops and restaurants, and they wanted a Jody Maroni's Sausage Kingdom stand. The rent would be expensive, but Jordan was wowed by the presentation and felt proud that such a great brand wanted to be associated with his. He said yes on the spot. Fortunately, Universal would build the space for him, so Jordan wouldn't have to borrow any money to make it happen.

The stand, on the Universal Studios CityWalk, succeeded beyond Jordan and Universal management's most optimistic projections, doing even more business than the Venice Beach location. Jordan felt good about all this business and his growing renown, but he was stressed by myriad problems. Appliances and machines broke down and had to be fixed immediately. He worried about hiring the right people for his factory and sausage stands and whether they were being trained as he wanted. Could he find a good backup for his supplier of chicken, who was turning flakey on him and missing deliveries? Could he negotiate an affordable new lease on his Venice Beach stand? And could he still take the time off to go with his family to Hawaii? Universal Studios was opening a new attraction and was expecting record crowds at CityWalk, and Jordan's supervisor for that location was in the hospital recovering from a motorcycle accident. Fortunately, Jordan's factory manager was doing a good job acquiring more customers for the sausage factory while expanding capacity to accommodate the demand from CityWalk. That part of the business, at least, was in good hands.

Jordan remembers this time as the high point of his entrepreneurial career. He was making more money than he had ever dreamed. He had moved his family to a great home in one of his favorite LA suburbs. He was a local celebrity. He was able to help the causes he cared about. He loved his life and "selling joy."

Up to that point, Jordan's fantastic run had been powered by his innovative sausages and his larger-than-life King of Sausages persona and brand. He had never taken a business course, and he didn't know what a balance sheet was or why anyone would bother counting inventory. Jordan's alter ego, Jody, was a people person, and the business he ran, Jody Maroni's Sausage Kingdom, relied on people, not processes, for its success.

Entrepreneurship researchers glean many of their insights about entrepreneurship by looking at what happens to some group of founders over a five-year period. What are the characteristics of those who survived versus those who did not? Other researchers study entrepreneurs who succeed at a particular moment and try to distill the common elements in their experiences. Eight years after Jordan had invested his modest savings in a food stand on Venice Beach, he would be considered by any researcher using any common standard, or anyone that knew him for that matter, to be a model entrepreneur.

Managing a business that makes and offers over two dozen different types of sausage, some pre-cooked, some fresh, some frozen, at two high-turnover food stands, half a dozen sports venues, and several dozen supermarkets is much more complex than running a single food stand where you make fresh sausages in the kitchen every day. Not surprisingly, Jordan made some expensive inventory mistakes, resulting in meats and even frozen sausages spoiling because they were not consumed in a timely fashion. After wasting what just a few years before would have seemed like a life's savings on bad inventory, Jordan finally taught himself inventory management, installed inventory tracking software, and trained some of his staff to use the software and take responsibility for processing orders to buy meat, schedule production, and control the inventory.

Jordan, like many self-made entrepreneurs, wants to feel he understands all aspects of *his* business. "Teach me" is a phrase he used and uses when there is something important he doesn't understand. But like other self-made entrepreneurs, Jordan didn't and doesn't want to take the time out of his hectic schedule to learn anything he doesn't *for-sure* need to know. That's a mindset that means mistakes will be made, and that as the business grows those mistakes will increase in size and costliness.

There are many far less expensive ways to grow a business than learning through costly mistakes. But Jordan and many other entrepreneurs do not like conceding that they need help, particularly if they're already making enough money or growing fast enough to keep themselves, their investors, and their banks happy. Most entrepreneurs regard their mistakes as one-time events. So they single-mindedly continue to focus on the customers who are asking for more, failing to consider how to handle the growing complexities of their businesses.

All of Jordan's behavior—working to expand, learning on the job, toiling tirelessly to train his team—was rooted in his desire to prove to his dad that he could be more successful, that he could make sausages that tasted better than anything his dad had produced, and that he could be as compassionate a boss. It was important enough for him to bet his life savings on it when he could have spent the money on a more comfortable lifestyle.

The desire to impress his father also explains Jordan's refusal to ask for help from more experienced advisors and mentors. Many people, not just Jordan, want to feel as though they can do it all themselves, rather than feel as though they need assistance. Jordan didn't want to dilute the praise he would receive or the pride he'd feel for making it—he wanted to figure out what to do on his own.

As long as the business continued to perform well, Jordan had proved to his satisfaction that he could run a successful business and gain his father's admiration. He felt accomplished, contented—and a bit bored.

Now another of Jordan's strong inner desires came to the fore: his wish to be loved and admired for who he was. He felt deeply satisfied when people complimented him for his work, driving him to do all he could to get his product into the hands of as many people as possible. The praise also drove him to give money to causes he cared about. "I loved the populist aspect of my business," he says.

Wanting to be loved by scores of people, whether Jordan realized it or not, led him to focus on actions that could bring him more recognition, sometimes to the detriment of making more money or reducing the risk of losing money. He fervently wanted to accept the high-profile expansion opportunities that were presented to him, even if they might be financially risky. Looking too deeply into the problems and potential risks associated with expansion could get in the way of reaching more fans. Besides, Jordan felt he could solve any problem that popped up, whether he had anticipated it or not.

Getting Below the Surface

Jordan did not understand the true nature of his dreams—his motivations—until decades after he founded the Sausage Kingdom. The fact is that most aspiring entrepreneurs do not understand the real reason they want to endure the traumas of starting a business—to their detriment. There is always a public explanation that people tell themselves and others about why they chose to be an entrepreneur. And then there is almost always a private reason, a reason that is sometimes so private and emotional that the entrepreneur may not acknowledge it or even realize it, let alone admit it to anyone else. As it is true for all of us, it is always the private reasons that drive our actions, particularly our entrepreneurial actions.

To better understand reasons that work and don't work for being an entrepreneur, it helps to invoke some key insights and findings about motivation from the field of psychology. Motivations are the mental processes that lead to us to take action—*all* action. Fortunately, thousands of studies, led by many brilliant researchers, have yielded valuable insights on why we do what we do, and why we do some things with more determination, passion, and intensity than others.

More specifically, motivations are the mental processes that determine what actions we will take to improve our state-of-mind, i.e., our well-being. We act in order to get what we desire or to alleviate some fear or discomfort. All our actions, all of the time, are ultimately driven by selfish motives—to improve how we feel about ourselves and our status in the world.

We all have a long list of desires, while at the same time we try to steer clear of our fears and any discomfort. Motivation—how our brain decides to take the actions it takes—is therefore an extremely complex process. But we can say that generally, our brain prioritizes actions to eliminate profound fears before it takes any other actions to achieve a desire, even an intense desire like sex. Once fears are under control, our motivations then shift toward achieving our desires, whatever they may be. We differ greatly on the relative importance of our desires, each of us making our own trade-offs between immediate pleasure and long-term feelings of well-being and purpose.

To understand our real motivations for wanting to be an entrepreneur, we need to home in on what we selfishly want most. Only those particular desires or protections from specific fears can drive the consistent long-term actions that will make us successful and satisfied entrepreneurs. First, we need to understand the difference between implicit and explicit motivations.*

Explicit motivations are those of which you are conscious and can describe easily. They are created in the front part of your brain, where reasoning takes place. Examples of explicit motivations could be that "I want to lose weight," or, "I want to start a company." We naturally understand and can explain our explicit motivations. People with an explicit motivation to lose weight can explain how they plan to satisfy it—by hitting the gym more often or cutting down on soda, and so on.

Most of us are pretty bad at fulfilling our explicit motivations if we can't do it quickly. Relatively few people maintain their resolve to go to the gym or lay off their favorite sodas. Maintaining consistency in the actions we plan over long periods of time is hard. Other explicit motivations compete for our attention and take hold on a day-to-day basis. For example, we might put our plans for losing weight on hold in order to have a long and relaxing meal out with an old friend or to drink a pick-me-up soda before a big meeting. It is almost impossible to be constantly thinking about our need to go to the gym or to stop thinking about how much we need a sugary pick-me-up. Too many other things are more pressing. Indeed, our explicit motivations are poor predictors of the long-term actions we take.

The actions we take to achieve our profound desires or avoid our most primal fears spring from our *implicit* motivations, not our explicit motivations. Implicit motivations are stored in the more ancient and inaccessible parts of our brains, near the back. Our brain is wired so that the primal parts have direct control over *all* our actions. For evolutionary reasons, those primal parts are hard to access—overriding what the brain had been programmed through evolution to do quickly and effectively for survival would have been dangerous and risky for early humans. Furthermore, our ability to

---

* Implicit and explicit motivations are different than intrinsic and extrinsic motivations and often get confused. I describe the difference in the Notes section.

negotiate on our own behalf could be compromised if our rival could figure out our most important desires and fears. They could use such knowledge to manipulate us—so we've evolved such that we ourselves do not even understand much of what drives us to do what we do.

Fortunately, our brain protects us from feeling too badly about failing to achieve all our explicit motivations. We construct and believe in ex post facto explanations that make us feel good about why we acted as we did. "I've been way too busy to go to the gym and too stressed not to have that glass of wine with dinner. I'll *try* again when this big project is over."

Entrepreneurs, too, are good at rationalizing when they fail to take any of the many incredibly stressful actions required to get a company up and running, to grow it, and ultimately make it self-sustaining: "I really didn't need to make the calls to potential new customers to see if they liked the samples I sent them. I know they'll love my improvements and it's more important that I follow up on some action items today than to get this feedback."

What might be happening is that the entrepreneur feels scared to call strangers. The explicit desire/motivation to have the product succeed with real customers is weaker than the implicit motivation/fear of humiliation or rejection by strangers (a fear many of us have for evolutionary reasons). Clearly, Jordan would have fared far worse if he hadn't summoned the courage to project a highly extroverted Jody Maroni persona to the world. Jordan was willing to suffer potential embarrassment and rejection by passers-by to increase his chances of showing his dad that he could run his own business. Many entrepreneurs risk the future of their enterprises because they do not have the implicit motivations to deal with their very common fears.

Creating a business and making it valuable and self-sustaining is a long and stressful project and requires motivations strong enough to get past plenty of fear, fatigue, and unpleasantness. Explicit motivations won't get anyone there. Explicit motivations just create short-term projects that are eventually abandoned or superseded. Successful entrepreneurs, whether bedrock or high-risk, are driven by strong implicit motivations. Lack of understanding of those core motivations can cause real problems. An entrepreneur is in a much better position to succeed if they are honest with themselves about why they *need* to be successful as an entrepreneur, because then they have a chance to do something about their motivational mismatches before they cause too much damage.

A classic solution is to find a partner who has a very similar vision for a successful business and who has complementary skills and personality traits. This works occasionally, but most often ends problematically when the partners' visions for the business diverge. Entrepreneurs with access to lots of money can hire people to do what they do not want to do, but this is expensive and usually results in poor profitability that stresses the entrepreneur. Sometimes entrepreneurs find formal or informal coaches or paid therapists that help them find even stronger core motivations that they have buried or overlooked. Self-awareness and mindfulness exercises can enable such discoveries. (I describe some exercises for finding deeply buried motivations at the end of the chapter.)

Academics have spent a great deal of time studying the explicit reasons aspiring and successful entrepreneurs cite for having taken on the burden of starting an enterprise. But they have shied away from investigating the private and emotional reasons—a deeper level of understanding that's hard to get to for researchers and entrepreneurs. There is also a sense among academics that "clinical" analysis is an imperfect science to be avoided, foreclosing an understanding of the dynamics of entrepreneurship. Not wanting to get "personal" with the entrepreneurs we study is analogous to a doctor giving a physical exam to a fully clothed patient. The patient may feel more comfortable, but the doctor is unlikely to find the rash that is a symptom of a disease that could be treated before it becomes fatal.

It's Not Money

Entrepreneurs often cite making money as their motivation. Making money can be either an explicit motivation that disappears when something more important comes along, or it can be a proxy for a poorly understood implicit motivation. For example, your making money might impress your parents, make you feel superior to a rival, or alleviate the fear that your loved ones could ever go hungry. Making money can also serve as a socially acceptable proxy for some less socially acceptable implicit motivation, like craving power over others.

Josephine Esther Mentzer's life was transformed by an insult. She was probably seventeen at the time. Estella, as she was then called, was great at engaging customers in conversation at the beauty parlor where she worked. She had learned some practical sales skills at an even earlier age, when she worked for an aunt who owned a neighborhood store that sold clothing and other sundry items. Estella loved to sell and bragged to her family and friends that "[They] bought more when I waited on them." Even as a young girl, she was proud of what she had accomplished as one of seven children of an immigrant family in Queens. She was therefore stunned when a woman to whom she was tending reproached her for complimenting her on her pretty blouse and asking where she had bought it. "What difference could that possibly make?" the woman asked. "You could never afford it."

Estella always cited that moment as pivotal in her life. She decided to dedicate herself to proving to the world that she could become wealthier, more glamorous, and more socially superior than any other woman in Queens. It wasn't money per se that motivated her; it was transcending a lifestyle she felt was demeaning.

Working in a beauty parlor came naturally to Estella. From an early age, she had loved being made up, and she loved to make up others—to the annoyance of her father. As with most children living in homes of limited means, Estella was expected to work from an early age, first helping out on weekends in her family's small hardware store. When she was a teenager, she was able to negotiate working at her aunt's establishment instead, where she was called upon to do everything from keeping stock, to arranging the store windows and selling.

After the humiliating customer experience, Estella dreamt about another life, a life away from Queens. She realized that she wanted, *needed even*, the life of beauty and high society that she had glimpsed through the eyes of the customers she served in both the beauty parlor and at her aunt's store. Estella's friends and family had long sensed her ambition and repeatedly teased her that she would probably open her own beauty parlor, or maybe even a dress store. But at that pivotal moment, Estella wasn't so sure—she was thinking, "actress."

Shortly before the beauty parlor put-down, an uncle from Austria immigrated to Queens and set up a chemical company that produced embalming fluid, delousing powder, eczema ointment, as well as lip rouge, fragrances, and skin care products. Because of her love of makeup, her Uncle John invited Estella to help him out after school. While embalming fluid was of no interest whatsoever, she was enthralled with learning how to make beauty products. Watching Uncle John attentively, Estella learned how to formulate her own beauty treatments, which she then applied to her high school friends in the evenings, watching for their reactions.

As Estella was finishing high school, she was swept off her feet by a handsome and witty twenty-five-year-old with a similar first-generation immigrant background. Joseph Lauter (the "t" changed only later to a "d") had just started a business importing silk. Joe fit into Estella's vision of a more beautiful and luxurious life. After they married and she had a baby, Estella put her plans to change her life into action by selling the face and hand lotions her uncle produced. But selling her beauty products to friends and neighbors did not satisfy her—she wanted to change her life in a bigger way.

Unfortunately, Joe's business failed and he was frustrated by his inability to find a job and a place where he fit. Estella reproached Joe for his setbacks and worked even longer hours selling her uncle's products, further driving her apart from her husband. These and other frustrations built to the point that Estella and Joe separated and finally divorced. Estella took her four-year-old son and moved to Miami Beach, where she felt she could be more successful on her own. She set up shop selling her beauty products in the lobbies and beauty parlors of luxury hotels—to a higher-class clientele than she had access to in the beauty parlors of Queens. As a glamorous, independent young lady, Estella attracted the attention of several of the well-to-do single and divorced gentlemen that vacationed or spent winters in Miami.

Living in Miami gave Estella a further glimpse into the life she wanted, but it still did not provide her with the means. Selling beauty products one at a time wasn't going to make her rich enough to be respected by upper-class women. So she took yet another tack. She would borrow money from relatives and sell her own products on a much larger scale, making and packaging them exactly the way she wanted. She would move back to New York and remarry Joe, who badly wanted to reunite, provided he would agree to the terms she set: He would have to quit his job as a salesman and be her partner in running a beauty business. She would be its chief salesperson and spokesperson, while he would manage and run the back end. And to be a glamorous leader of a beauty business, she would adopt a new persona, taking on the more aristocratic sounding name of Estée Lauder for herself and her new company.

Estée worked tirelessly to make her company a success. She spent over two hundred days a year traveling to sell her products, to train her salespeople, and to promote her brand. Joe processed batches of cream, put them into beautiful-looking jars, and shipped out the orders from morning till late at night. He also looked after the kids, including a second son that arrived a year after they reunited. Their older son Leonard helped his father after school.

Estée was relentless, especially when trying to get her products into a specific department store. Several days a week for months she sat in the reception area of Saks Fifth Avenue, waiting to present and re-present her case for the prestigious department store to carry her line. Since the cosmetics buyer didn't see the need for adding another line of beauty products, Estée thought up ways to get women to ask for her products at the store. The scheme that finally landed her at Saks was hatched when she offered to provide the party favors for a charity luncheon that was held at the nearby Waldorf Astoria hotel.

In each of the three hundred bags of party favors she put a tube of her best and most expensive lipstick, a lipstick she specially packaged in beautiful metal tubes, something that was hard to find at that time. She told the ladies at the luncheon that they could get their refills at Saks. Within weeks, Saks agreed to carry the Estée Lauder line.

Estée grew her company one department store chain at a time and spent weeks on the floor training salesladies. Insisting that her products be presented in a certain way, she pioneered many of the cosmetics sales techniques still considered the best practices today, like free gifts with purchase and cosmeticians at the sales counters offering a free make-up session to try out her products. These techniques were effective for her when she sold her uncle's products in beauty parlors, and she wanted every Estée Lauder saleslady to follow them *exactly*. It worked, and the company grew year by year.

But Estée wanted her company to be bigger and grow faster than the slow and steady progress she was making. Fortunately, the business was profitable, and both Estée and Joe were frugal in those early years, doing everything themselves and hiring workers only when absolutely necessary. She used the money in the bank to develop what she felt would make the company much bigger. At the time, perfume was considered a luxury, something only well-to-do women wore daily. With her many years of dealing directly with customers from around the country, Estée believed that scented bath oil could be an affordable and popular product. Youth-Dew was a sensation. The company doubled in size in a year, transforming Estée Lauder into one of the leading beauty product companies in the world and delivering to Estée the lifestyle and prestige she so desperately desired. Wealth was merely the means to that end.

Why Ideas Aren't Enough

Neither Jordan nor Estée were motivated to become entrepreneurs by an idea. They each had a core motivation they needed to satisfy, and they each used personal skills to create companies that satisfied that need. They invented new ideas—new sausage tastes, new scents—but these ideas were, like money, just means to an end.

William Shockley did pursue his idea, a truly great one at that, but he loved his idea so much that he was unwilling to change it to make it commercially viable. He also loved his idea more than he valued his relationships with the smart people he had hired to work for him. But his love for his idea was ultimately not strong enough to make him want to change. Shockley's motivation was to always be recognized as the smartest scientist wherever he was. He fantasized that commercializing his world-changing transistor would further increase his scientific prestige. But when commercial realities conflicted with his scientific priorities, the commercial realities were set aside. Shockley's love of the transistor did make him a great scientist, but it could not make him even a mediocre entrepreneur.

Contrary to popular opinion, ideas—even great ones—cannot generate in a person the passion required to lead a successful and self-sustaining company. An idea can cause strong feelings in people, feelings strong enough to create the explicit motivations that could drive them to found a company. While the actual founding of a corporation is quick and pretty straightforward if you put your mind to it, growing it into something that produces value and self-sustainability is not. Just as passion as an explicit motivation for marriage fades with time, so does passion for an idea. Passion for an idea fades with the inevitable loss of control that comes when you realize that customers actually want something different, and it fades with the hardships that must be endured to make even some semblance of the idea a commercial reality.

Building an enterprise takes a long time and requires founders to overcome many challenges and hardships. "Identifying an opportunity" and "doing something fun, or interesting, or instructive" are not strong enough motivators. If you become an entrepreneur because it's fun, then you'll stop as soon as the fun fades. Similarly, if you found a company merely to learn how to be an entrepreneur, then you'll feel OK about making mistakes, resulting in a demoralized and unstable team and some pretty unhappy customers.

It is Always a Test

The world does not care if any of us become entrepreneurs, no matter what we may have previously accomplished. Becoming an entrepreneur is ultimately a personal, selfish decision. While we may describe our motivations for starting our own enterprise differently, we are all ultimately subjecting ourselves to a test: "Am I worthy of the status I seek?" We may make or lose money on our startup, but far more important than the money is how the experience changes what we think of ourselves and whether we proved what we set out to prove. And we must always prove something to satisfy our core implicit motivations. *Core motivations always come with a test—they are two sides to the same coin. Passing the test is how you know you've achieved your core motivation.*

While you do not get to explicitly choose your core motivations, you can choose whether you want to take the entrepreneurial test. Most people never test themselves; they either are not self-aware enough, and/or may be too scared to fail. All of our entrepreneurial role models endured self-imposed tests, but it's likely that none of them understood the deep roots of their tests: being a better business person than their father, being more socially elite than anyone else in Queens, or being the best scientist of their age.

Whether or not you realize why you're doing what you're doing, you will stand accountable for making sure you've giving yourself the correct test, and that you test yourself correctly. William Shockley did not set the right test for himself. Somebody who aspires to be acknowledged as the best scientist on the planet should not be trying to produce products to sell. Jordan, once his Jody Maroni's Sausage Kingdom was larger and more successful than his dad's butcher shop, set himself a new test: being loved by the greatest number of people possible. The test of entrepreneurial success can be well aligned with this core motivation, as entrepreneurship is focused on making large numbers of people happy and getting money in return. But Jordan did not test himself correctly in two ways. First, he didn't care enough about getting the money in return, and launched into ventures without enough analysis on potential issues that could prevent his investment yielding a decent return. Second, as we'll come to understand later in the book, Jordan let others have too much leeway in delivering the Jody Maroni "joy" (i.e., happiness) to his customers, which diluted the experience and ultimately disappointed customers.

Getting at the Real Why

The experience of being an entrepreneur does not turn out as expected for most who try. The majority of people don't get very far and give up. Less than half who actually start a company survive five years. And only a small fraction of those who remain in business meet their explicit objectives for having started the business in the first place. Other than William Shockley, this book profiles entrepreneurs with core motivations adequately strong and well aligned to power them to success, whether or not they could accurately describe those motivations when they launched their venture.

A strong "why," a strong core motivation, is always present with great entrepreneurs, but rarely with entrepreneurs who muddle through. Uncovering and understanding those deeper motives is the first step toward succeeding as an entrepreneur or discovering that you are not cut out for its punishing demands—the personal sacrifices, inevitable setbacks, relentless work, crushing time pressure, financial uncertainty, and sleepless nights faced by 99 percent of entrepreneurs. You need to know whether your motivations are strong enough to carry you through an experience that can certainly be exhilarating, but also exhausting, calling on your deepest reserves of personal strength. You need to understand what test you must pass.

You could, of course, invest a great deal of time and money in therapy, but most ordinary entrepreneurs have little time or money for that. Besides, you don't necessarily need to resolve whatever issues underlie your motives; you only need to know what those motives are so that you can guard against their excesses. You can start by undertaking a simple exercise that I often use with aspiring entrepreneurs and students.

First, ask yourself why you want to be an entrepreneur. You've probably answered this question many times before, either for yourself or friends and family, and you've also likely come up with the usual platitudes. Nevertheless, write them down. Then ask and answer some deeper and far more specific questions:

- *What fundamental desire or fear would success as an entrepreneur satisfy?* This question, too, produces some answers that recur over and over. For example, many people fear being humiliated in the eyes of a parent or rival. Others discover that they have a deep drive for power or status, or to be listened to. They are deeply motivated by the wish to have no one ever telling them what to do, or to have a group of people become highly dependent on them. Many other people's deepest motives are driven by challenging childhoods—economic hardship, for example, or an alcoholic or abusive parent—and their deepest wish is to never again feel the way those challenges made them feel back then. Still, others have had their deepest motives formed by any of the many possible permutations of family dynamics.
- *What makes me so mad that I can't control myself?* Perhaps there are certain names or labels that make you flash into anger. Someone casually says something that suggests you're lazy or inconsequential and you erupt. That eruption is an indicator that you're getting close to a core motivation you don't fully understand. Suppose, for example, that you're infuriated when what you regard as your unfailingly diplomatic touch is seen by someone else as toadying or spinelessness. Your anger is out of all proportion to the offense. Why? Perhaps as a child, you were the peacemaker in a highly dysfunctional family, a valuable role that you are constantly driven to recapture.

Maybe there is some other deep reason. But the point is that your hair-triggers can tell you a lot about yourself, if you're willing to pursue the clues they provide.

- *What made me happiest when I was child?* Like anger, joy can point us toward our deepest motives. But if you ask people a generic question about what makes them happy, they will either name transitory things like a good meal, or long-term experiences like enduring relationships, family life, or spiritual satisfaction. Localize the question to childhood, however, and the indelible memory of specific situations that made you deeply happy and you can begin to hone in on highly specific motives. Maybe it's as simple as constantly wanting to recapture the feeling you had when you made the winning goal in an important soccer game. Or perhaps it is as complicated as the enormous relief you felt when your parents reconciled after a trial separation. But whatever it is, it will get you closer to uncovering what really drives you.

- *What's the test I need to pass?* It is critical that passing this test will give you a sense of well-being. The test will likely be tied to proving your self-worth and your ability to act autonomously.

- *How would I feel if I failed?* If the answer is, "as long as I felt I had given it my best, I could accept failure," then the chances are your motivation is not strong enough. The psychological consequences of failure must be significant enough to drive you to overcome, without hesitation, the hardships and traumas you will encounter. There must be nothing that is more important; otherwise you are likely to abandon the effort when the going gets really tough. And it's far better to find that out about yourself before you lose money, waste precious years of your life, and destroy a lot of valued relationships along the way. That doesn't mean you shouldn't join a startup where you can exercise skills you're proud of in exchange for some kind of payback. It just means that you probably shouldn't be the leading founder.

- *Would someone whose wisdom and guidance I value see my motives the same way I do?* Once you have examined and recorded what you believe motivates you, seek out a trusted advisor, someone who knows you well, who has seen you in action in a variety of situations, *who can be counted on for candor*, and is willing to ask probing questions. Do their perceptions about what really drives you align with yours? If not, then revisit your self-questioning and try to resolve the difference.

As you will understand when you complete this exercise in self-discovery, your strongest motivations arise from the things that are the source of your happiness or that protect you from primal fears. You therefore inevitably find you have a totally selfish reason for wanting to be an entrepreneur. There is no shame in that, and there is much to be gained by identifying it and admitting to being selfish. If you don't acknowledge it, you're likely to feel ambivalent about success and, as a result, sabotage yourself.

Does that mean you should adopt a "looking-out-for-number-one" philosophy and steamroll anybody who gets in your way? No, just the opposite. The most challenging requirement for entrepreneurial success is the constant need to change your leadership style as your business grows and changes.* Without a powerful motivation, you will not make the required changes within yourself, nor will you master the tricky balance of being selfish enough to be a driven entrepreneur and selfless enough to lead the people that sign up to help you achieve your dream.

---

* This will be discussed in great depth in the chapter "How Much."

Why Not

Wanting to see your idea become a reality is not a good reason to become an entrepreneur. If you have a good idea then patent it and license it to someone who has a selfish need to run a company—which may or may not be you.

Wanting to do something interesting or fun is not an enduring enough reason to become an entrepreneur. Go find a fun and interesting job instead.

Wanting to learn is not a good enough reason to become an entrepreneur. Go find a job or take a class that'll teach you what you want to learn.

You need a good reason to want to be an entrepreneur—and an enduring one, because succeeding will take a lot of time and inflict significant hardships.

You need a really selfish reason for being an entrepreneur because you will need to make the world want what you have to give it. Your selfishness will drive you to change, to care about your customers and teammates, and to take the steps required to get your vision accepted by others.

You must want to test yourself. That's the only way you can get good enough to feel satisfied about yourself as an entrepreneur. It's also the only way you can stay good enough to keep your customers happy.

With the self-awareness of what you really want comes the corresponding test of whether or not you can get it. Once armed with the knowledge of how and why you need to test yourself, you then have to choose whether a bedrock or high-risk strategy is best suited for you. High-risk entrepreneurship is capable of most expeditiously resolving whether you can pass your test, so let's understand what that entails.

CHAPTER 5

WHAT IF

What if you always dreamed of going to Mars, and somebody believed in you so much that they offered to finance your rocket ship? Wouldn't that be cool? Today, Jeff Bezos is spending hundreds of millions of dollars to build the rockets and the support organizations to enable him to travel to Mars. He is spending almost entirely his own money to finance his expedition because this is a project he cares about personally. When it comes to his space dreams, Jeff is a bedrock entrepreneur. Not wanting to rely on strangers or feel pressure to meet externally imposed performance or financial milestones, he is building his space company slowly and steadily.

But Jeff Bezos started as a high-risk entrepreneur. He now has the money to finance Mars missions only because he was able to get savvy people to invest millions into his startup and then more investors to buy hundreds of millions of the shares of Amazon once it went public. Investor demand for these shares has, in turn, made his shares worth tens of billions of dollars. Jeff is a thoughtful and strategic entrepreneur who understands exactly when to be high-risk and when to be bedrock.

Audacious dreams that you cannot finance and staff completely yourself require a high-risk entrepreneurial mindset. To really understand this mindset, you need to understand the Silicon Valley investment model and the people who run the system that enables high-risk entrepreneurship. And, yes, Silicon Valley is the proverbial home of high-risk entrepreneurship. The Silicon Valley model can be summarized as, "shoot for the moon and use other people's money."

High-risk entrepreneurs play a disproportionately important role in job and wealth creation; less than a fraction of a percent of all startups create slightly less than 10 percent of all the wealth generated by startups. With the support of venture capitalists (VCs), whether or not they're located in Silicon Valley, high-risk entrepreneurs launch companies that grow faster than an average company and are more likely to go public. Entrepreneurs backed by wealthy and experienced venture capitalists enjoy immense competitive advantages in business sectors where economies of scale or network effects dominate cost structures and/or customer acceptance. In business sectors where long-term studies are required to get regulatory approvals (like biotech), VC backing is virtually required to succeed. Without the Silicon Valley investment model, the United States would not be the world leader in enterprise software, semiconductors, social media, biotech, and e-commerce. The leading businesses in these essential industries all started as audacious dreams.

But not all businesses, and not all audacious dreams, find favor or gain competitive advantage from using the Silicon Valley model. Every entrepreneur needs to be able to decide for him or herself if their dreams need the support and favor of the highly experienced, busy, focused, and wealth-driven VCs. So, let's understand what's expected of high-risk entrepreneurs—and start by understanding why the fate of all high-risk entrepreneurs with audacious dreams that need or want the support of the venture capital community will almost certainly be determined on a Monday.

The Importance of Mondays

The entire field of venture capital works in almost perfect synchronization. It's a ritual. On Monday, almost all of the venture capital world holds "partners meetings" to decide the fates of thousands of entrepreneurs—both aspiring entrepreneurs looking for money, and existing entrepreneurs operating their enterprises under the watchful eye of one or more partners of the firm.

The meeting style differs from firm to firm. Some are formal, some informal; some include only partners in the meeting and some invite their senior analysts. The manner in which the meeting is conducted depends on the preference of the person or persons calling the shots at the firm. VC firms have cultures just like any other business. In fact, venture capital firms are just businesses started by entrepreneurs.

On Monday morning, usually not too early, the senior partner in the firm calls the meeting to order: "OK, let's get started." The agenda is virtually the same every week: review potential new investments, then review the performance of the companies in their portfolio, then discuss fundraising (which is almost always happening in successful firms), and finally discuss administrative matters such as hiring and firing within the firm, or planning events like the annual partners retreat or the annual limited partners meeting. The meeting can take most of the day.

Usually, before each meeting, a packet of information gets distributed to the partners. It includes some summary information about how the VC firm is running, and detailed information on any of the companies that the partners will be discussing for possible investment.

Each firm feels it has its own competitive advantage in how they find the companies they want to invest in, and it is important to the firm that they maintain this competitive advantage. One of the important metrics of venture capital is termed "deal flow"—an indication of the quantity and quality of the potential investments the firm has reviewed. If any senior partner senses a problem with deal flow then that becomes the first topic discussed on Monday morning.

Firms that are willing to invest in early-stage startups care about the quantity and quality of the startup deals they've been asked to invest in. An early-stage VC needs to see a large quantity of proposals for early-stage startups because the firm will fund only a fraction of the deals they look at—sometimes as few as one in a thousand. So if they want to fund six deals a year, then they need to consider as many as 500 proposals a month.

VC firms also want to feel they are receiving high-quality proposals, so they often track how the proposals came to them. Did a proposal come in from another VC firm they respect, a firm asking them to co-invest? (That's very high quality.) Did it come through a junior partner who has contacts with the business school faculty at her alma mater (medium quality), or was it received from a stranger over the Internet (poor quality)?

The partners of early-stage firms do not discuss the hundreds of pitch decks and information packets they receive.* Instead, each firm has a process for reviewing the information of the companies they've been solicited to invest in. The process usually starts with one of the junior analysts looking over the submissions, throwing away almost all of them, and creating a single-page summary consisting of the who, what, where, and how much of the few proposals he or she thinks their junior partner supervisor would like to see. After reading the one-page summaries, the junior partner may meet with one of the senior partners to discuss the firm's potential interest in one or more of the business plans the young analyst summarized. If the senior partner is interested, then the junior and senior partner will brain-

---

* In recent years the pitch deck with supporting information has replaced the business plan as the way entrepreneurs introduce their ideas and their teams to potential investors.

storm additional information they might want to know, and will then call the entrepreneur(s) who submitted the information. If the entrepreneurs on the call sound like they have a deep understanding of their moneymaking idea, they will then be invited to visit the VC firm to present their idea and their team in person.

In understanding how Silicon Valley super-sized dreams are made, you also need to realize that only about a third of venture capital firms actually invest in startups. Early stage investing is a specialty; most VC firms specialize in "growth investing." Two-thirds of all venture investment dollars go into more mature startups. Most VCs think it is too risky to invest in high-risk entrepreneurs with dreams. In order to deliver a good return to their investors, most VCs prefer to invest in young, perhaps not yet profitable companies, with already established products and happy customers, that are looking for additional investment in order to grow faster. In other words, most VCs invest in growth—not dreams. If you're just getting going, then you need to pitch your idea and your team to an early stage VC firm.

The opportunity for a venture capital firm to invest in these more mature startups, particularly those considered already successful and headed toward an IPO or "big exit," comes from having a reputation as a "hot" firm that has invested in other super-successful startups, and from having a personal relationship with the founders. On Monday mornings, senior partners share stories of how they met or socialized with founders and CEOs of "hot" startups and when and whether they think their firm will be invited to invest.

Almost all VCs that specialize in investing in more mature startups hire several young, extroverted Ivy League or business school graduates to make dozens of calls every day to CEOs of startups they have recently learned about. They try to get the CEO on the phone to flatter him or her with praise that the VC firm has been impressed with what the startup has accomplished. The young analyst's mission is to try and get beyond the startup's publicity and hype and obtain enough financial information to determine whether the startup has "momentum" (i.e., is growing fast). If the startup is growing fast enough, then the young analyst will brief a senior partner, who may bring the company and the financial information they've received to the attention of the partnership.

After all the tales of socializing, and assuming there are no issues with deal flow, the first official agenda item of Monday partner meetings is to discuss which of the interesting companies that the firm recently discovered—early stage or more mature—might be worthy of an investment. The partners review the potential opportunities and risks associated with a theoretical investment in each company presented. For those companies that could be an interesting investment, the firm makes plans to send a senior partner, along with a junior partner and maybe an analyst, to go visit and get an in-depth "feel" for the entrepreneur, the team, and the opportunity. The senior and junior partners will also be expected to call people they know in the general business area of the company they're investigating. If the company is in the information business, they might call up a person like me and ask, "Based on your experience, what issues would a company that wants to collect information on the tech world using social media encounter?" If they like what they see and hear from their visit and from their calls to people like me, they will report back to the partners with a specific recommendation. At the next partners meeting, they may be asked to get even more information, told not to proceed any further, or the partners may vote to give the senior partner permission to draft a Term Sheet for an amount of money the partnership would be willing to invest at a specific valuation.

The Term Sheet outlines the proposed terms of a potential investment the VC firm might make in the company. It is not a binding offer; it is a basis for further discussion and negotiation. Even after the Term Sheet is agreed on, it is still subject to negotiations over dozens of details, conducted between the lawyers for the company and the VC firm, as well as an additional investigation (called due diligence) into the company, its products, its finances, its top employees, as well as the company's customers, potential customers, partners, and suppliers. Assuming all this additional investigation and negotiation turns out satisfactorily for both parties, then a thick set of documents is signed by all parties, and money is handed over to the startup.

In debating whether to make an offer to invest ("deliver a Term Sheet"), the partnership considers if they should make a bet. No matter how much research and due diligence a VC firm does on any given entrepreneur and startup, they cannot tell if the company will be successful enough to make the investment worthwhile—a dilemma which necessitates the complex debates about how well the firm thinks they understand the risks relative to how much wealth might be created. They also debate how much to invest and what percentage ownership of the new company they want. The partners will then discuss what restrictions and constraints they will place on the entrepreneur: how much they will let him or her invest without asking permission, whom he can unilaterally hire, whether he can sign a lease, the size of the order he can place with his suppliers, or how large a contract he can sign. For some of these decisions the entrepreneur will be required to get the permission of the Board of Directors; for other decisions, the venture capital firm may reserve veto rights.

After an investment is made, the senior partner who worked on the deal is assigned responsibility for the investment and must report on the progress of the company at partners meetings. Such updates are typically the second item on the agenda of these meetings. The updates include a summary of the company's latest financial results, but more importantly, from the partners' point of view, they also include an assessment of what could be done to "help" the company do better and become more valuable. The discussion about how to help a company takes on a different tone depending on whether it's an early-stage or growth-stage VC. Partners at early-stage VCs will discuss whether they think the original premise for the company is still valid based upon the latest information they received on product testing or customer reaction. Their discussion centers around the changes they think management should make: "The prototype they sent to IBM for qualification failed testing, I think we need to insist they hire an experienced quality engineer to get better control over their supply chain."

If you're listening to a partners meeting at a growth-stage VC, you might hear more comments about the quality of the leadership than about the product—comments along the lines of, "The company is falling behind on their plans to introduce their improved product. I don't think the head of engineering really understands the magnitude of the challenge—he doesn't have the experience to manage a team of fifteen engineers. The CEO is too easy on him because he's not a software guy and is not confident in pressing for change. I think we need to insist that John (the CEO) start a search for a new VP of engineering, and if he resists then we need to think about replacing him."

You might also hear a senior partner at a growth-stage VC firm start another discussion along these lines: "*My* company is doing well but could be doing better. I am worried that their major competitor just got funded with another $50 million. They could start taking our clients away by offering rebates, which could slow our growth rate. I have talked to the CEO about my concerns but she thinks that her better customer service will make such a competitive attack a waste of money. I think this shows overconfidence and a lack of vision. I have privately discussed this with the other investors on the board and they're equally concerned. I haven't broached the subject of replacing the CEO with them but I plan to do that this week. I'm sensitive to how traumatic that change could be, but keeping her as CEO could mean the difference between the company being worth only $50 million rather than being worth $1 billion."

Because growth-stage VCs invest only in already fast-growing (but perhaps not yet profitable) companies, their focus is on how well the company's leadership team is growing the business. They're not focused as much as early-stage VCs on the viability of the product. It's when early-stage VCs bring in the bigger, growth-stage VC firms that the founder's job becomes at risk. Research has shown that the more successful a venture-backed startup, the more likely the venture capital firm is to try to replace the founder.

Near the end of this part of the agenda, the partners focus on investments that they are close to "exiting"—by selling the company or taking it public. The partners all want updates on where the firm's portfolio companies stand relative to the "process" of offering a company for sale, or of creating a structure and environment where a company's stock can be sold on public markets. They want to know from one another, "Where are you on choosing your investment banker?" "When will the pitch book (or prospectus, in case of an IPO) be done?" "Are they going to beat their numbers this quarter relative to the baseline projections used for our valuations?"

The partners are all focused on doing whatever they can to maximize the money they receive from selling or IPO-ing their portfolio of companies. Without successful exits, VC firms cannot survive, junior partners cannot get promoted, and senior partners can't make the big money they aspire to. The subject of exits therefore gets a great deal of their attention. Venture capital partners feel anxious when there are none to discuss.

After the partners debate how to best position the companies they plan to sell or IPO, VC firms move on to discuss fundraising. Almost all venture capital firms operate as a collection of ten-year partnerships. Each ten-year partnership controlled by the venture capital firm represents an independent business that has been created with the sole purpose of buying shares in startups and other private businesses. The partners in a venture capital firm are the "general" partners of these legal partnerships and get paid by all the other investors in the fund (investors are legally "limited" partners, i.e. silent partners) to invest the partnership's funds in such a way that before ten years has elapsed, each investor gets back *much* more money.

Of the money invested in the partnership, the VC partners are usually allowed to spend 2 percent each year on their own salaries and expenses, sometimes reduced to 1.5 percent after five years. So over the ten-year life of the partnership, the venture capital partners spend 18 to 20 percent of the original investment to pay, support, and house themselves, and only around 80 percent of the limited partners' original investment is used to invest in startups and other private companies. On top of the salaries and expense reimbursements paid by the investors, VC partners are also paid a bonus of 20 percent of all the profits made by the partnership. This can be a considerable sum of money for a successful venture partner. This compensation plan is known as the "two-and-twenty" model, and it generally applies to the functioning of venture capital firms, as well as to private equity and hedge funds.

The formula for how venture capitalists are compensated has significant implications for entrepreneurs who seek to score venture capital funding. It drives VCs to look for entrepreneurs who want to do something big, who want to "shoot for the moon." Very roughly, if a venture partnership has been given $100 million by its limited partners to invest over ten years—a small fund by today's standards—then it will look to invest in companies where it thinks a $5 to $7 million investment on their part can grow to be worth $50 to $70 million in five years or so. A $100 million VC fund gets $2 million a year to pay salaries and rent a nice office, as well as to pay for expert opinions, sundry legal fees (the startups themselves often agree to reimburse VCs for all or part of their legal fees), limited partners meetings, and dinners with other VCs. That translates into a fund this size having only a couple of partners, some supporting analysts, a couple of personal assistants, and a receptionist. A firm with staffing like that has the bandwidth to invest its $80 million (after 18 to 20 percent of the initial $100 million is allocated to expenses) in maybe fifteen companies. When divided up, this yields a target investment of $5 to $7 million per company.

Since most companies any VC invests in do not achieve their long-term goals despite the significant up-front analysis and due diligence, the firm needs their companies that do succeed to succeed big. In shooting for 10X returns with individual companies, the VC firm actually aspires to return to their investors about three times their original investment when the partnership dissolves in ten years. 3X equates to slightly less than a 12 percent compound annual return—a decent return for an investor who parts with their money for ten years with no guarantees.* 3X is what a VC firm needs to actually return to be considered "in the game."

---

* Because VCs often do not require all the money committed by their investors to be deposited immediately, actual returns can be slightly higher. For example, if a VC waited two years to call for the funds to

The implication of hundred million dollar VC firms looking to make 15 investments in the range of 5 to 7 million, each investment with the potential of being worth 10X what they invested, is that hundred million dollar VC firms only want to invest in companies that are going to be worth in excess of $100 million dollars in a few years time (very roughly, the VC will own only a portion of the company, so they will want their fraction of ownership to be worth $50 to $70 million). Unless an entrepreneur has a credible plan to create a business that can be quickly sold for $100 million, he's unlikely to find venture capital backing from even a small, early-stage VC firm.

Today's most famous VCs manage funds with at least a billion dollars to invest, meaning their targets are ten times the numbers associated with a $100 million fund. That is why today's brand name venture capitalists are interested in businesses that can grow to be worth over a billion dollars very quickly. Venture capital only makes sense for entrepreneurs aspiring to build big companies quickly, hence the adage, "Shoot for the moon and use other people's money."

Even though each partnership has ten years to operate, VC partners are on an almost constant fundraising treadmill. Almost all VC partnerships are structured so that the general partners can invest funds only in "new" companies in the first five years, with the requirement that the second five years be focused on optimizing the performance of the companies in which the partnership originally invested. The mantra is, "Five years of planting seeds, five years of harvesting." So if a VC firm isn't raising a new fund within three years of the launch of their last fund (experienced partners expect fundraising to take at least a year and a half), they will find themselves at the end of year five with no money for planting seeds—making them no longer a player. Fundraising strategy and results are therefore discussions that occur consistently in the partner meetings of the most successful VC firms, usually at the end.

---

be deposited and returned 3 times that amount 8 years later, it would equate to a modestly higher annual return of 14.7 percent.

As you might imagine, how a group of partners goes about balancing all these different factors relative to the companies they invest in can get complicated. Virtually no startup performs as the partnership expected when they make their initial investment. A few will do better than anticipated, but the overwhelming majority of startups stumble or hit some unanticipated constraint. While most of the companies with venture capital investments will ultimately make a profit, their unspectacular profitability and unimpressive growth make these companies difficult to sell. Every decision about how to increase the value of the companies they own can have a huge impact on the careers and pocketbooks of VC partners.

The truth is that the majority of venture capital funds fail to return to their investors more cash than was originally invested a decade or more before. VCs are secretive about their returns. The venture capital trade association sometimes discusses numbers that point to average returns for their industry in the 14 percent range, but these numbers are not tied to the actual cash returned to the investors. The Kauffman Foundation, a large non-profit dedicated to fostering entrepreneurship, even wrote a white paper about the disappointing endowment returns they received from their own limited partner VC investments. These reported financial returns include estimates of the value a VC firm feels it will eventually receive for their shares in all the companies that remain unsold. Investors often receive only a fraction of the estimated value of "zombies"—slow-growth, marginally profitable enterprises that continue to operate and are hard to sell. And once the VC does manage to sell them, it often takes years for the checks to show up in investors' mailboxes.* In reality, at the end of ten years, most venture capital firms return less than a compounded 13 percent ROI. After deducting the fees and bonuses

---

* Often to sell a mature marginally profitable firm with risky growth prospects the VC firm must agree that a large fraction of the sales price of the company depends upon future results, thereby delaying their receipt of any cash for years and making the amount of money received an unknown variable. These deals are called "earn-outs."

paid to the general partners, many more VCs do much worse. Few venture capitalists make the large returns they dream about, and most VCs raise money only once, going out of business when their first fund winds down a dozen or more years after being launched.

Venture capitalists are high-risk entrepreneurs themselves. That makes the few consistently successful VCs great partners for the high-risk entrepreneurs that they invest in. These VCs understand how to identify, prioritize, and control risk, and ultimately how to reduce and eliminate risk in businesses.

We need to be clear here, because *all VCs invest in businesses and not entrepreneurs*, no matter what they say. The shares the VCs own represent ownership of the company and not of the entrepreneur. Early-stage VC investors *do* care about the teams they invest in. They feel the momentum and passion behind an idea will likely dissipate if they fire whomever leads product development, so they are just as likely to shut down a company as they are to find new leadership. Once a company gains traction and has accepted money from growth-stage VCs, the entrepreneur will be fired if and when the VC feels the company could do better without him or her.* It is the share price of the companies they have invested in that determines the priorities of all successful VCs. Entrepreneurs are strictly a VC's means to achieve their desired end.

The data on venture capital investment surprises most people. As of 2015, there were 718 active venture capital firms in the United States. Only 238 of these firms invest in early-stage startups; the rest invest almost exclusively in companies that already have established customers and products but may not yet be profitable. The number of entrepreneurs and their companies that received venture capital in 2015 to help fund their initial product development was 147. This number has been dropping for five years straight and is at a twenty-year low. And this is at a time when interest in high-risk entrepreneurship is close to or at an all-time high. We do not know

---

* Often the fired founder is offered an honorary title to save face.

how many entrepreneurs aspire to use outside funding from strangers to help get their product launched, but the number certainly exceeds 100,000. Clearly, only a tiny fraction of these entrepreneurs will ever succeed as high-risk entrepreneurs.

From 1995 through 2015, VCs have invested in a total of 28,516 companies, an average of 1,358 new companies per year. In 2015, VCs invested in 1,444 companies that had not yet received any VC funds, a number that has changed little in the past twenty years. Venture capital is not a high-growth business—but it is volatile. This is not so surprising if we look at what has happened to those 28,516 companies that have received VC money since 1995. Over that time, slightly more than 2000 VC-backed companies have gone public on US stock exchanges. (Some of these companies may have received their first VC investment before 1995, so this number over-counts the number of IPOs of companies who received investments from 1995 onwards). Another 7,535 VC-backed companies were sold or merged with other companies during this same period. A little over a quarter of these mergers or sales were at a loss. Again, these numbers somewhat over-count the exact quantity of post-1995 VC investments that resulted in a sale of the company. That leaves at least 19,000 VC-backed companies, two-thirds of the twenty-year total, either remaining in VC portfolios or shutting down. The fact that VCs have invested in slightly less than 13,000 companies in the past ten years (the aspirational maximum of the time a VC targets for owning shares in any given company) implies that from 1995 and 2005 approximately 6,000 companies backed by VCs were shut down—more than 38 percent of the total funded during that time. The numbers also imply that many VC-backed companies take over ten years to exit.

Angel Dreams

There are also angel investors. Angel investors seek to invest their own money in startups. There are an estimated 300,000 angel investors in the United States. In 2015, angel investors invested $24.6 billion in 71,100 startups and small businesses, which works out to an average of about $346,000 of angel investment in each company. Because angel investors often invest in a company with other angels,* the actual check size for any single angel investor is usually much lower—typically closer to $50,000. On rare occasions the checks can be bigger. I know a wealthy angel with $6 million invested in just one company, but the angel's former chief technology officer runs the company—there are always special circumstances associated with angel investors writing large checks.

In aggregate, angel investors invest just as much money as VCs in startups, but in smaller amounts to many more companies. Angel investors fire founders infrequently, but they are often even more involved in helping the company. This extra "help" may or may not be appreciated by the entrepreneur. Just as with VCs, most angel investors do a poor job of investing their money, while a few angels do a great job and enjoy phenomenal returns on their money.

Angel investors can therefore be problematic for bedrock entrepreneurs who want to remain independent. Angel investors want their money back, so taking an investment from an angel investor sets an expectation that the company will be sold in three to seven years, even if angel investors wind up owning much less than 50 percent of the shares.

Angel investment can be a great source of initial capital, but high-risk entrepreneurs cannot rely on angel funding except to get started. Angel investors fill in the gap that VCs have created in not wanting to risk their money on startups that are not already established. Because angels don't write big checks, high-risk entrepreneurs are still faced with the challenge of being one of the approximately 1,400 companies a year VCs choose to start supporting. Angel inves-

---

* Angel investors often form formal investment clubs within their local area and thereby compare notes and ideas about companies before one or more angels decide to invest together.

tors are not an alternate path of funding for high-risk entrepreneurs; they are a bridge.

The same holds true for *accelerators*. Accelerators take a small ownership in companies started by teams (never individuals) in return for putting up to fifty teams at a time through a ten- to twelve-week program of mentorship, education, and networking. In the United States, there are about 300 accelerators, operated mostly by investors hoping to make large amounts of money from these ventures. Accelerators mentor and train over 4,000 teams, including more than 12,000 aspiring entrepreneurs, in their programs each year.

Accelerator owners are entrepreneurs (mostly bedrock as they usually invest their own money!). Accelerators can be profitable businesses by investing small sums—often in the range of twenty-five to a hundred thousand dollars per team—in a large number of start-ups.* To show a positive return, accelerators need only a few of these companies to eventually sell for modest sums. Because accelerator owners want to get their money back quickly, they nurture teams of high-risk entrepreneurs they think have a decent chance of growing fast. All accelerators are selective, and the best ones are highly selective, choosing less than one in ten of their applicants; after all, the accelerators want to make money. Accelerators are therefore hotbeds of high-risk entrepreneurs. Since most accelerators have only been around for a few years the overwhelming majority of accelerators have not yet generated any positive cash flow.

Interestingly, a number of large established companies recently started hosting accelerators with the objective of identifying new product ideas that they can keep track of and eventually own. Many universities also run accelerators to help teach students about entrepreneurship, and they usually do not take any ownership in their student companies. (Princeton runs a summer accelerator.) These

---

* Hence the adage, "VCs shoot rifles, angels handguns, and accelerators shotguns."

non-quick-hit accelerators can be good deals for both aspiring bedrock and high-risk entrepreneurs, if they can get in.

While accelerators help thousands of teams a year explore their entrepreneurial potential, these teams, when they've graduated, nonetheless still need to find investors in order to survive. Every accelerator invites groups of angel investors, and VCs if the accelerator is famous, to their "demo day" graduation ceremonies with the hope that some of the newly accelerated companies will get funded. A small number of accelerated companies from the top dozen most highly regarded programs (i.e., the top 2.5 percent accelerators) receive funding by VCs—Airbnb and Dropbox most famously.

But even with the help of accelerators and angel investors, there still are only about 1,400 companies each year founded by high-risk entrepreneurs that get the funding they need to reach their full potential. While this number has not changed much in twenty years, the number of high-risk entrepreneurs has. More high-risk entrepreneurs present their ideas to a growing number of angel investors, more apply to a growing number of accelerators, more send pitch decks to VCs, and more aspiring entrepreneurs than ever read and dream about famous high-risk entrepreneurs. Our society is leading a lot of proverbial entrepreneurial lambs to slaughter.

The implication is clear. *High-risk entrepreneurs must understand how to please VCs in order to get funded and then to keep their jobs.* Few entrepreneurs I meet understand this.

Bedrock entrepreneurs can have high aspirations, too. Sam Walton built what is today the largest company on the planet using bedrock values and bedrock financing. He borrowed money to build his companies from 1945 to 1970, when Wal-Mart went public. He first borrowed money from his father-in-law, and then from banks. He paid back his first loan from his father-in-law in three years; he paid back his first bank loan (for $1,500 to buy a popcorn machine) in two. By the time Wal-Mart went public, Sam was personally responsible for millions of dollars of personal debt. Wal-Mart sold 20 percent of itself to the public when it was listed on the stock exchange, and those proceeds were enough to pay off all of Sam's personal debts, and for Wal-Mart to raise enough money to open stores as quickly as they could find good locations.

Sam built his retailing business with partners. His closest partner was his older brother Bud, with whom he partnered in several stores. Sam offered small percentages of ownership of each store that he opened to potential store managers in order to lure them away from other competitive retail chains. He also offered to let a store manager buy a larger ownership if he (it was still only "hes" at that time) was willing to pay for some of the store's opening costs. To a successful store manager that worked for another variety retail chain—J.J. Newberry, for example—the chance to own a piece of their store was unheard of. The lure of ownership encouraged many successful store managers to leave their current positions so that they might work for Sam. As we'll describe in the next chapter, Sam had already gotten to know every manager he tried to lure away, so they weren't really strangers by the time they signed on with him. Because Sam was risk-adverse, he made it his business to know a great deal about the people he offered to partner with.

By the time Sam started thinking about taking Wal-Mart public, he had opened twenty stores. In addition to the thirteen Ben Franklin franchises he owned that remained very profitable, he had eight more Wal-Marts being planned and constructed. Each store had been formed as a separate company with a unique set of partners. And some stores had seen their original managers retire or move away, so there were often multiple partners in a single location.* In order to go public, Sam had to reconcile, with unanimous consent, how several dozen partial owners of individual stores would each come to own some percentage of the original Wal-Mart shares. This was not an easy task for even the most seasoned dealmaker, and we can see from Sam's original handwritten worksheets that he spent a large amount of time working out formulas for the allocation of ownership. It is clear

---

* Since the IPO took place in 1970 and the Bentonville store opened in 1950, some Ben Franklin stores had been open for twenty years by the time of the IPO and the stores had seen multiple managers.

from the several thousand numbers on his worksheets, with about a hundred columns itemizing store assets and initial investments, each hand calculated (long before personal computers and spreadsheets, Sam used a hand cranked adding machine for his totals—even today, a spreadsheet this detailed would takes many hours to lay out before even starting to load it with numbers) that he was concerned that this be done fairly and correctly.

Venture capital firms have bright young graduates with quantitative degrees from good schools to do equivalent analyses when they're about to sell or take public one of their portfolio companies. Today, a VC-backed company of the same relative size to Wal-Mart when it went public would likely have a similar or greater number of disparate shareholders. For a contemporary VC-backed company, the disparate shareholders would be comprised of a combination of angel investors, various distinct venture capital funds (remember that each VC firm may manage several distinct ten-year limited partnerships funds, each investing as a distinct entity), and employees that held options to buy shares—not to mention the founder(s).

In the case of Sam Walton, almost all the ownership outside the family had been given away to create closer ties with key employees, equivalent to what stock options do today. After the IPO, Sam Walton and his family owned 61 percent of the company shares, the public owned 20 percent, and the remaining 19 percent was owned by store managers and executives (4 percent of this 19 percent belonged to Sam's brother). Ultimately, Sam gave to his key store managers individually larger ownership stakes in Walmart than all but C-level executives would expect today through stock options in their startups. Sam thought about ownership as an exercise in creating closer bonds with people he considered his partners, not about raising money, let alone from strangers.

To get started, Stephanie DiMarco initially raised about $50,000 from a family friend who was financially savvy and therefore could legitimately be called an angel investor (whether or not he thought of himself as that). This same friend invested another $50,000 a year later to tie Stephanie over for the extra year it took for Advent's software to get accepted. A couple of years after that, the original angel investor introduced Stephanie to another sophisticated financial investor whom she felt comfortable letting buy the shares previously belonging to her former partner Steve.

Stephanie later raised venture capital, primarily to give her company more credibility in the anticipation of going public. She did not need the money when she raised it—Advent was already profitable and growing steadily. VCs love to invest in fast-growing companies that are profitable and do not need their money. Shares in profitable, fast-growing companies go up in value much more often than they go down, so are not as risky. The lower risk profile of Advent compared to other private companies of its age meant that the partners in the VC firm offered to invest with relatively few restrictions on their investment. Under those conditions, venture capital was an excellent proposition even for a bedrock entrepreneur, and Stephanie was savvy enough to understand that.

To further understand whether bedrock or high-risk is the better path to entrepreneurial success and satisfaction, you need to understand how success happens, how good you need to be, and how much you need to have—the subjects of our next three chapters.

CHAPTER 6

HOW TO

Advising entrepreneurs on how to succeed seems pointless on at least three levels. First, entrepreneurs differ more than they resemble each other, and what they do to make people happy is almost equally diverse. How do you extract any insight from countless unique entrepreneurial journeys? Second, a din of contradictory advice from countless self-proclaimed entrepreneurial experts comes in the form of books, blogs, and podcasts. If the "experts" cannot agree, why should aspiring or practicing entrepreneurs pay any attention?

Third, providing "how-to" advice plunges us back into the wilderness of definitions for "entrepreneur" discussed in chapter 2. Which definition you have in your head as you contemplate starting a company influences how you go about it. If you think entrepreneurship is about starting companies that you can promptly sell, then you will pay diligent attention to how corporations are formed and how products are developed and launched as quickly as possible. If you think entrepreneurship is about successfully running the company that you start, then you'll pay much more attention to operational issues, like how you make a ton of sausages. If you think entrepreneurship is about leveraging your disruptive state of mind, then you'll pay special attention to how to get yourself and everyone around you psyched up to disrupt whatever industry you decide to go after.

Unfortunately, every definition of entrepreneur, each with an implied criterion of success, leads entrepreneurs astray because each definition narrows the entrepreneur's focus when their challenges are actually quite diverse. How an entrepreneur decides what to do—start a company, lead the company to prosperity, and then make the company capable of standing on its own, all the while being a decent person who may or may not have a family to care for—is complex, challenging, and fraught with siren-like calls to add unreasonable risks.

How best to cut through all this confusion on who does what to whom to get what result? By looking for a single role model who succeeded using the simplest, most widely applicable entrepreneurial techniques—Sam Walton. He may be the purest entrepreneur who ever lived. As we discussed, Sam's upbringing motivated him passionately to want to be a respected leader in a small-town community in order to have a happy family. To Sam, entrepreneurship was how you win respect while making enough money to comfortably take care of your family. Sam's explicit motivation to make money aligned well with his implicit motivation to be different from his father by having a happy family while living the small time life. Sam Walton led Wal-Mart into becoming the greatest entrepreneurial value creator of all time. Equally important, Sam was also a great husband and father, as well as a community leader—everyone around him benefited from his entrepreneurial leadership. Only his competitors suffered. Fortunately for us, because he was an extrovert and a straight talker who craved respect, Sam was willing to openly and sincerely share his entrepreneurial experiences in his autobiography *Made in America*. The book is a great read, but it is not a "how-to." Luckily, however, Walmart and the Walton family granted me access to Sam's files and the many oral histories of early employees that had worked closely with him that illuminate how he worked. Hearing the stories while holding in my hands the documents Sam Walton used when he made such pivotal decisions provides valuable insight into his experience. In essence, we can construct his how-to.

Virtually all entrepreneurs learn on the job. Sam's story vividly illustrates how learning formal skills and developing new skills relate to entrepreneurial success. He first learned the basics of retailing by buying out a nearly bankrupt owner of a Ben Franklin–franchised variety store in the small town of Newport, Arkansas. To help franchise owners succeed, thereby increasing Ben Franklin's revenues and profits, the corporate organization trained and supervised franchisees. What Sam needed to know to run a store he learned from them. He learned how to fill out bookkeeping, ordering, and inventory forms, and he learned merchandising—where to display goods on the shelves to better sell them. Ben Franklin expected franchisees to follow their prescriptions to the letter, and the franchisees could expect to make a decent living running a store in a small town.

The store Sam bought had been poorly run and two other variety stores stood in the same town square, though Newport had only 3,500 residents. Sam was happy to find a store he could afford with his savings, and a loan from his new father-in-law. But he was extremely naïve about the poor prospects of the business. How could he know? He had no experience and consulted no one who did. After he took over he soon realized that, like the previous owner, he faced imminent bankruptcy unless he could figure out how to lure customers from his nearby competitors. Sam quickly corrected everything the previous owner had obviously been doing wrong—for example, he didn't let popular products go out of stock and he laid out the store differently so customers could see every product the store had to offer—and sales ticked up modestly, but not enough. He then started visiting his competitors' stores and copying techniques that seemed to be working for them. Sam's constant "visits" annoyed his competitors, but there was nothing they could do about it other than appeal to the loyalty of their customers. Sam soon started to visit other stores in other towns to copy their successful promotions. Sam quickly learned that letting customers know what bargains they could find at your store really made a big difference. Within a year his sales doubled, and within three years, he was outselling both of his competitors.

After four years, Sam was running the best performing Ben Franklin store in the entire region. In fact, the store was performing so well that the landlord wanted it for his son. Sam was screwed. When he had agreed to assume the previous owner's lease, he had neglected to ask the landlord for an option to renew. Without an option to renew, Sam had no legal right to remain. Location in the town square was essential, and there was no other space available. Sam was left without a choice—he had to sell his inventory and other store assets to the landlord to recover what costs he could.

Many entrepreneurs that enjoy Sam's level of success in their first startup spend their profits quickly because they do not anticipate disasters and crises. Sam survived this disaster because he had saved for "rainy days" just as his dad had done. Having lived frugally, even with his family having quickly grown to four kids, Sam had enough money socked away to buy another Ben Franklin store on the town square in Bentonville, Arkansas, on the other side of the state from Newport. The owner, looking to retire, was happy to sell, and Sam was eager to start the process of building a business over again. Even though he remained a Ben Franklin franchisee, he boldly chose not to use the brand name in renaming his new store. Instead, he called it "Walton's 5&10" to make it clear to everyone who was responsible for the store.

Using the same techniques that had worked in Newport, Sam made Walton's 5&10 the most successful variety store in Bentonville. Sam could have stopped with his one store and been financially secure, as had most typical Ben Franklin franchisees. But he was restless and driven to do better. He firmly believed he could make more money if he did things differently, but he couldn't see clearly what practices he should change, so he experimented further. He particularly loved playing around with merchandising. Some techniques he tried, like buying a popcorn machine and selling popcorn in front of the store, pulled people in. But not everything worked—a cotton candy machine installed inside the store attracted swarms of flies.

The techniques that increased sales he maintained, at least until he discovered a new technique that increased sales even more. All the while, Sam kept visiting stores in bigger towns to find new ideas. Sam didn't view himself as an innovator, and he felt no pride in saying an idea was his. Selling more and more was what drove him.

Like virtually all successful entrepreneurs Sam discovered how he could increase sales through experimentation. By experimenting with pricing on sale items, Sam found that low prices on women's panties brought in significant new business, mostly by word of mouth. By selling a thousand panties at $1.50 rather than selling one hundred at $2, he found he could get a big boost in store sales and personally make more money. And many customers who bought low-priced panties bought other things, driving sales up even more.

Selling products at a deep discount went against Ben Franklin franchising rules and the prevailing wisdom of retailing that focused on profit margins and not profit dollars.* Nothing but the law could stop Sam from doing something he thought could make him more money, which he realized meant making his customers happy by offering things they needed at surprisingly low prices.

Ben Franklin supervisors constantly reprimanded Sam for not following their rules. But as he kept finding goods he could buy at low prices and offer for sale in his store, profits grew month by month. Because Sam's stores were so successful despite his flouting of the rules, Ben Franklin was happy to let him franchise additional stores in new locations. Sam ultimately became the chain's single largest franchisor, owning fifteen franchises in total.** But after seventeen years of operating franchised stores, he wanted complete freedom in deciding what to sell and how to sell it. To achieve that

---

* Profit margin is the percentage difference between what an item is sold for and how much it cost.

** By the time Wal-Mart went public Sam had closed some of his Ben Franklin stores to concentrate his time and resources on opening new Wal-Marts.

freedom he created his own independent chain of pure discount stores—Wal-Mart.

When Sam opened his first Wal-Mart in 1962 in Rogers, Arkansas, the next small town over from Bentonville, a few large discounters, like Kmart and Target, already existed. Like Sam, they had concluded that discount stores could pull in large numbers of shoppers and still be profitable. Fortunately for Sam, major discounters focused on opening stores in major cities, not small towns. The closest small-town retailer experimenting with offering major discounts every day was in Texas, 400 miles away from Sam's store. But most discounters, whether part of a large chain or just a local store, failed back then. Most still fail today. The lesson: the majority of startups fail even after they find out how to make their customers happy. The founder is unable to execute on his or her insight. They may understand "the what," but they screw up "the how."

Even after opening his Wal-Mart stores, Sam continued to use Ben Franklin bookkeeping worksheets to track his sales, inventories, wages, and profits. Every week, he received reports from each store, initially as letters sent through the mail, about sales and wages. To encourage his store managers to experiment, he asked them to write on the slip they sent a single sentence describing an item they had offered at a new price that had sold especially well that week.

Saturday mornings, very early, Sam drove to work, sat at his desk, and copied each store's numbers onto a big worksheet. After filling in the sales and wages, he calculated how much bigger or smaller the figures were compared to the previous year. Personally copying the numbers into his worksheet and then calculating the percentages enabled Sam to understand what might need his attention. Looking at his spreadsheets and his notes, we can practically hear him thinking, "I need to find out why the Fayetteville store didn't rebound as quickly after last week's storm as Bentonville did." On those Saturday mornings, he also called store managers to ask questions and learn. "You sold 4 dozen napkins at 23 cents this past week, how did that work?" After filling in his worksheet and getting his questions answered, Sam had the numbers typed up, along with every store's best-selling item, and sent the results to the store managers. Each store manager therefore knew how well the company was performing. They were also able to learn from one another, exchanging ideas about items to feature to boost sales. Simple. Simple enough that there were no misunderstandings about what was expected.

But the numbers were not the only things that Sam relied on to help him understand. He visited his stores, several a week, for most of his life. No amount of time on the telephone and no amount of facts and figures could give him a sense of what was working and what was not. He needed to see, hear, and smell it himself. He visited stores unannounced and took copious notes on what he saw. The first thing he did was look for the manager—whom he expected to find somewhere on the floor, not in an office. He then walked through every department by himself, talking to customers and to each sales associate. He asked customers what they wanted that they weren't getting. For example, his notes from one store visit read, "Getting a request here from our older customers in this store. Why don't we have our aisles signed by departments, like in grocery stores? Why don't we tell them where to go? I keep hearing it and we aren't doing a damn thing about it!" And he'd ask sales associates what was selling and what was not. "Five dollar new baseball collection collage for kids. Who from? Made in the USA . . . It's a great item." He noticed everything that was done differently than he had expected, and he commended people for the efforts they had made to sell more items, "The thing I really like are the benches they have all the way through the middle for customers to sit in. It has a nice open appearance and they have the store looking real good."

All the while, Sam took notes to remind himself of things he wanted to tell others about each store he visited. At the end of a visit, he communicated to the store manager what he liked and what he wanted to see improved or changed immediately. And he made a point on returning to the store to make sure the improvements were made. Sam had an intimate understanding of each store, each manager, and for many years, every store employee. When there were too many employees for Sam to know personally, he promoted a trusted store manager to regularly visit the other stores around him and write up his notes for Sam.

Sam's strategy—keep things simple and controllable—manifested itself in the stores he opened over the next dozen years. The stores were all located within 130 miles of Bentonville—the distance that someone could travel on small roads, unload a truck, and still return home the same day. That distance was also prescient because once there were about ten stores, Sam could reasonably ask his store managers to travel every week to attend a Saturday morning meeting in his office. There they reviewed the weekly results, answered his questions, debated ideas, and made plans that could be immediately set into motion. The Saturday morning meeting became the driving force in how Sam controlled what became the largest retailer in the world. Today, twenty-five years since Sam passed away, Walmart still holds the Saturday morning meeting.

Sam hated wasting time. But he didn't feel that getting to know his employees, whatever their position in the company, was a waste of time. He was not cold, or terse, or abrupt. When he talked to people, he listened to them. He might cut them off if they wandered off the subject, but he always cared about what people thought, and he was always considering how their ideas might improve the company.

Sam's distaste for wasting time was manifested in how he wanted things done. For example, after he had opened half a dozen stores, Sam found himself spending much of his time driving between locations, often unable to visit more than a single store in a day. So he bought a used two-seat single-engine prop plane and learned to fly. Flying enabled him to visit multiple stores in a day. He'd fly into the closest landing field to a store and ask the first person he could find if he could borrow their car for a couple of hours in return for a few bucks. He also discovered that a plane enabled him to see clearly from the air in which direction a town center would expand based on parking patterns and where homes were being constructed, giving him a better understanding of good locations for new stores.

Sam's keep-it-simple-and-understand-it-yourself strategy wasn't an accident or a lucky call; it was a manifestation of how he thought and what he respected. It also kept costs down; Sam couldn't help but feel personally poorer for every penny spent, even after Walmart became the most profitable retail chain in the world. People travelling on Walmart business were expected to share the most inexpensive motel rooms they could find. At first, store fixtures were bought second-hand; only years later did Sam find someone who could provide new fixtures for less money than it cost to find, buy, and transport used fixtures to new stores.

Many entrepreneurs past and present have tried to adapt this keep-it-simple-and-keep-it-frugal philosophy, but were ultimately shackled by it. Sam, however, did not let his desire for simplicity stunt his company's growth. He appreciated that growth in the number of stores and the number of items sold required more coordination than any person could implement alone. Once Sam owned a couple of stores, he hired an assistant to organize all the information flowing in and out of his office. When he got to six stores, he set up a simple system, similar to a post office, by building slots in the wall near his desk so that his assistant could sort all the orders that stores needed filled. At first, Sam himself placed those orders with Ben Franklin and his other suppliers. But when placing orders got in the way of his two top priorities—visiting stores and reviewing the weekly numbers—he hired another assistant to organize and place orders in exactly the way he had. Only when that person was working long hours every day placing orders did Sam hire another.

While Sam's care, competence, and dedication inspired confidence among those around him, he always understood that his personal ability and capacity to make improvements were limited. He counted on everyone around him being appropriately dedicated and skilled to accomplish what he expected of them. He spent his time understanding what could be done to make his stores run more efficiently, and he expected to be able to delegate to others to make those improvements happen within their domains of responsibility.

To choose the people he could count on, he used a simple and effective process. Sam loved to introduce himself, greeting anyone he crossed paths with. And he clearly cared about them, because he listened and responded to who they were. "Hey, I've been to your town," he'd say, or maybe, "Where'd you get that good-looking jacket you're wearing?" Sam used this skill to walk into any store that caught his attention, especially stores belonging to competitors, and introduce himself to the store manager, "Hi, I'm Sam Walton. You run a really interesting store. Can I ask you a few questions?" The store manager, almost always flattered by the attention, would show Sam around his (rarely "her") store, telling Sam all he wanted to know, even answering detailed questions like, "Can I see where you keep your returned merchandise?" All the while, Sam took notes on a legal pad he carried with him (he later switched to a pocket tape recorder). By listening to what store managers were proud of in their stores, he picked up ideas, but he also noticed problems in organization, pricing, training, merchandising, and cleanliness. At the next Saturday morning meeting, Sam discussed with his store managers what was going well and what was going poorly at other people's stores so his managers could implement the good ideas and steer clear of the bad ones.

Introducing himself at the stores he visited was also a great way to find store managers who were successful, motivated, and highly skilled. And he stayed in touch with them, often inviting them out to dinner so he could meet their wives and learn more about what they liked—or didn't like—to do. Sam particularly favored non-smoking, non-drinking, church-going store managers who knew their numbers and took pride in their stores and employees. In fact, he hired most of his early store managers from the collection of store managers to whom he introduced himself.

By seeing a manager in action in his own store and by getting to know him personally, Sam reduced to near-zero the risk of hiring someone incompetent or immoral (nobody can remember a totally incompetent or immoral store manager hired by Sam). That didn't mean that every store manager worked out perfectly, but most worked out well. The few who didn't at least did not set their stores back too far before Sam replaced them. He understood the skills he was looking for and went looking to see people practicing those skills in real time—a great strategy.

After opening six Wal-Marts, in addition to operating fifteen Ben Franklin stores, Sam began to pay attention to the increasing number of late deliveries to his stores. The reasons for missed deliveries were also increasing: there were too many orders to place in a day, numbers were transposed or copied incorrectly or misread because of penmanship, somebody was sick, or maybe a supplier's truck broke down. Because his office was right next to the area where the orders from the stores were received and then placed with the suppliers, Sam could see, hear, and understand that there were too many products being delivered to too many stores for his then four assistants to administrate and trouble-shoot effectively. He knew that large chain stores used distribution warehouses, but the idea of owning a building full of products his customers couldn't buy repelled him.

From store managers working at other retail chains, Sam heard of a chain in the upper Midwest that moved items through their warehouse very quickly. He arranged a visit, taking along his most senior store manager and buyer to get their opinions on whether Wal-Mart could benefit from a distribution center. Observing in operation a warehouse where items were received and shipped out to stores the same day—and directly questioning the employees who worked there—enabled Sam to see that opening a warehouse would be a simpler, lower-cost way to manage the flow of products to his stores.

Understanding that designing and running a warehouse differed greatly from anything anyone at his company had done before, Sam hired an employee he knew and respected, one that had previous warehouse management experience, to set up and run his distribution center. Of course, he arranged to move his office next to the new distribution center so he could visit it every day when he wasn't visiting stores. He needed to see with his own eyes that everything that had come in the previous day had been shipped to a store by the following day.

Using a warehouse to manage the inflow of many thousands of items and redistribute them to a growing number of locations in exactly the right quantities necessarily centralizes a business. Transitions involving greater systemization in operating procedures and decision-making trip up many entrepreneurs. These transitions involve significant change in what people do, and change scares almost everyone. Asking key performers to do things differently results in a perceived change in their status along the lines of, "I used to be able to decide what to sell in my store and now I'm told what to sell." This transition wasn't easy to lead. Other than being open with people, Sam didn't have any magic formula for making them feel comfortable with change. Sam succeeded because he explained the need for a centralized distribution warehouse so that every employee understood why the transition was important. At Sam's Saturday meeting, every store manager could discuss what was working with the transition and what was not, and actions to mitigate problems could be quickly decided upon. Each Monday, the store managers briefed their own teams about what needed to be done next to make the new systems function as effectively as possible. Ultimately, everyone felt Sam was sincere in wanting to set up the new systems in such a way that store managers had the greatest autonomy possible.

Even with all the trust Sam had from his store managers and all the competence he had within his warehouse team (and soon thereafter, from his computer systems team), this was an emotional transition for many top managers. It proved so emotional, in fact, that some managers left the company. Critically, almost all the managers understood that the transition ultimately lifted the last constraint on how fast the company could grow. Because Sam had chosen extremely competent managers to design the distribution center (soon centers) and put in place its systems, Sam steered Walmart through a transition essential to its long-term competitiveness. Now a limitless number of items could flow precisely through the distribution center, get delivered to the correct store, and get placed in the right spot inside.

Sam believed in giving people opportunities, but he did not tolerate mediocrity and he set high expectations appropriately. He understood that if you set expectations so high that a person or team can't meet them, it demoralizes that person or team. If you set expectations too low, then the skill set of the team does not improve fast enough to overtake the competition. Sam set high expectations that he knew from experience could be met, perhaps with some help. If someone fell behind in opening a new store, then Sam sent in as much help as necessary to get it on track. If the person in charge learned how to plan store openings more effectively from the experience, then Sam was okay with that—and that person felt good about what he had accomplished and learned. Those who didn't learn from the experience or were unwilling to accept help soon understood that they no longer had a bright future with the company.

Sam used his team effectively. While he set most of the priorities for the company based on his continual search for better ideas, he was entirely open to ideas from anyone. Because he took no pride in ownership of an idea and was quick to give credit to others for good ones, everyone felt proud to contribute. Sam's hands-off delegation demonstrated respect for people's skills, making them proud and eager to perform to the full extent of their ability.

Sam was not only open to suggestions and ideas from others—he also sought out new ideas and techniques to fulfill his vision of selling more at a lower cost. Early on, when he realized that computers could possibly help Walmart, he took a weeklong class at IBM on using computers in retail businesses. He didn't become the expert himself, but he learned enough that he understood how to support the experts he hired.

Continually seeking out new ideas gets many entrepreneurs in trouble. Organizations cannot accommodate continual changes in direction, strategy, or processes. What is effective for others is not necessarily effective for everyone. A great deal of time, resources, and money can be wasted on implementing ideas that could never work in the context they were intended. Sam *experimented* with the ideas that appealed to him—he never bet the farm. Every new idea or technique he tried had a simple, straightforward, easy-to-understand and easy-to-measure objective—almost always an objective associated with sales going up, or cost or inventories going down. The ideas had to be straightforward because they had to be implemented by dozens, hundreds, thousands, or even millions of people.

Not every experiment worked. Sam tried opening up arts and

crafts stores. He also tried selling manufacturers' excess inventories. He experimented by testing an idea in a location or two, usually within already empty buildings that he didn't have to lease for a long period—similar to what we call a pop-up today, but on a larger scale and with the possibility that the location could stay in business if the experiment worked.

One experiment that worked well was Sam's Club, which was designed to mimic the super-discount Price Club.* After hearing about the Price Club's success at selling product in bulk directly to consumers, Walton flew to California to visit the store and learn all he could about how it operated. He even invited Sol Price out to dinner to hear whatever he was willing to tell. He flew back to Bentonville the day after his visit and created a team of three individuals who had reputations for liking to do things differently. He asked them to find some empty cheap building in a well-trafficked suburb within a day's drive to set up a copycat to see if the concept would work in the Midwest. Within months they were established and validating that many Midwesterners loved buying in bulk—that is, everything except bulk wine.

Sam, entirely a bedrock entrepreneur, likely could not have succeeded any other way. He didn't open up his first Wal-Mart until he had been in business for himself for seventeen years. No outside investor would have waited that long for Sam to finally create a concept that would take another eight years to go public. Further, Wal-Marts were not highly profitable at first—they didn't equal the profitability of Sam's Ben Franklin franchise stores until about the time Walmart went public. Most investors would have considered the first Wal-Mart a failure and resisted opening a second. In its first year of operation, the initial Wal-Mart lost money and was barely breaking even by the time the second Wal-Mart opened in Harrison, Arkansas. Sam's instincts and understanding about what he could do to improve on

---

* The Price Club was actually founded by a Mr. Sol Price.

the first store in opening a second were spot-on, in spite of opening day fiascos with exploding watermelons and donkey dung.

Until he took Walmart public, Sam relied entirely on bank loans to fund expansion. He even bought the local Bentonville bank thinking it would help him find the loans to grow the business. Most local banks knew Sam personally, and many had loaned him the money to buy inventories and grant mortgages for the stores he built. They supported him because his business was profitable and had been profitable from his first Ben Franklin store days. But they still insisted on collateral— Sam had to personally guarantee each loan he took out—something high-risk entrepreneurs are well advised never to do, lest they go personally bankrupt using other people's money.

Even after Walmart went public it remained a bedrock organization, with the Walton family and employees retaining control of 80 percent of all the shares. Sam could still experiment with arts and crafts stores and distribution centers and not worry that his job was at stake based on whether the experiments worked. Walmart retains its status as a bedrock organization today because the Walton family, its foundations, and its corporations still own almost 50 percent of the company's stock.

It's All About Skills

Every entrepreneur faces a unique set of hurdles in trying to take a particular idea about how to make customers happy and grow it into a valuable and self-sustaining enterprise. The hurdles differ, depending on whether you want to sell discount panties, specialized accounting software, sausages, autopsy services, iPhone apps, or whatever. *But the underlying skills required to get over all entrepreneurial hurdles and build productive, competitive, and self-sustaining enterprises are the same.*

Entrepreneurial success boils down to understanding how to put together productive, competitive, and self-sustaining enterprises. Sam possessed five core skills that we find in almost all accomplished entrepreneurs:

Self-awareness. Sam always listened and watched to see what could be improved and thought about what to do to make those improvements. He remained acutely aware of what he did and didn't know and what skills he did and didn't have. As soon as he realized he had a gap, he acquired and practiced the requisite skills. Self-awareness is itself a skill, not something you're born with. You can learn it—learn how to identify your capabilities and your personal modes of learning and self-improvement.

Relationship building. Sam was clearly an extrovert. Meeting people energized him. But being extroverted doesn't attract and build a team whose members dedicate their lives to achieving someone else's vision the way people dedicated themselves to achieving Sam's. Sam was highly skilled at building relationships—creating strong, shared objectives with others. It's a skill that you can learn and master, whether you're an introvert or an extrovert. (Walt Disney, whom we'll meet in the next chapter, was an introvert who could also create strong relationships with people whose help he needed.) The objectives that Sam set up to share with the people around him tended to be simple and based upon the results that were reported to him every week: sales, wages, and inventories. He also made it clear to his people that he sincerely cared about them and their families, and shared their objectives to be successful husbands, fathers, and community leaders. Sam constantly asked about what was happening with his employees' families, and his employees knew he cared about their answers.

Relationship building is rarely taught in school, though you can read about it in books. Some life skills coaches know how to teach and help people practice it. Where did Sam learn to build such strong relationships? We don't know, but he likely learned some of it from his mother, a beloved member of her local community. He also likely learned some of it from the coaches of the athletic teams he played on when he was growing up. Sam was usually team captain, a position from which you can practice relationship building while getting feedback and advice from a good coach. But Sam most likely mastered relationship building by deliberately practicing with people to whom he wanted to get closer. When he set a goal of getting to know somebody, he accomplished it and then figured out how he could do it better the next time (which is precisely the way I learned most of my relationship-building skills).

Motivating others. Sam was great at making people he had never met before or barely knew feel good about helping him. People often described Sam as charismatic, believing it to be an inborn trait. But the ability to motivate other people is a skill you can learn and practice. Sam's technique is classic: he made people feel good about themselves in the context of doing something important—for Walmart, or perhaps the church Sam and his family attended. He likely learned this skill captaining sports teams. You can imagine him saying something like, "it's amazing how well you penetrated the defense in last night's game; what's your new technique?" People on the receiving end not only feel good about themselves, but also want to rise to the occasion again.

Relationship building and motivating others are different skills. Sam didn't always compliment the people he worked closest with. He could be scathing when people failed to meet his high expectations. "Who bought those 500 women's jackets with the fake fur that all had to be returned because they're junk?" That doesn't build a new relationship, but it can certainly be motivating.

Leading change. From day one at his first store, Sam was always changing things, usually resulting in some sort of improvement. But people don't like change and will often passively-aggressively or covertly resist it. Most change is poorly envisioned and poorly aligned with what people think of as important, and so it's is viewed as confusing. The associates and managers of Walmart expected change, embraced change, and viewed change as positive—many changes every week, in fact. They embraced change because Sam explicitly let them know why each change was important, what was expected, and how they would benefit from it. They knew the entire organization would provide each and every person with the support and resources needed to make the changes happen efficiently and successfully. And because change was extremely well delineated, communicated, and supported, it was viewed as low risk. Sam avoided the management sin that many fall into, which is asking somebody to change something, change it perfectly, and change it without getting any support and without using any resources. Sam pushed through enormous amounts of change every week, but everyone knew the entire organization, and Sam personally, had their back.

Even extensive changes, like shifting to a centralized, quick-turnaround distribution center, were done so that everyone knew what was expected to happen. Not that there weren't surprises, or mistakes, or disappointments, but Sam's weekly meetings meant that adjustments and mitigations were made quickly. Under Sam's leadership, Walmart became the gold standard in relentless, speedy, positive change.

Sam mastered his change leadership skills by engaging in what is now referred to as *deliberate practice*. Every week, Sam outlined changes to be made, and every week he'd receive feedback from his management team about how the changes were implemented, what went right, what went wrong, and what could have gone better. Sam, who was always open to suggestions, improved his leadership practices based on his own analysis and from the advice he received.

Enterprise basics. This, too, is a learned skill, not one you're born with. Sam understood that he had to make a profit, and to do so he would make his customers happy by offering them unusually good deals. He created simple routines (i.e., processes) that made repetitive tasks, like ordering, as productive as possible, so he and the organization could focus on relentlessly implementing improvements (i.e., projects). He diligently created a culture of people who loved to undertake projects and use processes to make customers happy by keeping costs and prices as low as possible.

Understanding when and how to use routines, processes, and projects to create an effective retail operation is not rocket science. Back when Sam worked at a J. C. Penney, he learned about the routines that keep a department operating smoothly and productively. Perhaps he even experienced an improvement project or two that rolled through his department there. In the army during World War II, he got a further taste of projects and processes— experience that he likely applied by analogy to his stores.

In sum, every entrepreneur needs to become competent at these five basic skills to survive and prosper: self-awareness, relationship building, motivating others, leading change, and enterprise basics. With the exception of enterprise basics, these skills apply to all good leaders.

Industry-Specific Skills

Depending on exactly what type of business you're starting, you will also likely need some additional specific skills. How do you know what specific skills you need? Just study successful entrepreneurs in the field. If you are interested in starting a retail business, then study Sam Walton and Jeff Bezos. Write down all the things they appear to do effectively, day in and day out. You don't need to be as good as them, but you need to be good enough. "How Good" is the subject of the next chapter.

Three Ways to Acquire the Skills You Need

How do you learn these how-tos? Every entrepreneur learns and implements their skills in different ways, but almost everyone learns them on the job or in some intense group activity, like sports or volunteer organizations.

Virtually no one learns entrepreneurial leadership skills in the classroom. First, schools rarely teach them. Second, even students who may have taken a class that *did* teach one or more of these skills likely forgot what they learned. Chances are they never practiced the skill to the extent necessary to feel confident exercising it many years later in the intense atmosphere of a startup.

Sam began learning and practicing his leadership skills from an early age: playing on sports teams, observing and listening to his job supervisors, and participating in and leading volunteer organizations. When he was in high school and college, his peers and teachers saw him as a leader. Sam practiced leadership more than most of his peers because he volunteered to organize activities and events for practically every club or team he joined. He invested significant time and thought in becoming more and more adept at leading organizations. He always focused on results, and he was always short of time, which meant that he was always trying to get teams to work more effectively. And because Sam spent so much time on extra-curricular activities, he was a much better leader than he was a student.

A great deal can be learned from a boss or supervisor, even at a part-time or summer job—*if* your boss runs an effective business or department (a big if). You can also learn leadership skills by organizing activities beyond school or the workplace, as Sam did. For example, starting a local volunteer chapter of some national organization can give you direct experience in relationship building, motivating others, and leading change. If the national organization has a program to help people start local chapters, that's also a great way to get feedback and coaching. National Outdoor Leadership School (NOLS) teaches basic self-awareness and relationship-building skills to many.

The hard part about learning from a boss is choosing the boss and business to work for. Large organizations often do the choosing, and not the other way around. Just make sure that you choose an organization that embraces change and trains its people.

School can teach you *industry-specific* skills. Sam learned his retail operational skills from Ben Franklin. Culinary schools prepare chefs with the specific skills required to run restaurants. Many dental schools teach their students the basics of running a dental practice. Today, programming skills that you learn in many schools can be important for designing effective application software.

Besides learning on the job or at school, Sam used a third way to acquire essential skills. He hired already skilled people and gave them the authority and responsibility to take ownership of tasks they could execute with more expertise than he could. As we learned from Sam, *great entrepreneurs look to meet capable and skilled people and lure them to work for them as needed.*

Clearly, the lack of a decent education didn't hold back Vidal Herrera, the founder of 1-800-AUTOPSY, whom we met in chapter 3; he barely made it through high school. Like most entrepreneurs, he got his training on the job. He also was open to learning everything he could about how to succeed as an entrepreneur. Like him, you need just enough prior education to be able to quickly acquire the skills required to succeed in your targeted end market.

Progress, Not Perfection

Sam wasn't perfect. In particular, he was disorganized. To look at pictures of Sam at work in his office is to see great piles of paper—on his desk, on the floor, on chairs. Sam's well-organized assistants knew what out-of-date reports, legal pads filled with his illegible notes, or old copies of trade magazines and newsletters to take and file away in their offices, or else he would have buried himself in paper.

Sam also was insensitive about other people's time. He regularly pulled people away from what they were doing, at home or at work, to ask them questions that could have waited. He was notorious for standing people up, even people who had come long distances to meet with him. And he wasn't punctual either, except for his Saturday morning meeting, for which he spent hours preparing. Sam was so focused on thinking about how to improve Walmart that he operated strictly according to his own assessment of what was his highest priority at the moment.

Sam's relentless setting of higher and higher expectations burned out many people who worked for him, particularly store managers and buyers. He didn't promise lifetime employment, but his people knew that and didn't expect Walmart to keep them employed once they no longer felt enthusiastic about their jobs.

Perfection doesn't exist, and entrepreneurs who insist on it will make people uncomfortable because such bosses never offer praise. Certainly, some entrepreneurs who withhold praise have built successful businesses. But people feel most comfortable working for, buying from, and being with flawed people like themselves.

How to Split Up

A high percentage of founding partners cannot agree on what to do when their company starts to grow. When that happens, the performance of the company in question is always negatively impacted and often collapses. These transitions are perilous. Few entrepreneurs and nascent companies survive the loss of individuals with critical skill sets, let alone with the momentum they need to stay ahead of the competition. But Stephanie did.

How Stephanie DiMarco managed the fraught task of easing her partner out is rife with lessons for entrepreneurs about how to lead a successful startup. On forming Advent, Stephanie added a valuable resource that many entrepreneurs neglect to put in place—an experienced board of directors to help her overcome naiveté. As is almost always the case, with success came trouble: her partnership with Steve foundered and the company was in danger of stalling. Steve was and is a great engineer, but his love of engineering was greater than any desire to see Advent become a big, valuable company. He preferred to make things perfect rather than make them work economically, and he felt uncomfortable supervising anyone who felt otherwise. This mindset resulted in missed schedules among the company's engineers. As soon as Stephanie identified the problem she secured managerial coaching for Steve. When that produced no change, she wisely sought the advice of her board, ultimately working out an agreement to buy Steve out with the stipulation that he spend up to one year training his successor. Stephanie, with the help of the

Board, had found a graceful way to ease Steve out, a breakup that most entrepreneurs with partners find impossible to face. *Relying on other people's skills doesn't mean letting those people hold you back*—but this is true if and only if you understand how to deal with these tricky and stressful people issues. Like Sam Walton, Stephanie did not possess the skills critical to dealing with this situation, but she was smart enough to access those skills through her tight circle of advisors, mentors, and board members.

When it comes to entrepreneurship, skills matter; style and personality, not so much. In order to prosper, Sam and Stephanie got lots of help when and where they needed it. But without some minimum level of competence, of themselves and within their founding team, they would never have succeeded. We need to understand the answer to the question, "How good?" As we'll find out in our next chapter, the answer isn't so simple.

CHAPTER 7

HOW GOOD

Walt Disney barely made it as an animator and as a head of an animation studio. *Barely*. But when he finally put all the pieces in place, he redefined and reinvented several different forms of entertainment. That makes Walt Disney an excellent role model for understanding exactly how good you have to be to make it as an entrepreneur. Though he died years ago, you should get to know and appreciate his story. Because his impacts on art and entertainment are still strongly felt, he has been the subject of excellent biographies and a great deal of research.

As a child growing up in a family with limited means and little joy or affection, Walt found drawing a welcome distraction. He got started with a sketchbook and colored pencils that an uncle gave him when he was five. Friends, neighbors, and teachers praised him for his drawing skills and encouraged his pursuit, though his father thought it frivolous. Aspiring to be a newspaper cartoonist, Walt drew for his school newspaper and at every opportunity he could find. While in high school, he even took adult night classes at Chicago's Art Institute in order to learn professional drawing and cartooning skills.

Home was such a joyless and dispiriting place that Walt left home at sixteen to join the army. While the army rejected him for being too young, the Red Cross didn't look too closely at the age of the scrawny kid who applied to drive ambulances. He wound up in France right after the end of World War I and experienced a world very different from the Midwest where he was raised. He drew whenever he had the chance, passing up ample opportunities to meet the friendly and appreciative locals with his fellow Red Cross volunteers. He preferred drawing by himself and earning some extra money by sending cartoons back home to a local newspaper. At age eighteen, he came back from France as a strong, strapping young man brimming with confidence that he would soon be a famous newspaper cartoonist.

Not wanting to return to his parents' home in Chicago, Walt went to live with an older brother in Kansas City. His brother helped him land a job drawing for a local advertising agency. But there wasn't enough work to keep him busy and the job soon fizzled. Rather than look for another one, eighteen-year-old Walt teamed up with another draftsman laid off from the same agency, Ubbe "Ub" Iwerks, to start an agency based on the selling power of humor. In spite of being an introvert, Walt had no qualms about walking into downtown business establishments and telling anybody who would listen that he could get them more customers with humorously illustrated ads and flyers. In the first month Ub and Walt made some good money, but business tailed off quickly when the ads didn't bring in the promised throngs of new customers. To survive, they made their agency into a part-time business, and Walt took a job around the corner at an agency that created ads for movie theaters to run during intermission. Walt quickly got immersed with his new job, and the agency he started soon died.

With stars like Charlie Chaplin and Harold Lloyd, movies were already a huge, fast growing business in the early 1920s, attracting scores of entrepreneurs, completely analogous to the entrepreneurial attraction of today's Internet. Bigger cities each had advertising agencies that specialized in designing eye-catching ads to show specifically to movie audiences. Animation was one of the ways to make an eye-catching ad, and the agency Walt went to work for had a small group that did that. Walt was enthralled, and his interest quickly got him transferred to work with the animation group. He borrowed a camera from the agency owner and in the garage in back of his brother's house he set up a crude animation rig. He worked until past midnight virtually every night animating his own humorous versions of classic fairy tales. He took out the only book on animation he could find at the public library. He followed its every instruction, and then he'd experiment with his own ways of getting the effects he wanted. His animations were crude, but nobody at the agency or in all of Kansas City could do any better. Several successful animation studios already existed at that time, and millions loved cartoon characters like Felix the Cat. But all the famous studios and their animators were located in New York City, and Walt felt no pull to move there.

Not long after Walt started experimenting, he began to feel constrained and started to dream about being his own boss and making his own funny animated cartoons. He showed his work to the theater owners in town, but it took about a year before one of them agreed to show his series of short humorous cartoons during intermissions. The cartoons were satires of life in Kansas City. Although the local theater owner paid only a small sum of money, Walt felt this indicated that he could prosper from his talents. So after work was over at the ad agency, and before he went to his brother's garage to produce his weekly Kansas City cartoon satire, Walt began asking everyone he knew to loan him the money to start his own animation studio. Although his older brother and a successful uncle declined to invest, they introduced him to a prominent member of the local political elite who thought that it would be great to have a movie studio in Kansas City. He gave Walt a loan for the equivalent in today's money of around $50,000, and he urged his business and political buddies to invest, as well. Walt used this largesse to incorporate Laugh-O-Gram Studios (even though at twenty he was technically too young to incorporate a business in Missouri) and quickly hired eight people, including his former partner Ub Iwerks, and a salesperson, to start production on a series of five-minute animated fairy tales.

As soon as the first of the animated fairy tales was finished, Walt dispatched his salesman to New York to try and sell it to a distributor. Over the next several weeks, the salesman lived and entertained lavishly in New York, which, when combined with the all the Kansas City salaries and production expenses, depleted the money Walt had in the bank. Walt had no choice but to call his salesman back to Kansas City and start begging for more money. But on the day he departed New York, the salesman picked up a written commitment from a small regional movie distributor to buy six animated fairy tales for $11,100 (the equivalent of around $150,000 today), with $100 up front and the rest paid on delivery of the six fairy tales the following year! Although this was an absurdly bad deal because Laugh-O-Gram would take on all of the risk for a year's worth of work, Walt felt it vindicated his efforts and sent a clear sign that he should carry on and borrow more money wherever he could find it. Dozens of people loaned him small sums of money to help him fulfill his dream.

Moving several times in the dead of night to avoid bill collectors and to keep his equipment from being repossessed, Walt eventually made four of the six animated fairy tales. Unfortunately, within months the regional distributor went bankrupt, leaving Walt with no customer whatsoever for several of the animations he had already finished but not yet delivered. To get the money he desperately needed, Walt made a few other animated shorts for local businesses, using the opportunities to try out new techniques. But after a year of effort Walt was all alone and homeless (his brother had moved to Portland), his clothes were threadbare, and he was skeletal. Every night he slept on a different friend's floor. With debts that amounted to the equivalent of about half a million dollars today, he recognized that he had no choice but to declare bankruptcy. He sold his camera and packed his few remaining possessions in a battered cardboard suitcase and boarded a train for Los Angeles, dreaming of making it as a movie director.

At that time of the bankruptcy Walt Disney was the best animator and animated filmmaker in Kansas City, but the region had nowhere near enough customers to sustain a local studio. He failed to establish his reputation with any of the national distributors in New York that would have enabled him to break into the business. Walt knew he had to sell in New York and he tried, first with an expensive salesman and then on his own, but he was not yet skilled or savvy enough. He was a naïve businessperson, and he lacked the basic skills to manage money. Although Walt had initially hired a business manager, he used him basically as a bookkeeper until he could no longer afford to pay him. And although Walt was thoughtful about how he planned his animated shorts, he was not thoughtful at all about how he planned to spend his money—he thought money was just the means to his ends.

Walt learned a lot about animation from his failure. By the end of the experience, his animation production skills were as good as almost anyone's in New York. In fact, while experimenting with new techniques in his frenetic attempt to save the studio, Walt Disney developed a novel one for combining real and animated footage. He even made a short called *Alice's Wonderland* starring a four-year-old actress who played with cartoon cats. But by the time of Walt's bankruptcy, none of the New York distributors had offered to distribute the novel short.

When Walt launched his first studio, he was a pure, high-risk entrepreneur. He conducted the equivalent of a half-a-million-dollar experiment with other people's money, only to discover that he wasn't good enough to make his entrepreneurial dream come true. With crude skills and no coach, he chose to compete as a walk-on in the major leagues of animation. He raised his half-million dollars from naïve investors who enabled him to practice and improve his animation skills. Today, entrepreneurs undertake similarly expensive experiments with the money of friends, family, or strangers.

How good do you have to be at what you do to succeed as an entrepreneur? The answer depends on what entrepreneurial league you want or need to play in. In Walt Disney's case, he was good enough at the age of twenty to sell his animations locally but not nationally, so he went bankrupt.

Owning a small store in a small town may not require as much mastery of as many skills as founding an animation studio or founding a company that provides cybersecurity software to the world's top banks (one of today's most sophisticated businesses). And while the independent retail owner and the cybersecurity founder are both entrepreneurs, they appear to have little else in common. But in fact, the success of both of them results from decisions they make about how good they want to be relative to their fellow entrepreneurs. All entrepreneurs ultimately decide what league they'll try playing in— unfortunately, most choose unconsciously and choose the wrong one.

Succeeding as a small shop owner requires knowledge of where you can buy the goods you think you plan to sell at a low enough price that you can make enough money to pay your rent and salaries. You need to know basic math so you can calculate change or add up the total cost of a list of items. It would also be beneficial to understand what your customers want to buy and the price they're willing to pay.

If the shop owner proves competent at buying goods that customers want, at a cost lower than customers are willing to pay, *and* the owner is frugal and able to save the profits, *then* the shop owner may choose to use the savings to rent a larger space and sell a wider range of goods. To compete with other shops selling the same goods, the shop owner would then need employees to help and would need the skills to find, hire, and train honest people who knew enough basic arithmetic to make correct change or to count the goods as they were delivered from the wholesaler. To make a profit running a medium-sized shop, the former small shop owner would need more sophisticated merchandising skills, at least as strong as those of shop owners selling similar goods. The shop owner would also need some basic bookkeeping and inventory management skills to keep track of money, what goods to replenish, and what items were selling well.

When it came to skills, Sam Walton knew his limitations. While working for J. C. Penney after college, Sam had been trained to be a skilled department store salesman, but he understood that didn't prepare him to run a small-town store, let alone compete with established storeowners. As a young man just out of the army, knowing he lacked those skills, he chose to buy a Ben Franklin franchise store. He didn't want to risk his future on having to instantly acquire the skills required to source, inventory, and merchandise thousands of items. So he gladly agreed to forgo a significant portion of his potential profits in exchange for being trained to run a well-branded store supported with sourcing and distribution through Ben Franklin.

Walt Disney and Sam Walton took opposite paths in mastering the skills they would need to compete in the entrepreneurial leagues they joined. Walt chose to compete in the big leagues of animation, acquiring the skills to do so through trial and error and with no expert coaching. Sam chose to de facto pay a brand name coach to help him prepare to compete with the two other small-town shop owners in Newport, Arkansas. He had to work hard to implement all he learned from Ben Franklin's supervisors, which he then augmented by copying what he saw was working at other stores. Sam succeeded to the point where his profits allowed him to buy a new store when his landlord refused to renew his lease. On the other hand, Walt's choice created no value but lots of experience, and he lost lots of other people's money in the process, forcing him to leave town to get another chance.

On declaring bankruptcy, Walt felt his best opportunity lay in joining his Uncle Robert and his brother Roy in Los Angeles. Living off of Uncle Robert's good will, Walt ignored his uncle's expectations that he would quickly get a job, any job. Instead, Walt spent his time visiting movie studios and trying to sell versions of his Kansas City animation ideas to LA's even more sophisticated theatre owners. Fortunately, a New York distributor of cartoons began to have contract difficulties with one of the animators she worked with. So she decided to reconsider an inquiry she had received from Walt about her interest in *Alice's Wonderland*. She offered to pay Walt $1,500 for his novel combination of animation and live action, giving him a chance to get back into business.

Walt, who was never afraid to ask for help, made a decision to ask his older brother Roy to be his partner in a new business, Disney Brothers Studios. As we learned from Sam's experience, key partners can bring essential skills to an enterprise. Whether Walt realized it or not, Roy had essential skills that he lacked, including bookkeeping and money management. Roy had always been good with figures and at saving his money, as he had been a bank teller before being diagnosed with tuberculosis. Indeed, Roy was still recuperating in a tuberculosis ward when Walt snuck into his room in the middle of the night to wake him up and ask for his help. As his convalescence was coming to an end, Roy had been contemplating what to do next. He was delighted to help his beloved little brother with his business venture.

Roy's involvement and maturity made it possible to borrow $500 from Uncle Robert to rent space and set up the business, money they paid back with interest when they received the $1,500 for *Alice's Wonderland*. The distributor, who wanted Walt's cartoon idea to work as much as Walt did, was disappointed with it. She said its poor workmanship and dull story made it unusable. Nonetheless, she gave him permission to produce a second episode for another $1,500. Walt, who was always open to artistic criticism, produced a more appealing and better-executed second episode that satisfied the distributor and gave her the confidence to offer Walt a contract to produce a new episode every month for the next year.

Walt's animation experience made him effective at visualizing how he would produce his new series, and he immediately dispatched Roy to rent a bigger space while Walt negotiated for his former partner Ub Iwerks to move to LA to help draw the cartoon portion of each episode. Walt assigned himself the task of directing the live action. Roy's assignment was to operate the movie camera, pay the bills, and keep the books.

Walt's animation production skills and Ub's drawing skills rapidly improved with the steady work. Despite the distributor feeling as though improvements in the quality of production were still necessary, the contract was renewed for a second year. The distributor dispatched her brother to LA from New York for several months to oversee the improvements. Walt diligently adopted the improved production techniques, but the costs of doing so ate up all his profits.

With Walt having mastered the production techniques that made the *Alice* series equal in quality to other cartoons of the era, the distributor asked him to pitch a new cartoon series that Universal Studios would be able to market to theaters to show along with its movies. Walt proposed a series based on a smart-alecky rabbit with long ears named Oswald—an innovative concept at the time, since everyone in the business had always used cats as their protagonists.

Oswald landed them a contract to produce twenty-six episodes over the coming year. Jubilant and emboldened, Walt cajoled his small team to double their production, producing another *Alice* along with the new *Oswald* episode in the following two weeks. But, as with the first *Alice*, the first *Oswald* episode was rejected by Universal for having jitter in the opening sequence, a confusing story, and Oswald's bottom-heavy appearance. Walt, understanding that working with a major studio would require him to produce even higher-quality product, agreed with most of Universal's criticisms (but rejected their suggestion that Oswald don a monocle). The second Oswald was accepted and received favorable reviews from the movie press.

With the *Oswald* contract from a major motion picture studio, Walt had been accepted into the big leagues of his profession. Sam Walton similarly climbed from the small-town league of shop owners to the global retail big leagues through a relentless focus on process improvements. To run multiple stores, Sam had to develop and master crude processes for simultaneously tracking the status of sales and inventories in multiple locations, a process for replenishing items for each store, plus a process for managing the logistics required to get the items delivered to the right store. Sam developed his first crude processes with the help of Ben Franklin. He tacked pieces of paper with numbers he needed to know—like store reports or invoices— onto a bulletin board in front of his desk. Each bunch of papers held together by a tack represented a different action he had to take each week. Sam was visually oriented and seeing bunches of papers grow in size gave him an additional sense of how things were selling and helped him prioritize next steps. These crude processes worked for Sam in running a half dozen Ben Franklins, at which point he moved into a bigger office space with cubbyholes for each store's paperwork, which he reviewed on a weekly basis or when a cubby filled up.

Because Sam was not well organized, these basic and crude processes were critical for his success. If he had not religiously sorted his paperwork, transcribed critical numbers onto big worksheets, or sorted papers into cubbyholes, he would have lost control over the stores he owned, irrespective of whether he visited them constantly. Relentlessly working with store managers to make incremental small improvements to merchandising and store procedures improved almost every one of his stores, each becoming the best in its locale.

But the store managers could only have been supported with the inventory and merchandising they needed because Sam forced himself to implement some basic processes for tracking store performance and for ordering. As these processes became routine, Sam could train others to take them over, thereby incrementally freeing up time and attention that could be invested in adding more stores, until he no longer needed Ben Franklin's costly support and could gradually begin to compete with more sophisticated and better financed retail chains.

Walt's initial processes to successfully deliver his *Oswald* cartoons were equally crude by today's standards. But in both cases, these processes were absolutely required for Walt and Sam to compete in their respective entrepreneurial leagues.

With the *Oswald* contract in hand, Walt Disney, at the age of twenty-three, started to dream big. Walt instantly ratcheted up the demands and pressures on his team to produce better crafted, funnier, and more inventive *Oswald* episodes. To get even more production and higher-quality work out of his team, Walt developed several important productivity improvement techniques over the next year, including working out story and timing details using rough animations before committing to more detailed and costly final drawings. With a growing fixation on quality and detail, Walt became increasingly critical of his team's work and demanded longer hours, resulting in his animators no longer feeling appreciated. On the other hand, Walt and Roy felt successful for the first time and used their *Oswald* profits to build identical houses for themselves on neighboring lots near their studio.

As tensions rose at the studio, the distributor, Charles Mintz, was also feeling increasingly anxious about working with Walt.* Mintz felt Walt was losing his skill as an animator and adding little value as the producer. Walt spent most of his time improving the quality of *Oswald* in ways that only cost more money and that audiences wouldn't even notice. As the time approached to renew the contract, the distributor and most of Walt's disgruntled animation team secretly schemed to take over the production of *Oswald*. Walt Disney traveled to New York for what he thought would be a routine renewal of the *Oswald* contract. The contract negotiations went nowhere and Walt wound up spending several months in New York trying to convince the distributor or Universal to renew. The magnitude of the revolt was finally revealed when Roy, back in LA, received the mass resignation of almost the entire animation team. Only Ub Iwerks and a few junior animators remained loyal to Walt.

Defeated, stunned, and depressed, Walt headed back to LA. On the return train trip, he sketched out on cocktail napkins and train stationery ideas for a new cartoon character based on a mouse. While the traitorous animators remained working at the studio for another two months to finish up the first *Oswald* contract, Walt and Ub worked secretly late into the night to produce the first *Mickey Mouse* episode. But no film studio was interested in distributing it. With no money coming in, Walt and Roy mortgaged their new houses to raise enough to make a second episode. Still no takers.

A few months before, *The Jazz Singer*, the first talkie, had premiered, throwing the film industry into turmoil about where and

---

*   Charles Mintz had married Walt's original distributor Margaret Winkler. By the time of the *Oswald* contract Mintz had taken over all dealings with Walt.

how sound would apply to movies—and cartoons—in the future. *Mickey Mouse*, as originally envisioned by Walt, was silent. After the second episode failed to sell, Walt and Roy decided to gamble everything they owned to add sound to *Mickey Mouse*. A few cartoon makers had experimented with atmospheric sound as a general back-drop to action, but no studio had yet figured how to synchronize sound with animation. Walt and Ub created a *Mickey Mouse* story, *Steamboat Willie*, where all the gags, and even Mickey's swagger, were tied to sounds. A junior animator suggested using a metronome to time the soundtrack, triggering Walt to develop novel timing tricks for scoring a synchronized soundtrack. The technique was tested with the small team remaining at the studio. While the film was projected, each person banged, squeaked, and mooed at appropriate times to synchronize exactly the sounds they planned to add. The team found tying the cartoon to their actions so hilarious that they continued to repeat their simulation over and over until they collapsed from exhaustion late into the night.

Walt headed to New York with the written sound score and a reel of animation in search of a sound studio that could add sound to their film. The big companies that owned competing sound technologies were not excited about adding sound to a short cartoon when their business of adding sound to full-length features was growing quickly and demanding their full attention.

As with hot technologies today, back in the late 1920s, new technologies such as adding soundtrack to film spawned scores of new startups, each of which offered supposedly unique products. Naturally drawn to people who showed appreciation for his work, Walt was most impressed with a sound-to-film entrepreneur named Pat Powers. Walt probably knew, but chose to overlook, the fact that Powers was notorious in the film industry for double-dealing and strong-arm tactics. Completely ignoring Roy, Walt decided to license Powers' Cinephone Sound System for far more money than they had. Walt then gladly accepted Powers' offer to find the best sound effects men in town and arrange for a sound studio (Powers just provided the equipment). The recording session cost $1,000, which was the last of the cash Roy had raised from the mortgages and from selling some assets. The session was a complete disaster, as the musicians ignored Walt's instructions on how to synchronize the score to the cartoon.

To obtain the money for a second recording session, Roy had no choice but to do what they had avoided doing up until then—taking out a bank loan. If *Mickey Mouse* did not succeed now, Walt and Roy would have to declare bankruptcy. To make sure the second recording session would work, Walt thought about how to make his instructions dead easy to follow. Over the next two weeks, Walt inscribed a ball that bounced at the implied beat of the action onto each frame of actual film the musicians watched while they played—and the second recording session hit its mark, so to speak. (Walt's "follow the bouncing ball" technique is still used on karaoke DVDs today.)

But Walt still didn't have a distributor, so Pat Powers convinced Walt, again without consulting Roy, to make him Disney's exclusive sales agent for 10 percent of all future fees. Powers then arranged for Walt to show *Steamboat Willie* to some top studio executives, most of whom loved the cartoon—but no one offered to distribute it. Fortunately, the manager of a large and famous New York City movie theater who had been invited to one of the *Steamboat Willie* screenings loved it and offered Walt $500 to show the cartoon for one week at his theater. Walt desperately needed more money to make payroll back in LA, so he countered with $1,000 for two weeks, and a deal was set.

Audiences loved *Steamboat Willie*. So did the critics—even the critic for the *New York Times*. Audiences flocked to the theater to see the cartoon (not so much the feature film *Gang War*). A sensation with the public, it was also immediately recognized as a revolutionary cartoon, with everyone amazed by the new dimension sound added to storytelling. (It would take over a year for any other animation studio to figure out how to enhance their stories as effectively with sound.) Practically every distributor immediately offered to distribute *Mickey Mouse*, and many of the large studios offered to buy Disney Brothers outright. Walt was not interested in selling, and instead insisted on unprecedented fees and rights, which established distributors refused to accept—so still no deal.

Pat Powers stepped forward with another offer. Again, without consulting Roy, Walt accepted, agreeing to let Powers oversee the regional distribution of *Mickey Mouse* in exchange for 10 percent of the gross receipts. While the national distributors and movie studios balked at Walt's demands, regional and foreign theater chains jumped at the opportunity to show *Mickey Mouse* while agreeing to pay unprecedented fees for the cartoon. Money started to roll in, more money than Walt or Roy had ever dreamed of seeing.

Walt and Roy bet their personal financial futures to enable Walt to develop new skills that they hoped could be commercialized. In roughly seven months, Walt had catapulted from being an inconsequential owner of a small animation studio producing a single cartoon series for a much bigger studio to being the most respected and successful animator in the world. He jumped from playing backup in the big league of animation to starring in the World Cup of talking cartoons. Walt's breakthrough came when he actually invented new techniques: synchronizing animation, synchronizing sound scores, and using sound to amplify the impact of stories. He trained others in these skills so he could reproduce the innovations with each new cartoon, churning out products as innovative and globally impactful in their day as the iPhone was when it debuted in 2007.

All the fame and accolades Walt received fueled his desire to make each new *Mickey Mouse* episode better than before. Consequently, each episode took longer and was more expensive to produce than the previous one. Even though Disney Studios received more money for *Mickey Mouse* than any cartoon in history to that point, the studio made less and less profit on each episode, to the point that a few years into the series, *Mickey Mouse* episodes *lost* money.* It was two other cartoon series that didn't draw as much of Walt's attention, *Donald*

---

* Walt dropped "Brothers" from the name of the studios, without consulting Roy, when Oswald became a hit.

Duck and *Silly Symphonies,* which kept Disney Studios profitable enough to expand.

Walt and Roy made another "all-in" bet when Walt decided to make the first animated feature length film, *Snow White and the Seven Dwarfs*. Walt worked intensely with his animators and story editors for five years writing and re-writing, drawing and re-drawing the story of Snow White. The arduous process of creating the first full-length feature cartoon required more money than any cartoon studio could fund from its cash flow. Walt insisted on total control of his ideas, which they both understood meant that there could be no outside investors to whom they would have to answer. Roy understood his position in the partnership was now to borrow the money to make the story of Snow White possible. Disney Studios would be financed by debt for the next thirty years.

Roy had to prepare sophisticated projections that met the standards of banks large enough to provide them the millions of dollars they needed (today's equivalent of many tens of millions of dollars). He became highly astute at understanding financial statements and projecting cash flow. Roy also mastered how and when to bring Walt into his discussions with bankers so the bankers would understand his creativity but not worry about his spendthrift ways.

Snow White was considered by many to be the best movie ever made, and to this day it is always listed among the best. It was a global blockbuster; nobody had ever seen anything like it. Not even the first *Star Wars* movie can compare to its impact on audiences, let alone on critics. Once again, Walt and Roy were able to pay off their loans and still be flush with cash.

But the next three very expensive feature animated films, *Pinocchio, Fantasia*, and *Bambi*, were financial bombs even if many admired their artistic contributions. The losses from these movies consumed all the *Snow White* profits, all the cartoon profits, and all the money Roy was able to borrow. Roy even had to sell public bonds in the early 1940s based upon the fame of the Disney brand, a de facto IPO, just to finish the movies in production. With the studio in financial distress, outside Board members representing the public bondholders and bankers refused to loan another penny for making any new full-length animated feature, grounding Walt. He wasn't fired— nobody had the power to do that—but he was prevented from moving forward in the way that he wanted. Bedrock entrepreneurs may never have to give up ownership, but if they don't generate profits, they cannot do whatever they want, no matter who they are or what league they play in.

Walt Disney and Sam Walton took opposite approaches to achieving their bedrock entrepreneurial success. After *Oswald*, Walt relentlessly drove breakthrough innovation. Walt's repeated successes, each with its close encounters with bankruptcy, catapulted Disney to the top of the major leagues of the entertainment business. But the profits of each breakthrough were used to finance new breakthroughs, so when the profits from past breakthroughs were spent and not replaced with profits from another innovation, Walt had to stop. He still controlled the place and he could still get involved in whatever project sparked his interest at the studio, but he couldn't make films the way he wanted, when he wanted.

It took Disney Studios fifteen years to build its profitability back to the point where Walt got another shot at innovating entertainment. During those fifteen years, Roy and Walt even sold a portion of the studio to the public to relieve pressure on their large debts. Over this time, Walt's reputation subsided from wunderkind genius to formerly great innovator. He became less insistent on dictating every creative decision at the studio. Roy had a freer hand at managing the budget and finances, which helped him to maintain his focus on cash and profits. Limited by the studio's focus on producing films in already established formats, Walt's attention waned and critical and artistic acclaim eluded him.

Walt badly needed creative release to feel good about himself. Since he could no longer feel creatively fulfilled at his studio, Walt developed new hobbies. He became fascinated with miniature dioramas, medium-scale operating model railroads, and moving, lifelike figurines, and his projects grew larger in scale and scope with time. When finances at the studio were finally stable enough, Roy arranged for Walt to receive a generous royalty income for the studio's use of his name. Walt immediately invested this extra income back into his hobbies, which then grew further in scope to become so expensive that Walt even mortgaged his house to finance them.

Walt's hobbies enabled him to master a new series of skills. He was aggressive in hiring experts to help and support him in creating ever more sophisticated dioramas with moving figurines to accompany his scale model trains. Walt honed his skills to the point where he was able to envision an entirely new entertainment experience, which he called "Disneyland." He brought more and more people to his personal studio/laboratory, where everyone loved his ideas and encouraged him to turn them into a reality.

With Walt's excitement in Disneyland growing , Roy girded himself to place yet another "all-in" bet for Disney Studios to be able to create and build the park. And he didn't finance it by selling stock—a move that Disney's outside investors would have thought way too risky. Roy, working again in tandem with Walt, landed financing by getting huge advances from the ABC television network for making shows for the wildly popular new entertainment medium, something no other studio was willing offer as they thought TV competed too directly with movies.

Disneyland, as with all of Walt's major breakthrough projects, went way over budget, putting Disney Studios again on the brink of bankruptcy. But Walt's conceptualization of an entirely new type of themed family entertainment, promoted brilliantly through his popular TV shows for more than a year before the park opened, was an instant success. The park was such a hit that its profits enabled Disney to pay off their loans in full, and once again put Walt in control of his company's destiny.

Disney's journey is typical of the challenges faced by highly technical or highly creative entrepreneurs that insist on realizing their personal visions. As Walt's entrepreneurial career progressed, he developed increasingly sophisticated production and technical skills in order for his entertainment products to compete at a national level, and then internationally. Walt's example is pertinent for entrepreneurs that aspire to create local or regionally competitive enterprises. Many businesses require their leaders and workforces to master highly sophisticated skills even to compete locally. Cybersecurity software would be an extreme example of a demanding and competitive business for an entrepreneur to enter at any level. Developing cybersecurity software for big banks requires an entrepreneur who can assemble a team that knows as much about the security of banking systems as the most sophisticated hackers in the world. Staying ahead of both competitors and hackers requires a relentless pace of learning, which in turn requires sophisticated skills to be able to prepare and deliver world-class training to key individuals in a rapidly growing enterprise using rapidly evolving technologies. An entrepreneur who knows how to create such an enterprise can make even the most sophisticated banks in the world happy, gladly paying lots of money for something they are incapable of doing themselves.

I have a friend, Barry, who founded and runs a successful, self-funded firm that manages the cybersecurity of small- to medium-sized enterprises on the West Coast. Barry knows much more about cybersecurity than his customers do; he was a star student in the subject area when he got his bachelor's degree from a university with a great cybersecurity program. He sells his products and services to firms that don't have cybersecurity experts on their staffs. They therefore don't expect as much of Barry and his firm as would a major global bank. His customers like and respect him and his firm, feeling he gives them great attention and provides them expertise they could not afford to hire directly. Since Barry launched the firm fresh out of college, it has grown steadily. Along the way, he has had to learn new skills to motivate his growing team, to market his services more widely, and also to keep up with the latest cybersecurity techniques and technologies. *Nobody can grow their business without a dedication to mastering new skills.*

Today it would be unrealistic for Barry to ask a large global bank to hire his firm to provide cybersecurity consulting or support. He and his firm lack the expertise to understand the computer vulnerabilities of banking systems. But what is important is Barry's motivation—

his "Why"—whether he wants to grow his firm to be a bigger West Coast provider of cybersecurity services to small- and medium-sized enterprises, or whether he should invest his profits into hiring world experts in banking systems and banking system hackers. Expanding on the West Coast will still require additional skills, likely in sales and marketing. Since these skills are more readily available on the talent market, this is a less risky growth strategy. But Barry's personal motivation may drive him to achieve a higher status that can only be achieved by capturing a global "big league" banking client. It is entirely up to Barry to decide if being a leader in providing security to medium-sized firms on the West Coast feels satisfying. The risks and challenges of competing against more experienced and better-funded companies for this type of business greatly increase the chances of losing money and perhaps even failing entirely. Because Barry owns 100 percent of his company, the loss would be entirely his. If he had major shareholders, then the stakes would be different; if he failed to get banking customers after having invested considerable money and time in the effort he would also risk losing his job. In essence, Barry's position is similar to when Walt got a local theater owner to hire his studio to make simple animations for local audiences. That wasn't a big enough market and challenge for Walt, but it might be for Barry—time will tell.

As in sports, entrepreneurship has graduated leagues. Most sports have leagues to suit every level of skill, from amateur after-work and summer leagues, to professional minor leagues, to big leagues for the best competitors in the world. To play, you need to be better than the worst athlete playing your position in the league. Learning a sport is initially frustrating. It takes practice to become decent enough to compete in a league. Some people play sports with almost total dedication in order to prove to themselves that they can be *the* best at something, while some people play merely to have a good time.

The same is true of entrepreneurship. Breaking in and learning the ropes of entrepreneurship is challenging for everyone. It takes dedication, practice, and usually some coaching. Almost all entrepreneurs learn their business skills by trial and error on the job; the vast majority learn how to run and manage straightforward businesses like a sausage stand or a retail shop. Entrepreneurs can choose to compete locally—for example, by selling sausages on Venice Beach, or providing security to small businesses in LA. Barry, Jordan, and Sam started by competing in the entrepreneurial equivalent of a neighborhood after-school league, and Sam had a franchise owner helping him break in. Once established locally, entrepreneurs can practice and seek coaching to hone their skills, thereby enabling them to be highly compensated for serving the most demanding and sophisticated customers in their field. Some people sell things they produce for fun, turning hobbies into endeavors that generate some cash. But as with sports, *entrepreneurs can only succeed and feel satisfied with their success if they compete in a league suited to their level of skill and ambition (i.e. motivation).*

What is an entrepreneurial league? Entrepreneurial leagues are determined by competitors who want to deliver to your customer the same product or service that you do. If you run a local coffee place, then your league contains the local Starbucks, as well as the other places to pick up coffee in the neighborhood. It does not include Starbucks the parent company. In essence, leagues get tougher as the number of potential customers expand and the number of companies that compete for these customers increases in scale, scope, and sophistication. Think of each of the over 1,000 government classifications for industry mentioned at the beginning of chapter 3 as a different sport, with each having leagues that start at the local level and others that reach up to national and multi-national leagues. This is true for practically all types of businesses. You can even compete in local car-making leagues. As of 2013 the Census Bureau reported 249 different "Automobile and Light Duty Motor Vehicle Manufacturing" companies in the US—far more than the number of brand name car manufacturers. This list includes companies that produce customized cars and specialized performance vehicles, like racecars or electric vehicles. You do not need to compete with Toyota and Ford to get into the car business. Elon Musk originally founded Tesla as a boutique manufacturer of a few dozen all-electric versions of an existing

Lotus roadster. He did not jump immediately into the big leagues of automotive manufacturing.

Which leads us to an important realization: *Almost anyone with skills that make some group of people happy can succeed as a local entrepreneur, while no entrepreneur who is unskilled can succeed on a national or global level.* This has several valuable corollaries that expose some widely accepted myths about entrepreneurship:

Myth: *You need to disrupt an existing industry.*

Several famous and wealthy entrepreneurs and venture capitalists have written bestselling books claiming that all entrepreneurs should shoot for the moon or else the effort is not worth it. They explain that being an entrepreneur is hard, so there's no point in doing something small. Some go on to claim that to really succeed, entrepreneurs must be innovative enough to disrupt an entire industry; otherwise, entrenched competitors will run you out of business. They claim that failure is good, so you might as well shoot high because it doesn't matter if it doesn't work out—the more audacious your goals, the more experience you'll get. All these claims are made by people who have already made it big and who want to associate themselves with other people that they think are going to make it big. All these claims are self-serving—and misleading.

As we have seen, most successful entrepreneurs started small and grew big only after they had demonstrated they could make money. Only a handful of high-risk entrepreneurs, virtually all of them with previous experience and highly developed relevant skill sets, can persuade venture capitalists to fund their high-stakes, winner-take-all, invest-as-much-as-you-can-as-fast-as-you-can-build-it-out   business ideas. We are talking less than 0.1 percent of all entrepreneurs. If you say all entrepreneurs should eschew starting small, and instead immediately compete with well-established global competitors or well-financed and highly experienced and skilled entrepreneurs, then you're needlessly leading lambs to slaughter, and you're ignoring history and precedents that are as relevant and vital as ever. Every entrepreneur profiled in this book started in some form of an entrepreneurial minor league. So did Elon Musk, Mark Zuckerberg, and Bill Gates.

Myth: *Fresh ideas about how to disrupt a market spring from the beginner's mindset.*

All entrepreneurs must have a minimum skill set to have the credibility required to assemble capable teams with the necessary skills. Without credibility, you can't put together a team with the skills to know what's wrong with an industry, let alone with the skills to fix it. Credibility is a signal that other people can trust you as a leader, and it comes with experience. Credibility also comes with a mastery of the skills that other people recognize could enable change in industry best practices. No one with significant experience is interested in working with somebody they don't think will succeed.

That doesn't mean you must have direct experience in a market— as in having made a similar product or delivered a similar service—to successfully enter or change the market. A different mindset, free of the hidden assumptions that constrain the operation of almost all established markets, is an almost essential element in creating valuable innovations. High-frequency customers and suppliers form pools of people with considerable knowledge and expertise about how value is created at the enterprises they do business with. Estée Lauder was an innovative entrepreneur because she understood cosmetics from the perspective of a power user and a power salesperson, as well as someone who had been tutored in cosmetics' formulation and production. Estée's greatest innovations were in how to sell cosmetics, something she understood better than the department stores she sold to.

From time to time, entirely new businesses are created where no leagues yet exist and there are no hidden assumptions about how business should be transacted. This is analogous to new sports being formed. As a new sport emerges and becomes accepted by both players and spectators, the skills required to excel at the sport evolve and develop. The new stars of the sport are virtually always those with the physical and mental traits that align well with the sport, and who also have the motivation to train more diligently and shrewdly than anyone else. While there were no leagues in personal computer software when Bill Gates and Paul Allen began Microsoft, both of them possessed considerable skills in programming. They also invested more hours of their time than any others to become the world experts in developing programs for computers with small memories. Such emergent industries offer great opportunities for diligent and motivated entrepreneurs to develop new world-class skill sets—new industries just don't emerge very often.

Far more entrepreneurial opportunities arise because of the constant changes experienced by every business in existence and the fact that no business is able to react to every change in such a way as to please every customer. Every change creates at least two niche opportunities. One, to find and take away those customers who are dissatisfied by the changed condition and are no longer satisfied with the existing product or service and want the product or service modified: "I want bigger, less expensive packaging." "I want smaller serving sizes." Addressing these dissatisfactions can be challenging, but they are always there and they are always growing. Sam Walton captured these sorts of opportunities, as did Estée Lauder.

Two, opportunities always arise to help existing businesses adapt to the changed environment, maybe by providing a new service or a new product (like a new software program). Changing is difficult for established businesses. If you can help them adapt more but change less, then you're going to make them extremely happy. Stephanie did this very well; so did Vidal.

Fortunately for entrepreneurs, the almost infinite number of new opportunities start out as niche products or services. As a result, an entrepreneur can develop skills, assemble teams, and confirm profitability as the niche demand develops, while often not being perceived as a threat by the entrenched players in the broader market. This positions the entrepreneur to enter "adjacent" markets once the company has become profitable as well as reliable in the eyes of customers. Again, Sam Walton did that; so did Jordan Monkarsh.

Myth: *To compete as an entrepreneur, you need masterful programming skills.*

Walt Disney's experience is telling. He started in animation by producing the animations himself, but did not achieve any traction or notoriety until Ub Iwerks actually took over the drawing and Walt focused his efforts on producing and managing the relationship with the distributors. Animation skills to Walt are directly analogous to what programming skills can mean to a software entrepreneur today; they can help you get started in a software business and help you understand how to manage other programmers in such businesses, but they are not what will make or break the business. As we saw with Stephanie, even in a business that creates and sells sophisticated software, the success of the entrepreneur and the enterprise rests not with the coders but with the people that understand the needs of the customer. Even the big leagues, software and otherwise, never require the entrepreneur to have world-class coding skills. Programming skills support just about any business of scale today, but programming does not in itself make anyone happy, other than maybe the programmer. Entrepreneurs tell programmers what to program.

As we've seen from Walt, Vidal, Jordan, and Estée, starting out in the entrepreneurial minor leagues requires very little in terms of assets, though it certainly imposes no limits as to how successful you can become. There is, nonetheless, a minimum set of required assets every entrepreneur needs to possess in order to launch a successful business, regardless of league. That's what we need to discuss in the next chapter.

CHAPTER 8

HOW MUCH

Aspiring entrepreneurs are continually asking me, "How much money will I need to make sure my ideas succeed?" or, "How much money should I raise?" Money is quite literally the last thing an entrepreneur needs. Money is the fill in. Money is what you need after you've pulled together all that's already available to use to start your enterprise.

As we saw with William Shockley, the Nobel Prize–winning inventor of the transistor, if there's something critical you lack, no great idea and no amount of money can make you successful, not even with the best idea of the twentieth century. Shockley had more than enough of everything he needed, except for two essential qualities: leadership skills and motivation. Without those, neither money nor all the smart, dedicated people he hired could help. Shockley lacked the motivation necessary to create a company that focused on customers rather than on him. He couldn't accept ideas that were not his, nor could he invest the time and emotional energy required to master new skills. Any entrepreneur without enough of all the right stuff is in danger of losing everything.

How Much Depends on the Test

Whatever you want to prove to the world as an entrepreneur, and however you want to change the world, you must, *to some degree*, possess the following assets:

- A strong enough implicit motivation to succeed,
- An idea that makes a large group of people happy,
- Leadership skills,
- The attention of a large number of potential customers,
- A team with mastery of the skills required to reliably deliver and market the product or service,
- Enough time to grow the idea into something that creates value, and
- Enough money to develop the idea into a product or service that can be reliably delivered and ultimately makes lots of people happy.

To estimate specifically how much of each of these things you need, you must first understand your motivations.

How Much Motivation

As we discussed in chapter 4, no one is forcing you to start an enterprise. In becoming an entrepreneur, you are asking the world to change to suit *your* needs. The world will get along just fine without you. Entrepreneurship is ultimately a test that you impose on yourself to satisfy some core implicit motivation. The quantity and quality of the assets you need to pass your test depend on the test you feel the need to put yourself through.

It would be best for you and for the world if you ultimately balance the severity and riskiness of the test you choose with the amount of emotion, effort, time, and money you're able and willing to invest. This is equivalent to saying that it's best for everyone that you choose to compete in the entrepreneurial league where you have a good chance of succeeding rather than failing. If you create a rational balance between what you are able to invest with the amount of change you feel compelled to make in the world, then you will create the most good and the least waste.

Many entrepreneurs strike an ill-advised balance because they do not understand what they're trying to prove or because their desire for status makes them take unnecessary risks. Walt Disney went way beyond what he needed to spend in Kansas City to see if he could commercialize his animation skills. Sam Walton and Estée Lauder challenged themselves to demonstrate their commercializable skills before expanding beyond their modest original forays into business.

How much motivation do we need to prove to ourselves we are worthy? Researchers have developed some scales to estimate the strength of motivations. The most popular scale in use right now is the "Grit Scale." It measures how dedicated we are to accomplishing whatever we commit ourselves to do. Because we typically commit ourselves to doing things to satisfy our *explicit* motivations, the Grit Scale measures how well our *explicit* motivations align with our *implicit* ones.

The existence of the Grit Scale yields a valuable insight: We can increase the chances of our entrepreneurial success by making our explicit motivations more consistent with our implicit motivations. If we can align our explicit and implicit motivations, then our actions become significantly more aligned with what we need to feel worthy. The difference in our ability to succeed once we align our own explicit and implicit motivations is analogous to the difference between the energy delivered by a 100-watt light bulb and a 100-watt laser. Both generate the same amount of light, but you can safely stare at a 100-watt light bulb, whereas looking into a 100-watt laser that focuses its light onto a single tiny spot would melt an eye in its socket.

Unfortunately, the Grit Scale is untested relative to determining an absolute minimum value of motivation required to be a successful entrepreneur. Rather than looking to measure a metric we have not yet discovered, I have found it is most effective for an aspiring entrepreneur to honestly assess how well their implicit and explicit motivations align, and then to diligently improve the alignment. If an aspiring entrepreneur seeks to improve his or her motivational alignment over a sustained period, then he or she has the motivation to succeed. Simple.

We can improve the alignment of our explicit motivations with our implicit ones in two different ways. First, through self-awareness, our motivations can become more focused and have more impact. By specifically understanding our implicit motivations, we can then focus the short-term actions controlled by our explicit motivations. For example, I have a burning desire to be needed that I did not become aware of until my mid-thirties. Up to that point, I had been a mediocre leader because I always acted in such a way as to prove to people that I should have been included in any activity that interested me. If I felt I had been left out, I became judgmental, disparaging whatever the person or group with whom I'd wanted to align myself did. I didn't realize this, and neither did the people I was around. I was just labeled as moody and difficult. I thought these were traits I had been born with, instead of realizing they were symptoms of my motivation, characteristics that I could train myself to mitigate. When I finally discovered the source of these mysterious mood swings and counterproductive actions, I was able to channel my motivation so that my actions helped, rather than hindered, the work of my colleagues.

Second, we can use techniques such as cognitive reappraisal to mitigate our irrational fears, or phobias, that interfere with our achieving our core implicit motivation. Many of our fears are rooted in the evolutionary development that makes us hyper-aware of things that could hurt us, so we can take action to avoid them. But we no longer need most of our evolution-based fears in order to survive. Social anxiety and fear of public speaking are common, and there are others that can dampen otherwise strong selfish entrepreneurial desires. Programs such as Toastmasters can often help people control their fear of public speaking or fear of public humiliation. Similarly, cognitive therapies prescribed by psychologists can help people mitigate a social fear of groups and strangers. Many fears today can be mitigated through cognitive routines and do not need to stand in the way of an aspiring entrepreneur doing what needs to be done.

Being a truly motivated entrepreneur has much in common with being a Zen master. Buddhist monks and Zen masters meditate without changing position for many hours, overcoming what we would experience as great pain. Through marathon meditation, monks demonstrate the strength of their motivation to be masters of their minds. Nobody is born with a motivation to be a Zen master. It must develop, and in most people it only does so later in life. As an entrepreneur, you must be strongly motivated to succeed, and you can develop and shape that motivation through the application of self-awareness to the point where you can endure great hardships. Entrepreneurship requires a quasi-religious dedication to giving up almost all worldly pleasures in order to master the additional challenging skills required to achieve your true selfish desires and ambitions.

Self-awareness skills, particularly mindfulness, can play a role in the discovery of hidden implicit motivations, sating desires or fears, and aligning explicit motivations. A great mindfulness coach or a skilled therapist can help you get your self-awareness skills to the level needed to align your actions with your implicit motivations.

Today's media hype encourages too many aspiring entrepreneurs to try to "shoot for the moon and use other people's money." This exhortation mistakenly implies that it takes moon shots and loads of money to satisfy implicit motivations. It does not. Dreaming about fortune and fame is an explicit motivation, not an implicit one. And *misaligned explicit motivations, particularly those tied to fortune and fame, can lead unsuspecting entrepreneurs to take on significant risks that are ultimately inconsistent with why they really needed to be entrepreneurs in the first place.* As a consequence, more entrepreneurs fail than would otherwise be consistent with the magnitude of the challenges they set. You should strive to understand your true implicit core motivations, control your distracting explicit motivations and irrational fears, and set your goals accordingly. If you have the grit to strive to align your motivations, then you likely have enough grit to succeed as an entrepreneur . . . if you can assemble the rest of the assets you need.

How Much of an Idea

How much of an idea you need is really a reflection of how much selfish motivation you have and what it will take to sate it. You only need an idea that *over time* will prompt enough happy people to hand you enough of their money that you'll be satisfied with the result. You need an idea that is good enough to let you prove what you need to prove to yourself.

If your mind and body pulsate with the intense need to prove to your billionaire father that you can be as successful as he is, then you're going to need an idea that can make huge numbers of people with lots of money very happy. If you're Jordan Monkarsh, you'll need an idea that will create a business that ultimately serves at least as many customers as your dad's butcher shop.

The strength and value of an idea doesn't have to be measured in monetary terms. If you're Josephine Mentzer Lauter, alias Estée Lauder, then you need an idea that's big enough to not only generate significant wealth, but to attract the prestigious friends and real estate that will get you accepted in high society. To Lauder, selling beauty cream would not have satisfied her if it only made her rich. She needed her business to win her acceptance in a higher social class, something money alone could not buy.

You can measure the strength of your idea by conducting quick, low-cost experiments. These experiments are sometimes called minimum viable products, MVPs, or prototypes. A prototype enables you to test customer receptivity to what you want to sell—in other words, to test how much happiness your offering generates. With virtually no investment, Estée Lauder was able to sell her uncle's beauty creams in beauty parlors and test what it would take to get a customer to buy. In conducting years of experiments with thousands of customers, there was no question that Estée was motivated to succeed.

Furthermore, after more than a decade of testing herself, she also came to understand that she needed to create her own brand and sell it widely in order to have an idea big enough to satisfy her ambitions.

How Much Leadership

Leadership skills are essential—you simply cannot accomplish much alone. No leadership skills, no success—period. The level of mastery you must achieve in practicing your leadership skills depends on how many people you need to help you and how much stress these people might be expected to endure.

When Steve Jobs founded Apple at the age of twenty-two, he was a visionary, but he wasn't a leader. Like many other successful entrepreneurs, he found partners who brought the requisite level of leadership skills to Apple. Jobs hired Mark Markula to be Chairman of the Board and Mark Scott to be CEO of Apple, and he let them handle all people-related tasks while he focused on development. Markula and Scott had the leadership skills to grow Apple faster than any company in history.

Entrepreneurs who want to create a fast-growing business need masterful leadership skills at the outset. They won't have time to develop those skills on the job because their enterprises will be in a constant state of flux as they grow.

By contrast, Vidal, like many successful slow-growth entrepreneurs, acquired his leadership skills on the job, picking them up as the enterprise developed. But even slow-growth entrepreneurs need rudimentary leadership skills, if only to hire the right people and to make sure they're productive. They must become students of leadership skills as soon as they form their company.

Leadership is a skill and not a trait—it has nothing to do with charisma. Leadership is measured by how much stress, cumulatively and peak, followers are prepared to endure to support their leader in the attainment of his or her vision. Some followers are willing to endure the ultimate in peak stress—death—to support their leader;

fortunately, that's never a requirement for entrepreneurial leaders (unless you lead a drug cartel or other illegal enterprise).

Some leaders use extrinsic motivators—e.g. money—to get their followers to do what they want and need. Other leaders, particularly entrepreneurial leaders, use some combination of the skills we ascribed to Sam Walton in the How To chapter. As we discussed in that chapter, Sam acquired many of his leadership skills by leading sports teams under the guidance of good coaches, and by leading student organizations. For Walton's entire life, the employees of Walmart were willing to do whatever "Mr. Sam" asked.

Walt got to experiment with leading, something he had not done while in school or even when working for the Red Cross in France, when he hired the staff for his Laugh-O-Gram Studios. That didn't last too long, as nobody was willing to work for him once the money ran out, but it was very valuable experience. He had to entice older people to work for him when he was only twenty years old, which required him to at least understand his employees' explicit motivations. His skills were basic enough to attract Ub Iwerks (once Walt offered to pay him the salary he demanded) to want to move to California, as well as many other talented animators and artists. Walt became adept in creating a vision of his company that talented artists felt would enable them to excel at their crafts. Animators that worked with Walt on *Snow White* considered it the high point of their career. Walt was open to everyone's ideas, and they all felt they were breaking new ground on an almost-weekly basis. Walt—and Roy—spared no expense in letting everyone experiment with new ideas on how to portray emotions in drawings that moved on the screen.

But Walt was considered tyrannical whenever he was under pressure or when he felt things were not working out as he had envisioned. Almost all his *Oswald* animators rebelled when given the chance. Later, even Ub Iwerks left Walt when he felt Walt no longer cared about what he had to say. Disney animators even went on strike after *Snow White*, as Walt refused to listen to their issues.

Walt had a vision that attracted great artists to want to work with him, and he was skilled at making major changes happen to enable the implementation of his ideas. But Walt's self-awareness never developed to the point where he selflessly cared about those that helped him. Roy mitigated some of Walt's leadership issues with the non-artists that worked for Disney, but after the strike, Walt was never able to recreate the open and productive working relationship he had with his animators during the production of *Snow White*— nor was he interested in doing so. Walt was not a great leader, but he had enough leadership skill to attract major talent to his vision of new forms of entertainment. It was good enough to get him his breakthroughs, but it wasn't good enough to continuously sustain the creativity he aspired to inspire.

You can find many different leadership measures and assessments. Most of them aren't very good. The best measurement and assessments will come from asking those you admire and trust to help you lead others. Many people in positions of power do not want other leaders in their areas of influence. You would not want to ask Walt Disney, if he were alive, to help you learn how to lead creative artists—but Roy likely would have lent a hand. This paradigm often applies to parents as well. Some parents have agendas for their children that they're not entirely aware of, and are unconsciously biased in answering a child whom they may or may not want to see start their own business.

Even with help, leadership ability will always come down to practice and skill development. Opportunities to practice leadership skills abound. Practicing leadership can be something as simple as putting together a fun group event. If you're not willing to reach out to people you do not know and help them do something they could not have done without you, then you should expect to be doing most of the work in your startup yourself, or with others in a very uncoordinated and unmotivated fashion. And your business results will be accordingly mediocre and disappointing.

How Much Attention

You cannot sell anything without the attention of potential customers. Every successful entrepreneur needs potential customers to focus on their product or service for enough time to internalize whether it could make them happy. If the entrepreneur offers a product or service that the customer feels will make their life much better, then the customer will take the necessary actions to hand over the money they were asked for.

If you're looking to sell good-tasting sausages, it makes sense to rent a stand on Venice Beach to capture the attention of passers-by—just long enough to get their gastric juices flowing. Jordan's yelling, "Hey, Handsome, want to impress your girlfriend . . ." was the perfect approach for the men strolling by his sausage stand. Many dozens of places on Venice Beach compete for customer attention—without the shout-out, Jordan couldn't have built his business as fast as he did.

But you must to do more than simply make someone aware your product exists. Jordan needed only to wave a mouth-watering sausage at potential customers, who then decided whether they were going to bite. On the other hand, if you plan to deliver software that automates accounting for asset management firms, getting customers to a buying decision could take weeks or even months of work. You first have to directly answer the questions and concerns of all the "influential" people inside the firm who will use or access the software. You then need the undivided attention of the CEO of the firm and other key employees over several meetings to make them feel happy that spending the company's money on your software will help their careers, directly enrich their lives, or both. Furthermore, those meetings should take place without the distractions that could generate unhappy feelings that could accidentally become associated with the product (I had a potential customer with whom I was supposed to meet on 9/11 to sign up for the services of the company I had founded. Of course, our meeting was cancelled, but their traumatic associations with our meeting that hadn't taken place never dissipated enough for them to engage). You need the focused attention of many people for long enough to implant feelings in them that your product can simplify a complex process at an easily affordable price.

As the opening vignette in the book describes, Sam Walton

did a great job of getting the attention of potential customers by initially offering product for excitingly low prices. Estée Lauder pioneered giving away great-looking samples of beauty products to attract attention. Today, it is standard to try and get attention by offering a free entry-level version of an app or software products on the Internet. Indeed, the practice is now so common that most free stuff gets ignored unless you're giving away something with significant tangible value.

Entrepreneurs are almost always deficient in how they plan to get enough customer attention to give themselves even a chance of success. The math is simple, and the research you need to have on-hand isn't all that hard to come by, either:

A. How long will it take for someone who doesn't know anything about your product or service to fall in love with it enough to give you the money you ask for it in return?
B. How many customers with the disposition to fall in love with your product or service do you need to make a profit?
C. How many potential customers do you need to get the attention of to find enough customers who actually fall in love with your product and give you the money you ask for?*

Multiply A times C (where C is much, much bigger than B) and you'll likely find that you require many thousands of hours of customer attention to have any chance of succeeding.

Well-financed entrepreneurs almost always hire experienced marketing executives to attract the attention of potential customers. But even experienced marketing executives can't reduce the amount of attention that's required for a potential customer to internalize how they feel about your product. That amount of time is dictated by how complex, and how visceral or inspiring, your product or service

---

* If the customer is a business then you'll need to count everyone at that business with enough influence to veto the buying decision.

is. Experienced marketing executives can make sure that you create the most positive experience possible once you're in front of potential clients. They can also figure out how you can get in front of the most potential customers for the lowest cost. Experienced marketing executives can make sure you don't waste any of the precious time in front of the customer. Nonetheless, there is a minimum amount of customer attention required for their internalization of the corresponding positive emotion that will be required for any product or service.

How Much of a Team

Sam Walton built his team one person at a time. His first official hire when he started over in Bentonville was a stock boy. By the time he opened his second store, he needed to find a store manger to run it. He hired an already experienced and successful store manager to run Fayetteville while he concentrated on running Bentonville, ordering goods from Ben Franklin, and finding deals from other suppliers that he could use to lure customers into their stores. He built his initial constellation of profitable Ben Franklin franchised stores by using the simplest metrics and the simplest processes implemented by proven, savvy store managers.

Twelve years later, when Sam opened his first Wal-Mart, he was still using the same basic processes—the only difference was that he had more helpers. But five more years and six Wal-Marts later, Sam was sensing that things would get out of control if he didn't install far more sophisticated processes to manage his stores. And for that he realized he needed to augment his team in a major way. He brought in Ron Mayer, whom he met at an IBM workshop on how to use computers to control retail operations. Ron was a young head of finance for another small retailer of the time. He also hired Bob Thornton, someone he knew excelled at managing a distribution center for a large national retail chain. He let Ron and Bob coach him in how to control Wal-Mart so that it would continue to grow.

Their recommendations included bringing on additional staff, more sophisticated processes, and eventually, a distribution center and a mainframe computer.

Assuming you have the leadership skills to inspire a team to work productively together, or maybe have somebody working for you as a CEO that has that skill (like Steve Jobs did with Mark Scott), then the success of the enterprise hinges on *evolving* the team with increasingly sophisticated skills. Evolving and enhancing the skills of a team—particularly a startup team, which is always in flux—is extremely challenging. This evolution unfolds in four distinct stages:

Stage one. The team must possess the skills required to develop a product or service that customers want badly. You need jack-of-all-trades, get-it-done, creative types to figure out how to develop and configure a product that makes customers as happy as possible so they'll hand you as much money as possible. In some businesses one person can do all this set-up stuff, as with Vidal, Jordan and Sam (with help from Ben Franklin), but sometimes it requires a team with creative skills or other specific abilities, as with Stephanie and her partner, Steve. Steve, a creative, all-purpose, get-it-done computer engineer, was an ideal co-founder at this stage.

Stage two. Once customers start buying the product, the team needs to grow large enough and skilled enough to 1) deliver the product reliably, 2) sell to more and more customers, 3) make sure customers are happy, and 4) make sure the company operates properly (pays salaries, accounts for monies flowing in and out, fills out regulatory paperwork, keeps the space clean, etc.). Performing these four distinct yet equally critical tasks requires different skills than those used for the initial product development. You and your team must figure out how to turn these four tasks into routines, otherwise the product and a great customer experience cannot be reliably delivered to a growing number of customers, and you can't be sure the cash will be in the bank when you need it. This means that every startup in stage two needs people with process design skills. Even Sam, who started by relying upon some basic Ben Franklin ordering forms, needed to develop his own simple processes (remember the thumb tacks and eventually the cubbies in his office) to actually operate effectively and to make sure everything was ordered correctly and accounted for. Having these routines allowed Sam to continue to spend most of his time in front of customers to make sure they were happy with his store and its service. As he got more stores and delegated much of the inventory management and filling out of ordering forms to his experienced store managers, these processes became somewhat more sophisticated. Sam could then spend an increasing amount of his time visiting stores to meet customers and the sales associates that knew what their customers wanted.

Entrepreneurs, particularly entrepreneurs building sophisticated new products and services, can't keep things as simple as Sam, and often run into trouble in this stage. Stephanie ran into trouble with her partner Steve at this stage because Steve was not as responsive to requests to enhance his software as their customers expected, which created unhappy customers. Steve was unable to delegate any of his favorite software development tasks to others, even if customers were waiting for the new feature. Stephanie could have just settled for running a small software company, basically ceding the market she developed to anyone that could set up a more effective software development process than Steve's. Many entrepreneurs in Stephanie's position accept the limitations of their partners. Many entrepreneurs also break up with their partners at this point, but are unable to attract the equivalent level of commitment and expertise from their new hire, making matters even worse. As we describe in the How To chapter, Stephanie, with the help and support of her Board of Directors, handled the issue in a very effective manner, making it work out for everyone.

Stage three. But competitors come after almost any business that's successful, and the team needs to evolve and expand again to the extent necessary to put in place processes and systems required to make the company scalable, productive, and flexible enough to compete effectively and grow. Sam's ambition to expand and his ability to compete with Kmart and Target was ultimately limited by his processes of using his office cubbies to figure out what orders to place. Sam realized he needed expertise to help him develop the processes Wal-Mart required to scale up and compete. So he brought into the company retail executives experienced in running distribution centers and computer systems. And they developed as good or better processes than any other retail chain had at the time, which enabled Wal-Mart to expand faster than any retail chain in history.

But potential for conflict amongst the team grows at this stage because the highly skilled people brought in to run and improve operations, sales, customer service and/or money management/finance want to hire their own people. They may need to create mini-cultures within their departments to enable their processes to be practiced at the highest level of performance. The incumbent team may not have their new teammates' skills and may not be sensitive to their needs—and the new teammates may not be sensitive to the needs of the incumbents. Only savvy leadership can prevent schisms between early team members and these more recent highly skilled hires.

This stage-three transition was extremely challenging for Sam. His store managers felt de facto demoted because many decisions they previously could make were then being made by the Home Office. Sam spent a great deal of time facilitating understanding between these two groups and ultimately his sincerity, his clear description of the need for the new systems and processes, and his relentless focus on fixing the issues brought up by his store managers—and the managers at the Home Office—enabled Wal-Mart to become the most efficient retail chain on the planet.

This is the transition that gets many entrepreneurs fired by their VCs and replaced with professional managers that have previously succeeded in making a similar changeover work. Many bedrock entrepreneurs try to bring on new expertise but themselves become uncomfortable with what they perceive as a loss of control to people more expert than they. So many bedrock entrepreneurs fail to assemble teams capable of this transition, and their companies stagnate and are eventually overtaken by competitors.

Stage four. The team must continue to evolve even after the company is highly competitive and scalable because the business must innovate in order to become truly self-sustaining. Every company needs to be able to do more than replace the customers it loses due to external forces beyond its control. This final stage in the evolution of an enterprise requires a sophisticated team that feels comfortable taking risks while remaining focused on delivering the most cost-effective, high-quality product possible. However, the team that feels responsible for making the company competitive and successful with its original customers can feel threatened by team members working to develop very different products, once again calling on the leadership skills of the entrepreneur.

Making sure the key players on the team have the right skills *and* the right level of skills, and that everyone on the team is motivated to practice their skills in harmony with everyone else, is perhaps every entrepreneur's greatest challenge—no matter the size of the company.

The challenges of building and leading a capable and productive team through these four stages remain the same for both bedrock and high-risk entrepreneurs, but the consequences of lacking the right skills and the right people working productively and harmoniously as a team loom larger for high-risk entrepreneurs. They spend money and effort to accelerate growth through larger and more experienced teams—experience being a surrogate metric for the level of mastery of specific skills. High-risk entrepreneurs also invest more heavily in systems like equipment and software used to automate processes than do risk-averse bedrock entrepreneurs. Mistakes in team formation are therefore more costly and demoralizing in high-risk ventures and require greater leadership skills to mitigate. High-risk entrepreneurs backed by VC money will get fired for those mistakes. There's too much money being spent too quickly in high-risk ventures to make it worthwhile to coach the founders on how to be more reliable and skilled leaders.

Bedrock entrepreneurs must either live with their mistakes in team building or try to undo them. Many bedrock entrepreneurs live with their mistakes and accept the resulting stagnation and lower productivity. Other bedrock entrepreneurs take the initiative to learn from mistakes. They seek out and invest in advisors and coaches who can help them rebuild their team and reinvigorate growth.

Time Versus Money

The question, "How much time?" is actually two questions: "How much time do I need?" and, "How much time can I get?" We also have to make sure we understand that these "how much time" questions do not mean, "How much time will it take to get into business?" Instead, all these questions are about, "How much time will it take to become consistently profitable?"

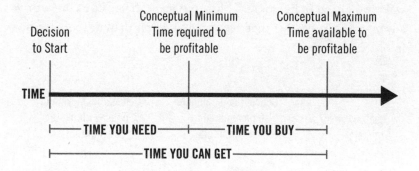

Every business needs some amount of time to set up, to develop their product or service, and then enough time to get some minimum number of customers happy enough to buy the product so the business becomes profitable. Some businesses can be set up and launch their product or service quickly and achieve profitability quickly.

1-800-AUTOPSY was profitable almost instantly because Vidal had a large initial customer and he could perform his autopsies at the VA's facility.

Nonetheless, most businesses need considerable time to develop before they become profitable. Medical and healthcare businesses take time to get regulatory approvals, while other businesses can take time to build up the large numbers of users required to attract advertising or to build large manufacturing capacities necessary to compete.

Furthermore, it's hard to predict how long some tasks will take, particularly when doing something for the first time. And unpredictable external factors can come into play; my business' ramp up was set back by months because of 9/11. All entrepreneurs need more time than they think, but that costs money.

Money can accelerate or slow down the passing of entrepreneurial time—the time it takes to achieve profitability. Here's how:

Money can reduce the estimated time to achieve critical cash flow milestones. Money accelerates entrepreneurial time by eliminating constraints. It enables you to get more people, more publicity, more space, more locations, and more of whatever is available, taking you where you need to be, sooner. More money is therefore a competitive advantage in businesses that need to grow faster than the competition in order to survive.

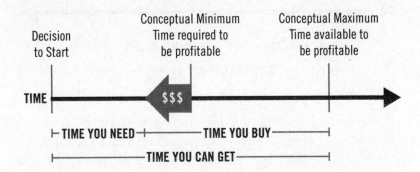

Money can buy you more time to reach profitability. More money means an enterprise can survive longer before reaching profitability. Money is therefore a competitive advantage in businesses that require a significant amount of time to set up.

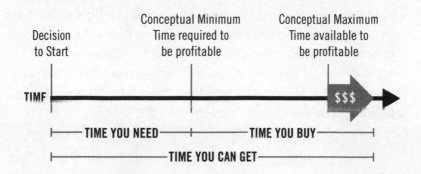

Money can also buy entrepreneurial time in two indirect ways:

Money can almost always buy needed skills and resources. Money can buy you people with skills or contacts you need to compete. Rather than taking the time required to develop a new skill, you can hire the highly skilled people you need, or you can engage them as consultants.

Nonetheless, sometimes a required skill or contact can be so specialized that no amount of money can buy it. In the early days of a new technology, few people may understand it or know how to work with it. If your team lacks a critical skill and no one with that skill wants to partner or work with you, then you will have to devise a plan for someone to learn it. This is one of the few cases where money cannot buy time.

Money can mitigate the fatality associated with many types of entrepreneurial mistakes. Money also increases the time available for undoing mistakes.

Time and money are inextricably linked for all entrepreneurs, but in different ways depending on whether your venture is bedrock or high-risk. Bedrock entrepreneurs and high-risk entrepreneurs perceive time and money differently:

Bedrock entrepreneurs make decisions to reduce the risk of personal loss—of money, status, and relationships. Bedrock entrepreneurs believe money is something that's easy to lose and time is something that's easy to waste. They therefore take actions to minimize the chances of losing either. Bedrock entrepreneurs therefore focus on starting businesses where the time needed to reach profitability is minimal.

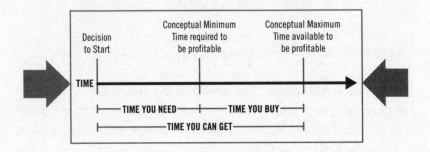

High-risk entrepreneurs base their decisions on maximizing personal gain—money, status, and networks. High-risk entrepreneurs believe that money multiplies potential outcomes and that time can be bought as necessary.

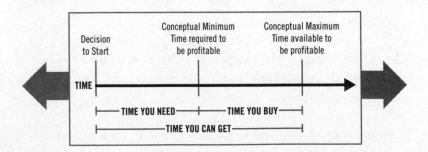

If you are in a race with competition to achieve scale or install a network, then your time is fixed by external factors associated with how fast factories or networks can be built. In these cases, you want to use money to accelerate time.

How much time is often just a consequence of the patience of the entrepreneur. Because many entrepreneurs never were really motivated to make scores of people happy and ask for money in return, they lose motivation to be an entrepreneur with time, and stop their efforts even when there's the cash in the bank to keep going.

How Much Money

Money is last on the list of things you need. You can decide how much money you need only after you understand how much of everything else you expect to be able to put in place, how much time is required, and how much time you already have. In many cases, once you've thought about how to best set up the other prerequisites, you don't need much money.

Money does matter in entrepreneurship, but not as much as you might think. Vidal Herrera started with literally nothing. Stephanie DiMarco and Estée Lauder started with next to nothing. Sam Walton borrowed just enough money to buy a bankrupt business, and as the story of William Shockley so vividly illustrates, no amount of money and no amount of everything else will be enough if you're not motivated to do what it takes to succeed.

Money is rarely ever the critical issue and is often a distraction. When you're a highly motivated, competent leader who has assembled a team that actively works toward delivering a reliable, desirable product or service, you will find the money. In fact, once you demonstrate how you and your team can make lots of people happy, the money often finds you—which can also cause problems.

Theoretically, you need only enough money to develop a working product or service, find your first customer, and then deliver the product or service in exchange for enough money to enable you to deliver the same product or service to your next customer. Beyond what you have to spend to build the physical product or deliver the service, you will always incur extra expenses, but they don't have to be much. You don't need a fancy place of business to begin. Stephanie DiMarco started with a tiny rented office (as did I). Michael Dell put together computers in his dorm room until he had saved enough money to rent a bigger space. Vidal Herrera worked as a contractor for the VA and used their tools to start his business. Jordan needed to rent a food stand on Venice Beach. Setting up work surfaces with doors on sawhorses or with used furniture costs little. In short, starting businesses that are inherently profitable can be done frugally.

You do need enough money to establish your product or service. Stephanie had to buy computers and networking software so that her partner Steve had the equipment and systems he needed to develop their sophisticated accounting software. She also had to fund almost two years of Steve's salary. Jordan Monkarsh needed money to buy some sausage-making equipment.

Plenty of digital-age companies continue to use the same model of developing and offering a product that makes the customer instantly happy and the company quickly profitable. 37signals and MailChimp are two well-known companies that fit this model.* Jason Fried, the founder of 37signals, developed excellent productivity tools for his web consultancy that his customers asked to use. He charged them, but the customers loved the software so much they told others about it. Jason soon made so much money from selling the software that he decided to shut down his consultancy. Ben Chestnut and Dan Kurzius took a similar route after being laid off of their corporate web design jobs. To keep money flowing in, they offered web design services to clients. The email tools they developed for their customers worked so well that the word spread. Seven years into their business, they shut down the web consultancy to focus exclusively on their

---

* 37signals has been renamed Basecamp after the company's most successful product.

MailChimp business, which is profitable to this day. Many other famous digital-age companies have been profitable immediately by design: GoPro, GitHub, Zoho, and most of the companies on the *Inc. Magazine*'s annual list of 5,000 fastest growing companies.

Most successful entrepreneurs and almost all bedrock entrepreneurs choose to start businesses that are inherently profitable. Think of "profit" as meaning the same thing as, "each sale brings in more than enough money to build and deliver the next one." Every entrepreneur profiled in this book chose a business, whether software, computer, retail, food, investment banking, entertainment, or otherwise, that they expected to become profitable quickly. They felt they would be able to provide such great happiness to their customers from the get-go that they could receive in return more than enough money to pay their employees, feed their families, and grow. Most of these entrepreneurs spent frugally and hired conservatively (Walt Disney being an exception before he teamed up with Roy). They planned their businesses based on how much money they had immediate access to rather than planning the business and then finding the money. They all chose, including Walt Disney, not to take the high-risk path.

Some businesses can only become profitable after many years of investment. Drugs, medical devices, and businesses that build physical or digital networks require extensive investment and years of losses before they can become profitable. They are among the riskiest of all companies, but if they succeed, they often wind up with few competitors. These are excellent businesses for high-risk entrepreneurs.

How Many Mistakes

Because virtually all entrepreneurs learn their leadership skills on the job, screw-ups are inevitable. Key team members can also screw up when called on to perform an ill-defined task under pressure.

Because we recognize screw-ups only after their unexpected and unfortunate consequences appear, they often require large amounts of money and time to repair. The loss of that money and time can result in a significant and enduring competitive disadvantage. Some screw-ups can be fatal. Most are survivable.

As we saw in chapter 6, Sam Walton's failure to get an option to renew the lease for the bankrupt store he bought was near fatal. Fortunately, Sam had saved the profits he made in running his store, anticipating that someday he would open a second one. An entrepreneur in a similar situation who had not saved his profits to grow the business and cover his mistakes might have enjoyed a better standard of living for a couple of years, but would have lost it all in the end.

That's why savvy entrepreneurs sock away their profits to cover for mistakes. Consider the worst possible scenario that could happen to your business once it's established, and put away enough of your profits to be able to fix the problem or start over.

How Much of a Jerk

There's a common myth that goes along the lines of, "To change things you have to break things." I hear this often in the entrepreneurial world, particularly in the high-risk world—to succeed you have to be a jerk. Don't believe it. There are many empathic and kind entrepreneurs.

Some entrepreneurs behave like jerks to compensate for their inability to lead change. As we discussed, in order to succeed, an entrepreneur needs to be able to lead many other people to change, and to change fast. That's a tough skill to master. Indeed, mammals, particularly dominant males, have evolved to react with emotion and anger to get others in their tribe to do what they want. Fear can work. The less skilled you are in leading change, the more of a jerk you need to be to get other people to change quickly to accommodate your needs. Walt Disney was often a jerk, and his animators felt stress when he was around. They put up with Walt because they felt he could help make them successful animation artists or film directors, and some of them were right about that. But not all successful entrepreneurs have aggressive, domineering personalities. Sam and Stephanie didn't, nor did Jordan or Vidal; they all focused on making and fixing things rather than breaking them.

All entrepreneurs need a collection of assets to be successful in the entrepreneurial league in which they intend to compete. Where an entrepreneur starts can also make a difference, but not in the way most people think. Let's explore the impact of location in the next chapter.

CHAPTER 9

WHERE

Silicon Valley doesn't come close to being the most entrepreneurial place on the planet. Uganda and Peru are far more entrepreneurial, with over 70 percent of the population between the ages of eighteen and sixty-five running their own, albeit small, businesses. Due to a lack of available jobs at established businesses, the people in these countries are forced to be entrepreneurial in order to survive. In general, entrepreneurship takes hold wherever jobs are scarce or where the number of jobs is shrinking. This inverse relationship between jobs and entrepreneurship holds everywhere, in both developing and developed countries. This relationship makes sense because many people, wherever they are in the world, prefer to have a steady job in an established business than deal with the stress of a startup and being their own boss.

Even in the United States, Silicon Valley is still not close to being the most entrepreneurial place. We find the highest density of entrepreneurs in Miami, Florida, with a rate of entrepreneurship 50 percent higher than in Silicon Valley. Because Miami is a major tourist center and the gateway to the Caribbean and Latin and South America, entrepreneurial opportunities, large and small, abound there. Miami's new businesses might not grow as fast as the VC-backed firms in Silicon Valley, but Miamians are certainly entrepreneurial. And for sheer numbers of entrepreneurs, the greater New York metropolitan area ranks number one. That's not surprising—the city attracts a steady flow of people from all backgrounds and from all over the world looking for a better life.

Silicon Valley is not even the top place to start a fast-growing company. That honor goes to Washington, DC. Why? Political parties require lots of help tuning their messages. The US government constantly needs new consultants, contractors, and research to support its initiatives in health, education, and defense. If you're tuned into what's happening in the government and in politics and are willing to set up shop in DC, then you're in a good position to create a business that can grow quickly and profitably.

Nonetheless, Silicon Valley is the best place in the world to start high-risk venture capital-backed companies. But as we saw, the odds are heavily against you winning big in Silicon Valley.

While these statistics may be interesting, they are ultimately irrelevant for any given individual. After all, entrepreneurship is about being different. Where you should embark on your business is therefore an intensely intimate question. It deserves an individualized analysis, not a recitation of statistics. And it's actually a two-part question: Where is it best to prepare to be an entrepreneur? Where is it best to start your own business?

A good place to begin your search for the skills, support, and mentorship you think you may need is right where you live.

Where Mentors Are Plenty

Estée Lauder the company sprang into being as both a reaction to, and a result of, the life and events Estée Lauder the person experienced growing up. As with Jordan and millions of other entrepreneurs, entrepreneurial identity is often discovered and molded within the extended family. Estée found what she wanted to do—and not do—by working with her aunts and uncles. From her aunt, she learned how to sell. From her uncle, she obtained an expert knowledge in the chemistry of the skin and skin creams, though she had only a high school education. But from working in the store, she also glimpsed what it would be like to be part of a higher stratum of society. And as we saw, a personal insult shocked her into taking control of her life.

You could say that the "pre-Estée" Estella was merely lucky to have relatives who taught her critical skills and opened her eyes to possibilities beyond her neighborhood. But that misses the point. Estella saw opportunity wherever she was and with whomever she encountered. More importantly, she grasped opportunity whenever it presented itself. She made herself; the world didn't make her.

Where do you prepare to be an entrepreneur? *You prepare wherever you can work with highly skilled people who excel in an area that interests you and who will let you practice your skills in an innovative environment that embraces change.* This is true whether you are a bedrock or a high-risk entrepreneur.

Learning to be an entrepreneur always starts with the opportunities that surround you, wherever you may be. And if you don't like the opportunities you find nearby, you can do what millions of others do and look elsewhere.

Where Challenges Are Met

Ken Marlin broke the news to his shocked parents: he was dropping out of college after less than a year. He had received good grades, but the work didn't answer his deepest question: "Who am I?" He sought the answer by enlisting in the US Marine Corps. He loved and excelled at the challenges of being a marine, and as a result he was invited to enter officer training. As an officer, he learned how to lead people under stressful conditions, how to distinguish real strategy from wishful thinking, and how to make judgments of character that could directly impact the success of a mission. Every time Ken was promoted the Corps offered to augment his education, enabling him to complete college and business school over the course of his military career.

Feeling he finally knew himself after ten years, he left the service. Former Marine Corps officers with combat training and business degrees typically have plenty of job offers from businesses, especially when they're still young, like Ken. From among several interesting offers, he chose the most personally compelling: becoming a member of a small group that assisted the CFO of Dun and Bradstreet (D&B) overseeing projects the CFO considered most critical to the company's success.

When Ken joined Dun and Bradstreet, it was an old and venerable firm going through a major restructuring—a big reason that Ken took the job. He knew he would learn different skills every day. A significant part of the restructuring involved D&B buying other companies that the CEO thought would enable them to expand their data-gathering expertise into new businesses. At first Ken merely supported the CFO by following up on action items required to make deals happen. Soon, he began to anticipate the CFO and CEO's needs and initiate relevant actions, sometimes even completing a task before he was even asked to undertake it. Within three years, the CEO let Ken lead major aspects of transactions. Ken sometime worked with investment bankers, but other times he orchestrated deals without them. He even helped develop strategies as part of the process of deciding which deals to pursue. And many of the acquisitions Ken worked on were international in scope.

Making deals, developing strategies, and ensuring they were properly executed were the most exciting things Ken had ever done. But after ten years, D&B's focus began to shift away from acquisitions, and the CEO offered Ken the presidency of one of D&B's divisions. He turned it down. He felt he was ready to be a CEO of his own company, so instead he found a job running an independent, fast-growing US-based division of a major Swiss financial information technology firm.

After several months in the position, time enough to have settled in and to have gotten a feel of the people he now worked with, Ken discovered that his definition of an "independent" division differed sharply from that of the Swiss owners. As a trained marine, Ken didn't leave, but instead hatched a strategy to induce the Swiss to sell him a part of the US division—a part they didn't seem to care much about. Because Ken was adept at structuring and financing deals, he was able to find Wall Street financial partners willing to back him, and the Swiss were happy to let him buy their non-strategic asset.

Although Ken had considerable experience working with Wall Street investment bankers in fashioning deals to buy and sell companies, this was his first experience working with venture capitalists, private equity firms, and other "financial sponsors." To get his company off the ground, he had willingly taken money from a fund that had been recommended by a close friend. Ken was happy and proud that he had struck a deal to make him the undisputed leader of his own company, but in putting together the financing, he had willingly taken money from strangers without doing much investigation on who they were, their financial goals, and the culture of their investment firm. It was only after completing the purchase that Ken discovered that his new financial partners were not actually willing to support his aggressive plans to grow the business—they wanted to grow slowly. In Ken's view, growing slowly would lead to failure, and that was incompatible with his philosophy.

The relations with his financial partners quickly became contentious. Ken's marine training again came into play as he consciously chose which battles he would fight with the investors on his Board and which battles he would leave alone. Instead of viewing the circumstance as a long-term assignment to grow his company into something large, profitable, and dominant in its market, Ken would focus on making his company more valuable so he could sell it. Three years after buying the business, he sold it to another big financial technology firm for about three times what it had cost him. His financial partners did well with the deal and Ken did all right, too, but he didn't make enough to retire on, and being his own boss had not been the experience he had expected.

Ken realized that he had been naïve. He had not done his home-work on his financial partners before taking their money. He had not properly understood enough about the intricacies of how finan-cial sponsors structure their investments to get control. So after his employment contract with the acquiring firm expired, he decided to try being a financial advisor himself. With his experience of making money for financial people, and having been involved with dozens of deals, Ken had no problem in finding a small boutique investment bank that was willing to offer him a partnership. But Ken received his offer shortly before the dot-com bubble collapsed in 2001, after which all dealmaking stopped.

We read a great deal about all the money to be made in invest-ment banking. In reality, investment bankers earn little in salary and make a lot of money in the form of large bonuses, but only if they personally initiate large transactions. If there are no deals to be had, investment bankers starve.

Within a few months of the bubble bursting and with no imme-diate prospects for making big bonuses, Ken took matters into his own hands. He launched his own investment banking firm. Most of Ken's colleagues thought he was crazy. On Wall Street, conventional wisdom holds that starting an investment banking firm requires a large amount of money. Investment banks need fancy offices with fancy furniture, expensive artwork, and an army of Ivy League–trained analysts to impress potential clients. And that's not to mention the hundreds of personal relationships with major CEOs that any firm needs to be "in the game."

But Ken wasn't looking to create a normal investment bank. Knowing few CEOs outside of the information business, Ken decided to concentrate there. No other investment bankers focused only on the information business, considering it way too small a market. Also, in contrast to standard investment banking practice, Ken rented a single office from a New York law firm that had just laid off a bunch of their lawyers and didn't need the space and wanted extra income. In the single office, Ken set up his business with three junior colleagues who all were willing to work only on commission (no salary!). All four of them spent their time making phone calls to find CEOs that wanted to meet with an investment banker who could tell them where to find investors or buyers. When a prospective client wanted to meet, they met at the CEO's office or a restaurant.

Ken calculated that he could survive for two years without doing a deal. He also projected that within that time, many information businesses, in order to survive, would have to find investors or bigger companies to acquire them. He figured he just needed to stay in close contact with the CEOs he knew, and perhaps others he could meet, in order to make some deals coalesce. But it didn't happen that way. In the next three years, Ken landed only four small deals, and the fees he earned covered neither rent nor expenses. But being a marine meant that he was disciplined. Ken stuck to a strict budget and spent money frugally. Fortunately, his new wife Jacqui fully supported his efforts and was happy to make sacrifices. In order to afford to paint their small house, Jacqui returned their wedding presents. Eating pasta for dinner almost every night, Ken and Jacqui figured they could survive even another year.

The pasta dinners came to an end in 2005, when Ken started to win a steady stream of deals. The CEOs he had cultivated during the downturn were convinced that Ken knew more about the information business than anyone else, so he became their go-to person to help them put together their deals. I was one of those CEOs.

In 1999, I had founded iSuppli to sell information and services that would enable companies in the electronics market to more effectively mange their supply chains. For the first nine years, we didn't need any outside capital or investment bankers to help us with the few small acquisitions we made during that time. But in 2009, we did need help to buy some additional companies that possessed proprietary information that would complement the information we had already developed about the tech world. So in late 2009, I unconditionally recommended Ken to the Board of iSuppli to help us raise the funds. As it happened, our fundraising didn't actually turn out the way we expected. Instead of buying other companies, we wound up receiving an offer to buy us that was just too good to turn down.

Ken helped us get a deal that became a legend in our space and that led to even more clients and deals for him.

Today, Marlin and Associates is one of the most influential and lucrative boutique investment banks on Wall Street, now dominating M&A activity in three areas of specialization. Though the business is lucrative, Ken remains frugal—there's still no expensive artwork on the office walls, no big expense accounts, no lavish spending of any kind. At heart, Ken Marlin is still a marine.

Contrary to popular belief, big organizations like the Marine Corps can train entrepreneurs. The armed forces taught Ken Marlin a great deal, including how to focus on clear objectives, develop domain expertise, lead and motivate others, operate with limited resources, and manage with discipline, as well as many other skills that are directly applicable to leading a startup. In fact, countries such as China and Israel consider fostering entrepreneurial ambitions in their recruits a strategic objective of their armed forces.

Many large organizations inadvertently train entrepreneurs. Pleasing a superior in a big hierarchy with a culture where initiative is recognized and rewarded is much like pleasing customers, particularly in a service business like investment banking.

Not all large organizations breed future entrepreneurs. Learning management skills in a highly regimented culture encourages instincts that impede entrepreneurial success. Highly regimented organizations are excellent at teaching the skills and instincts required to eliminate risk. But entrepreneurs cannot afford to eliminate risk *entirely*. While entrepreneurs do reduce risk through prototyping and experimentation, attempting something new and different always entails *some* risk. Highly regimented organizations school their staff to become intolerant of risk, impeding the development of entrepreneurial leadership skill sets. The clear lesson for aspiring entrepreneurs: *Learn your leadership skills in a culture that embraces change and succeeds at innovation.*

Where to Tech

Like "entrepreneur," "technology" is a loaded term needing definition. Most people imagine that technology requires manipulating electrons and atoms to make humans more and more omnipotent—which is sometimes the case. Other people think of technology more broadly as anything produced under the supervision of engineers and scientists. To still others, technology is a universal force that advances what humans can do.

For the purposes of both aspiring and existing entrepreneurs, technology can be more usefully defined as a synonym for innovation—a new action, product, or piece of information that some user group feels is more useful or insightful and that offers a better way of doing what they do.

My grandmother and my father provide great examples of where entrepreneurs learn to leverage technologies to their advantage. My grandmother on my mother's side was a British lady who did not suffer fools or discomfort lightly. Fools were what she considered most of her teachers at her proper British ladies boarding school to be, so she ran away and made her way to Hollywood, where she hoped to make it as an actress in the brand new field of moving pictures. My grandmother never made it in Hollywood beyond being an extra, which she found irritating, but not as irritating as the costumes she was made to wear. She hated putting them on, particularly because they often required that she bind her breasts—Hollywood directors at the time wanted to make young ladies in films look sexy by wearing low cut gowns and dresses. Ladies with unbound breasts beneath their dresses or ball gowns were considered too sexy to be shown on screen, so before donning their gowns actresses had to tape their chests. My grandmother considered it a barbaric practice, so she did something to eradicate it—she invented the backless bra.

It took several attempts to get all the forces at play to balance out in a design that was both comfortable and "reliable." Even though my grandmother had never finished high school, her design was a great example of mechanical engineering using soft fabrics. In her next role as a sexy extra, she wore the backless bra she had just invented. The garment caused a sensation—all the other aspiring starlets on the set wanted one. It was a perfect demonstration of technology and innovation at work. Inundated with requests, my grandmother set up her own company to make her "Maxwell Bra" (Maxwell was her maiden name). She eventually sold the company to Maidenform.

My grandmother's story is essentially the same as that of Sara Blakely, the inventor of Spanx, and of countless other entrepreneurs who tinkered with existing materials, tools, and techniques to create products others found useful. My grandmother's story is also the story of Stephanie DiMarco, who used a new tool—computers—to eliminate the tedium and inconsistency of asset management accounting. Tinkering with existing materials and tools to solve a real problem for a group you know well is tech entrepreneurship at its classic best.

My father serves as a more typical example of entrepreneurship meeting new technology. He grew up in the Baltic region of what was then Russia and later Poland. A good student, he was admitted to the Berlin Technical University, at the time perhaps the best technical school in the world. During a lab assignment devoted to a new phenomenon involving the transformation of light into electricity, my father accidentally burned up the tiny photoelectric device he was experimenting on. In those days, students had to pay for whatever they broke, and my father was forced to turn over two months' allowance in order to remain in class. He survived the rest of the school year by eating oatmeal.

My father always said that he figured that any small device that could be that valuable must be a good business. So he decided to learn as much about the technology as he could. A few years later, he fled from Germany, shortly before *Kristallnacht,* and made his way to New York City. He entered through Ellis Island with just the proverbial suitcase and a few dollars. Because nobody was interested in hiring a German-trained electrical engineer who couldn't speak English, he took a job provided by a distant relative—loading tires onto trucks.

After learning English and progressing through several unsatisfying jobs, my father answered a newspaper ad for an engineer who understood the photoelectric effect—exactly what he had studied. He applied, won the job, and within days boarded a train to Los Angeles to take up his new position. Upon arrival, after his five-day trip across the country, he was informed at the train station that the company had gone bankrupt. Even back then, high-tech companies had a high mortality rate. The company had developed a machine to quickly develop photographic film, but movie companies, the biggest consumers of film at the time, were content to do it the old way and didn't want to diddle around learning a new technology. Even today, user apathy about the benefits of technology remains a primary reason that so many technology companies fail.

The bankruptcy, however, created a unique opportunity. My father teamed up with the sales and operations managers of the defunct company. Using my father's technical skills and the managers' savings, they bought the bankrupt company's equipment to inexpensively start their own business. They focused on potential customers—camera manufacturers—that the sales manager believed would be more interested than moviemakers in using photoelectric cells. The new company started making photoelectric cells that would automatically control shutter speeds. The cells that my father developed were the best available in the United States at that time, so he quickly found customers. With subsequent development by my father and many others, the cells eventually morphed into the semiconductors and other solid-state electronic devices the world has come to rely on. With profits, mortgages, and, only many years later, money from investors, my father created one of the pioneering companies in the semiconductor business.

So where should you prepare to be a high-tech entrepreneur? The same place you should develop any other skill that will eventually make people want to buy what you make: *You prepare to be a high-tech entrepreneur where you can learn the technology from a master.*

It makes a great difference where you learn the skills that enable you to do things better and differently than everyone else. When you start your enterprise, you can only count on being as expert as the bosses and colleagues who taught you what they knew and supervised your practice. Jordan Monkarsh learned sausage-making from his dad, a skill he augmented with recipes he learned while travelling the world. Stephanie DiMarco learned asset management accounting from experienced practitioners and was then allowed to experiment in developing asset management software directly with people who used it. Vidal learned to perform autopsies from the Los Angeles County Coroner. Sam Walton learned how to manage a retail store from Ben Franklin franchise store supervisors and trainers. Estée Lauder's uncle made great skin creams, and her aunt was a great sales mentor. Ken Marlin learned how to put together complicated acquisitions by working on behalf of Dun & Bradstreet on a dozen deals with top lawyers and investment bankers. My father, like many high-tech entrepreneurs, developed his skill at a major research university. My grandmother learned what she needed to know about fabrics and mechanical engineering from the seamstresses and movie set designers she worked with at the movie studio. There was plenty more each of these entrepreneurs learned on the job after they started their companies, but the skills that differentiated them from their competitors were initially learned from highly skilled and savvy coaches.

But in every case, in every industry, and particularly with high tech, *the entrepreneur's technical skill matures and becomes practical through direct feedback from the people the entrepreneur aspires to entice into using the technology.* For my grandmother, that took place on the movie set. For my father, it happened where he could both get access to the right equipment and team up with a knowledgeable sales manager who could introduce him to high-end camera manufacturers willing to try a leading-edge technology. Commercializing technology happens only in direct contact with some needy group; it doesn't happen in the laboratory.

Where There's Culture

Each year, Princeton arranges a field trip for our entrepreneurially inclined students to the startups of Silicon Valley. We don't send them there to show them where they can learn new or better skills—their skills are already impressive—we send them there to soak up the culture of the place. Working in Silicon Valley differs from working in most other locations around the world; it focuses much more intently on achieving results quickly. Status, and therefore motivation, is based on the magnitude of your ambition for your enterprise. The culture attracts a disproportionate percentage of the world's most ambitious software programmers, product managers, and venture investors. Such highly ambitious people feel more respected and motivated in Silicon Valley.

The culture in the Valley also pushes entrepreneurs to develop high-value and proprietary capability—their own secret sauce. The high cost of living in the area puts pressure on everyone to "shoot for the moon" and "do it fast." Silicon Valley embraces, nurtures, and supports high-risk entrepreneurship writ large while burning out almost everyone else.

Silicon Valley culture also erects higher hurdles for success. Because salaries and rents are so steep, businesses in the area are at a cost disadvantage compared with similar businesses located elsewhere. Companies that set up in Silicon Valley suffer higher turnover of their key personal. But these higher costs and higher rates of employee turnover may not matter to companies that control valuable information and networks. They don't require large numbers of people to operate. Instead, they need relatively few people with mastery of highly specialized skills.

Unsuccessful firms die faster in Silicon Valley than they do elsewhere. Companies judged by Silicon Valley inhabitants to have poor chances of success cannot attract either the people or money they need. Businesses whose structures require time to mature and create value are penalized if they locate in Silicon Valley, relative to their competitors in less costly locations. Unless Silicon Valley confers special advantages to your business, you are actually disadvantaged there. So the answer to "where to prepare?" may not have the same answer as "where to start?"

When it comes to software, social media companies, and companies with business models focused on exploiting network effects, Silicon Valley is what I call a *vibrant entrepreneurial ecosystem* (VEE). It attracts people who want to leverage their software, electronics, and technology marketing skills to make money and to work on projects they consider interesting and fun.

But Silicon Valley is not the only VEE. If you want to start a company that makes movies or other entertainment content, then Los Angeles is the place to be. That's where you'll be able to most easily find talent, support services, funding, and partners. New York City is a vibrant entrepreneurial ecosystem for financial startups. Wisely, Ken Marlin started his investment bank in New York, not Silicon Valley or LA, even if his business concentrated the bulk of its attention on information companies not located in New York. If you want to make a difference in international high fashion, then Milan or Paris may be the best places to start. In Shenzhen, China, electronics manufacturing expertise and support services abound.

Many vibrant entrepreneurial ecosystems are local. Streets with heavy pedestrian traffic and shopping malls provide restaurants and movie theaters with large numbers of potential customers specifically looking to enjoy themselves. Public transportation is convenient and plentiful around entertainment and shopping destinations, which makes it easy to hire low-wage employees who don't own cars. Local entrepreneurial ecosystems often form around clusters of car dealerships, with many automotive support and service businesses located nearby, and attract customers from great distances. Similarly, marinas are where you find businesses that provide support to boat owners.

Beware of VEEs

Vibrant entrepreneurial ecosystems attract people who want to start new businesses much like the ones that have prospered there. If you are looking to start a business where a VEE confers competitive advantage, and you have the big-league credibility to steal the talent you need from competitors, then starting your company there makes sense. Moving from Boston to Silicon Valley worked for Mark Zuckerberg and Facebook because he had already attracted the experienced and well-known Sean Parker to lend him the credibility he needed to compete for money and people. Without significant credibility, like prior experience and an impressive team, starting an enterprise in a VEE is often a mistake. It's a big challenge finding the talent or money you need among people located in a VEE because they're all looking for those who already have what it takes to succeed in that particular big league.

Sam Walton could have started his first store in Chicago, which was a vibrant retail VEE at the time. Marshall Fields, Sears Roebuck, and many other prosperous major retailers were located there. But Sam knew better than to try to launch his business in Chicago, and his wife instinctively asked him to kill his plan to launch a store in St. Louis. He was still taken to the cleaners in Newport, Arkansas by his landlord, who hijacked Sam's store for his son. Though Sam was a fast learner, it took him seventeen years of opening and running fifteen other Ben Franklin stores before he felt confident that he could open, run, supply, and merchandise a discount store of his own.

Successful first-time entrepreneurs do exist in Silicon Valley, but almost all of them have been executives with significant and relevant responsibilities in related businesses. *They started with credibility.* Similarly, most successful restaurants on highly trafficked pedestrian malls were started by restaurateurs who already had significant food service experience.

Where's the Family?

I started iSuppli in Los Angeles, which was definitely not a vibrant ecosystem for information businesses or other businesses that served high-tech customers. Few customers for the information we were selling were located in the greater LA area. Few local investors would have been interested in investing in my venture. Nor were there the people with the highly specific expertise the company needed. I started iSuppli in LA because my wife and two sons were comfortable and settled there, and I didn't want to uproot them, especially at a time when my entrepreneurial aspirations were creating enough turbulence in our life.

For most entrepreneurs, family is the dominant factor in their decisions about where to start their business. Starting a business close to family and friends has major benefits because it adds emotional support during an extremely stressful time. And if you start a business similar to the business you've just been working for, then starting nearby can give you the advantage of already knowing where to find competent labor and support services.

Did founding iSuppli in LA hurt my chances of succeeding? I had plenty of competitors, so succeeding was not easy. At iSuppli we compensated for not being able to attract industry experts to LA by being flexible, letting the experts we hired work from their homes or in offices we set up in and around the major technology centers of the world. Our flexibility and extra efforts resulted in higher costs and more time wasted in travel. But our headquarters location didn't prevent us from succeeding because our competitive advantage came from the uniqueness and value of our information, which allowed us to sell our datasets for large amounts of money that more than covered those extra costs.

In summary, the lessons about where to learn the skills you need are clear-cut:

- **Successful friends and family are every entrepreneur's most accessible source of support and mentorship.** The extra attention friends and family are willing to give you can enable you to acquire valuable skills faster and more competently than at school or a job.
- **You can learn valuable entrepreneurial skills in big organizations.** Pleasing a superior in a big hierarchy within a culture where initiative is recognized and rewarded is much like pleasing customers, particularly in a service business like investment banking.
- **Learn your leadership skills in a culture that embraces**

and succeeds at innovation and change. Avoid organizations, large or small, that have highly regimented cultures. If you learn management skills in such a culture, you will develop the wrong instincts, which could take years to unlearn.

- **Develop and practice your leadership skills anywhere.** Even if you have never led a team or organization you can always find ways to lead people in the same way entrepreneurs do. Some of these exercises were described in the chapter "How Good."

There is not necessarily a clear-cut answer to the question of where to locate your business. But there are a number of critical factors you should weigh:

- **Vibrant entrepreneurial ecosystems (VEEs) are everywhere, but not for everyone.** Each VEE offers significant advantages to certain types of businesses through a combination of preferential access to customers, talent, technology, and/or supply chains, as well as cultural expectations that help shape beneficial business behaviors—but almost always at significantly higher costs. VEEs are therefore an entrepreneurial drag on businesses that cannot or do not leverage the preferential access or the cultural norms.
- **For most industries, no vibrant ecosystem exists.** Of the more than 1,000 distinct industries tracked by the US government, most can be entered from almost anywhere in the country without any competitive advantage or disadvantage. In my case, I started an information business where the location ultimately didn't matter.
- **Most bedrock entrepreneurs prefer to locate near their homes, families, and friends.** The emotional support can be invaluable during such a stressful time.

Once you've weighed all of these factors, the question becomes *when* to start your business, the subject of the next chapter.

CHAPTER 10

WHEN

"I just thought of this wonderful idea and I need to start a company to capitalize on it. What should I do next?" I am frequently asked this question. Most aspiring entrepreneurs assume that an exciting idea is the "trigger" to starting a company. As we've seen, the notion that great ideas make successful entrepreneurs is a myth. It is therefore incorrect and dangerous to assume that the answer to "when" is whenever you come up with a great idea.

I'm frequently asked other questions about the right time to found a startup: "Should I drop out of school? Should I wait until after my toddlers are in school or until I learn more about business, become more expert in my field, or find a complementary co-founder?" These questions, too, miss the point. In essence, if you ask any form of the "when should I be an entrepreneur" question, then you've already started. In the act of asking the question, you've already answered it: *now*.

Ray Kroc never asked "when?" He was fifty-two years old when he decided to change his life. He was already an entrepreneur—he and a secretary constituted both employees of a company that sold milkshake blenders. In his late thirties, Ray had felt under-appreciated by his bosses for his ability to sell Dixie paper cups, so he decided to leave the company and be his own boss. As a great salesperson, Ray knew lots of people in the food and food service business, particularly in the upper Midwest. He began to take note of things his customers did that he thought could be sold to others. One of Ray's customers for paper cups had been White Castle, one of the original off-the-highway multi-location restaurant chains. One of its founders had invented soft-serve ice cream. The popularity of soft-serve ice cream quickly increased the demand for milkshakes, and the increased demand for milkshakes led the inventor to develop a high-volume milkshake blender. Ray saw the opportunity to sell soft-serve ice cream makers around the country, but the White Castle owners wanted to keep that innovation exclusively for themselves. They suggested instead that Ray sell the patented blender. Eager to be his own boss, Ray agreed, confident that he could sell a blender to every diner and soda fountain in the country. He started a company whose sole business was selling the milkshake blender. Over the next fifteen years he sold the unit to just about everyone who could possibly need one. Milkshake blenders are a niche and limited market, and after fifteen years, the business was well past its peak and in decline.

At the age of fifty-two, Ray knew he had to find something else to sell or he'd slowly go bankrupt. A few years before he had bought the rights to a folding table design he thought he could make and market. But the table proved too expensive to produce and too heavy to be portable, and Ray was forced to scrap the idea.

Though he was now perpetually in a bad mood, Ray still travelled constantly to meet prospective and existing milkshake blender customers, even though the travel resulted in fewer and fewer sales. It was nevertheless natural for Ray to have wound up in San Bernardino, California, to visit his biggest customer, the McDonald brothers. The brothers had developed what was then an already famous method for producing high volume hamburgers. During his visit, Ray was awestruck by what he saw: the McDonald brothers were serving hamburgers and milkshakes ten times faster than he had ever observed in any other restaurant he'd visited.

Immediately Ray felt he knew how to change his life. His experience selling blenders and paper cups had given him complete confidence that he was a good judge of which restaurants could make money and which could not. He decided then he'd do whatever was needed to convince the McDonald brothers to let him open up large numbers of McDonald's all over the country. The next day, Ray went back to sell the McDonald brothers on the idea of making him their exclusive licensing agent for their fast food method—basically the same deal he had for selling the patented blenders. The brothers were impressed with Ray's decades of experience selling blenders. Furthermore, the person who they had employed to handle the flood of franchise requests they received had just had a heart attack. Nonetheless, Ray was forced to accept the brothers' onerous take-it-or-leave-it terms to get an exclusive agreement. Deal in hand, Ray felt he was ready to move into the food service industry equivalent of the big leagues.

Ray Kroc serves as an excellent example of how a lifetime of experience can prepare us to be successful entrepreneurs. All the entrepreneurs profiled in this book were constantly testing themselves to see what they felt confident they could accomplish. Ken Marlin tested himself when he joined the marines, again when he joined D&B, and again when he bought the company from the Swiss. Stephanie DiMarco tested herself in finding a computer science partner and then producing a program that her boss liked to use.

Estée Lauder first learned how to sell, then how to make creams, and then how and where to market beauty creams before she borrowed money from friends and family to start Estée Lauder. Walt Disney tested to see if he could get a customer before starting Laugh-O-Gram and again before starting Disney Brothers Studios.

In entrepreneurship, *when* is *always* and *when* is always *experiment now*. Recall the Austrian School's definition of entrepreneurship from the start of chapter 2: we are all entrepreneurs because all people who support themselves continually assess their risks and accordingly make decisions about what to do next. Even if you choose not to use their definition, their observation is valid—we are always assessing our entrepreneurial opportunities whether we realize it or not.

Sam Walton didn't know he wanted to go into retailing as a college student. He didn't figure that out until after he had worked at J. C. Penney and after he had found a supportive partner in his wife Helen. But throughout college Sam had pushed himself to be the leader of every organization he belonged to, all the while keeping up his childhood newspaper delivery business by hiring other kids to help. Sam was always testing himself to see how much of an impact he could have on the people around him. Whether he realized it or not, he had been preparing to be an entrepreneur since he was a teenager—as do we all! Sam just prepared much more effectively than anyone else.

Entrepreneurship opportunities are always opening and closing. The opportunity to meet potential partners, customers, suppliers, or people willing to loan you money could come at any time. The same goes for market openings. Every company in existence is constantly buffeted by change, and large organizations change more slowly than their markets or slower than the technologies that could be put to use in those markets. Established companies are regularly cutting back on their services and making customers unhappy, thereby opening up an opportunity for entrepreneurs to take customers by providing better service. The status quo is constantly challenged, if not by some new technology, then by changing tastes, new markets, evolving supply chains, and shifting demographics. When it comes to change that opens up opportunities, our digital age is nothing new.

Mapping Out a Starting Point

Just asking any question about when you should consider being an entrepreneur means you want to be an entrepreneur. Your journey has already started. That doesn't mean quitting your job to start a company right away. But it does mean that once you've asked the question, your responsibility to yourself is to be deliberate about mapping out your entrepreneurial journey—even if you don't know where you're going yet. *If you do not have the motivation to be deliberate about mapping out your journey, then you likely do not have the motivation you will need to succeed.*

Start by writing down your ideas for getting the skills you think you'll need, how you'll test these skills to make sure you are good enough, and then how you'll collect enough of the necessary assets that we discussed in chapter 8. *Think of this list as a list of experiments.* Experiments are not something that succeed or fail. They are deliberate, thoughtful steps you take to acquire information that you did not have. These experiments will give you new information that is valuable enough that you're willing to spend the time, and maybe a bit of money, to conduct them. Whatever you discover makes you more knowledgeable about the opportunities available to you and thereby increases the chances of your seizing them. These experiments reduce your risk, although they could also lead to the conclusion that you need to do another experiment.

I strongly advise against taking this journey alone, but most people do and many of them still succeed. Nor am I advising you to find a partner or a stranger to give you money. The fact remains that no one is ever the best person to know what he or she is capable of doing. Because we are all programmed to fabricate stories that make us feel the way we want to feel about ourselves, we are best served by finding objective sounding boards for our ideas.

I suggest assembling an informal council of role models—people whom you respect for what they've done with their lives. Invite them over for a meal or set up an equivalently respectful way for you to spend time with them. Devote the evening to asking them about why they did what they did. Ask them their advice on how to get where you want to go. Write down what they say because it can help sketch in a big part of that map you need to make. Ideally, your council will tell you things you did not know and will give you advice you did not know you needed.

Sam Walton's council consisted of his wife and her father. Helen was ambitious and smart and saw the world from a more practical perspective than her ever-optimistic husband. Helen's dad was a financially savvy small-town lawyer and rancher. Their advice proved pivotal to Sam's entrepreneurial success.

Helen, as we noted, steered Sam away from having a partner and from opening a store with that partner in St. Louis. Her dad helped Sam understand his financial options, including immediately creating a family corporation that would own the shares of the stores he would open. Instead of Sam and Helen directly owning stores or any shares in Walmart, a family-controlled corporation held the shares, providing far greater flexibility as to when and how they received taxable income. This structure made it possible for their heirs to retain 50 percent of the shares of Walmart in spite of it being the largest corporation in the world. Because Sam sought and listened to the advice of Helen and her dad, he was able to preserve wealth in the most sophisticated manner available, guaranteeing the financial freedom of the Walton family for many generations to come.

You don't need to take any of the advice of your council, but you can still benefit from their views. After his Laugh-O-Gram bankruptcy and his move to Los Angeles, Walt Disney sought the counsel of his older brother Roy and his uncle Robert. He listened to their advice because he needed their support to survive. They told Walt to get a job and start paying rent, but Walt wanted to persevere trying to sell the animations he produced in Kansas City. Roy and Uncle Robert's contrarian perspectives on Walt's prospects made him even more diligent in pursuing every possible angle.

Once that New York agency offered to pay an advance to distribute *Alice's Wonderland,* Walt asked Roy to be his full-time partner. Uncle Robert then agreed to help out, something he had refused to do when Walt himself asked. With Roy's bookkeeping help and financial advice, Walt set up the Disney Brothers Studios more prudently with far greater chances of success than when he had set up Laugh-O-Gram Studios on his own. Although Walt's personality and perfectionism always made him want to spend more money than he had, Roy's influence acted as both a conscious and subconscious governor on spending, even though Walt only reluctantly acknowledged its benefit. Without Roy's counsel and support, and initially Uncle Robert's, Walt Disney would not have made it.

Entrepreneurs have succeeded without mentors, advisors, or outside sage advice—it's not required. Asking advice or counsel from someone you do not respect is a waste of time. The point is to get a broad set of perspectives and become as well informed as possible so you can cut down on the number of experiments you need in order to acquire the essential knowledge, experience, and skills of a credible entrepreneur.

Anecdotally, I've found that entrepreneurs who take a systematic, deliberate approach to considering their entrepreneurial opportunities do much better than those who just leap at them. Deliberation isn't about writing a business plan, but about carefully figuring out how you might get to where you want to go. Developing a "map" and reviewing it based on the inputs from the people you respect is the most cost-effective and success-enhancing way of assessing and minimizing risk. Here's how:

- Write down what you'd like to do and why you want to do it.
- Make a list of what you'll need to do to get what you want.
- Write an explanation of how you'll get what you want, where you'll look to get it, and how much of it you think you might need.
- Set a goal for when you think you can get it.
- List what you don't know about what you need.
- Prioritize the list of what you don't know and think of actions you can take or experiments you can perform quickly, inexpensively, and reliably to find this knowledge.

Go over this list with your advisors. Listen. Ask questions. Amend your list accordingly. Now you're ready to conduct your experiments. Think of these experiments as mock-ups or simulations of the experiences you're going to deliver to your customers to make them happy. Cook up the sausage you plan to sell even if it doesn't yet have the exact look and feel of what you plan to serve. If your sausage elicits *oohs* and *aahs* from strangers, then it makes sense to refine the recipe, preparation, and appearance to see if that makes the sausage irresistible. If your talents are digital, you can lay out what your screens might look like for your app and just pretend with potential users what will happen to the information on the screen as they touch one button or another. Don't bother writing the program until you know for sure that people are excited by it and want to use it. In my design-thinking world these experiments would be called rapid prototyping; they're less real and much less expensive than minimum viable products (MVPs).

If done thoughtfully and deliberately, your experiments will give you knowledge that may be unique in the world (even if it may be the knowledge that your idea wasn't exactly what your potential customers wanted). Keep notes on all that you learn, and summarize these lessons at least monthly. Assess your progress on understanding your *what, why, how, where,* and *how much.* Every few months, or any time you make a breakthrough, present to your council how much closer or farther you are from committing money and full-time effort to achieving your entrepreneurial aspirations. Then listen and ask questions and amend your plan again.

Family Matters

Founding a company always profoundly affects your family. You can succeed as an entrepreneur and as a spouse and parent, but you have to integrate your family's timetable with your timetable. Savvy entrepreneurs strategize their family objectives and projects with the same intensity they bring to planning their business needs. The possibilities and pitfalls are many; and for bedrock entrepreneurs, a family that stays happy or a family that respects the actions of their entrepreneur can be the difference between fulfillment and disappointment.

Indeed, families are the key to the question of "whether?" as we'll discuss in our next chapter.

When to Quit

I am frequently asked, "Should I keep going?" or "Should I sell?" To fully answer those questions you must understand the difference between feeling happy and feeling fulfilled. Many entrepreneurs I have known came to me to ask for more money to keep their enterprise and entrepreneurial hopes alive with the typical refrain, "I just need a bit more time to do . . ." Some of these entrepreneurs have asked multiple times, and lead lives where entrepreneurship has become the equivalent of an addiction. They sacrificed friends, family, and others to keep their entrepreneurial hopes alive. These addicts don't care what people that have more experience think, because they *need* to have the prestige and control that comes with running their own business. It doesn't really matter if the business is viable or if it can support them—showing the world they are an entrepreneur is more important than eating. Walt Disney started out that way in Kansas City, and he was literally starving when he threw in the towel, declared bankruptcy, and moved to Los Angeles to be supported by his brother and uncle.

I am one-for-two as a founder and entrepreneur. I closed my first venture, Table of Contents, after trying to make it work for two years. This was an experiment in whether I knew how to run a business that differed from International Rectifier, the semiconductor company founded by my grandfather and father. I fantasized about creating a retail chain that sold plates, glasses, and other tabletop items. The experiment failed, costing me personally about two million dollars along with another $250,000 from business people I knew who invested with me. I put in the second million after my first million had failed to get our store to profitability.

At the time, I was a semiconductor executive, not a retailer. I didn't quit my semiconductor job to found Table of Contents and

I didn't run the store. But I was involved as a major investor and an opinionated owner. I did recruit an experienced board of directors and advisors, who thought that our store could be made profitable (though maybe they didn't have the guts to tell me otherwise). I nonetheless decided to close down Table of Contents after the second million dollars and a change in store management produced only an incremental increase in sales. My thinking at the time was, "I will look stupid to everyone that knows me if I go broke pouring money into a losing business." In short, I had founded Table of Contents to make me feel happy, not fulfilled.

Entrepreneurs with the foresight to have set up a panel of experienced advisers and counselors can make rational decisions about whether more money will allow an enterprise to turn the corner or not. But nobody can be completely rational when faced with deciding whether to risk financial ruin in order to prolong the chances of finally succeeding—no matter how rational they feel. You need objective help in assessing the actual risk versus potential reward of keeping on or quitting.

To answer the question, "is it the right time to call it quits," you must ignore immediate emotions and answer a more pertinent question, "*How do I want to feel about my life when I'm too old and feeble to work?*" Let me explain, using myself and my second startup as an example.

To start iSuppli, I quit my job as CEO of International Rectifier (IR), a global semiconductor company listed on the New York Stock Exchange. At the time, I had more than 4,000 people working for me in nine countries around the world. We were a profitable global leader in our technological niche and I was highly paid and well respected. But I wanted more, and it wasn't money. I wanted to prove that I could create lots of value on my own, my way.

The fact that IR was a company founded by my father and grandfather over 50 years before was for me both a blessing and a curse. I had not planned to work for IR after I graduated with a PhD in Applied Physics from Stanford. I was interested in lasers, not semiconductors, and I wanted to do what interested me. But when I had been working for about a year for the leading laser company of the era, developing cool new types of lasers, my father said he needed my help to save IR. That's tough to say no to.

My joining IR was not well received by almost everyone else in the company. I was widely considered a nepotistic interloper, even though my family's ownership of the company had been diluted to small single digits by the time I came aboard. My way forward involved avoiding many landmines, often deliberately put in my way. But these are stories for another time. Eighteen years later I became CEO with the unanimous vote of the Board of Directors after having led the transformation of multiple parts of the company from producing disappointing results to becoming the best in the world at what they did. Five years after I took the reins, IR was performing better than it ever had, and I felt I had accomplished what I had been asked to do. It was time to start my own venture, my own way. So at age forty-five, I did something few successful public-company CEOs ever do: I left a successful and profitable operation to start a company from scratch.

When I founded iSuppli, I had about as many unfair advantages as any founder could ever have. To begin with, I knew first-hand the problem I wanted to solve: help all electronic companies, IR included, better control their manufacturing and inventories by giving them improved tools and visibility into end-customer demand and the status of all the industry's supply chains.

As the CEO of IR, I had constantly asked why things couldn't be more efficient and why we didn't have all the information we needed to make expensive investment decisions. What I wanted to do was complicated, even relative to the highly technical world of the electronics industry. But this complex industry needed complex solutions to manage the billions of electronic parts that moved around the world every day, and I had some clear ideas about how the industry could save billions of dollars in inventory and distribution costs. My ideas were based on direct experience and best practices, and resonated with the more sophisticated players in the industry. It was my first unfair advantage: the problem was real, and I had a credible solution based on direct, high level, and firsthand experience.

Second, I had broad experience—I had run operations, sales, marketing, R&D projects, and supply chains at one time or another. Since earning my PhD, I had led a large company and I had started divisions from scratch, both close to home and in far-flung places around the world. Having raised over a hundred million dollars on Wall Street, I was financially savvy. And having learned much from my unsuccessful attempt to launch Table of Contents, I was the opposite of naïve.*

Third, I knew people and people knew me, and I had a reputation for being ethical, practical, and smart. Important people in the industry—potential customers and capable, experienced employees alike—were willing to take my calls and listen to what I had to say. That's not to say that everyone simply signed up for iSuppli's services on my word alone. What I was proposing was expensive and complex. It needed to be carefully evaluated before being adopted and implemented. But getting a hearing was still a huge advantage. And it helped me assemble a Who's-Who Board of Directors and board of advisors. Within weeks I had recruited an incredibly capable team of individuals widely respected in their areas of expertise. (Many other people were willing to come work for me instantly, but I didn't recruit from IR, which I loved and didn't want to harm.)

Finally, I had the unfair advantage of being very well off financially. My twenty-three years in the semiconductor industry had resulted in substantial wealth through stock options. At the time I started iSuppli, I had the financial means of never having to work another day in my life if I so chose. I could send my kids to college; I could take care of relatives; my wife and I could do whatever we wanted; and I could personally invest to get iSuppli launched.

---

* My experiment with founding Table of Contents happened about five years before I was made CEO of IR. It was an early reflection of my inner desire to do things my way—even though only as a hobby and with a startup that was run by others.

Nevertheless, I did ask some venture capitalists, some of whom were strangers, to invest in iSuppli and be my partners. Why? I thought I could remain in control because I thought I would have the funds to retain majority ownership. I reasoned that I could use "other people's money" to grow faster than any potential competitor who might copy my ideas.

iSuppli did have competition. We were solving a big, costly problem and it was the middle of the dot-com bubble, so there was ample money available to fund other people attempting similar solutions. There were plenty of smart, credible people in the semiconductor industry, and the list of potential competitors was long. My solution hinged on iSuppli building out a global supply chain faster than anyone else, which convinced me that I needed to take the high-risk route with strong financial backing at the outset.

But, as is true for just about all entrepreneurs, things didn't work out exactly as planned. For despite the many advantages with which I had begun, key advisors and investors suggested on four different occasions that I shut down iSuppli. But, as is true for most *successful* entrepreneurs, I felt that I wouldn't be able to live with myself if I failed.

The first time I was advised to throw in the towel typifies the existential crises most entrepreneurs face early on in the testing out of their business idea. To explain how to make the electronics supply chain more efficient, I made a cute diagram that showed how the two intertwined flows of money and parts could be more effectively synchronized. The diagram saved me explaining a complex concept and it got me plenty of attention. But as often happens when you're selling a business-to-business concept, the bosses at your potential client company understand your idea, while the people who will have to implement it feel threatened by it, doing whatever they can to make its implementation look impossible. After shaking hands with the Executive VP of our potential first client on a deal to implement our ideas for one year on an experimental basis, we were stymied for weeks. In every implementation meeting we were peppered with objections, showered with alternative interpretations of facts, and treated to many emotional outbursts. I also remember a dismaying, middle-of-the-night phone call from our experienced implementation team leader at our potential client's factory in the Philippines. "We've failed; it can't work," he said. "Let's not waste any more money fitting our round pegs into everyone's square holes." There were real technical issues; the problem wasn't just fear and reticence on the part of the client's implementation teams. We were afraid we couldn't deal with all the issues that had been thrown at us. Even the potential customer's EVP who had liked my ideas was losing patience with us. I thought, "If I fail with iSuppli, everyone will think I'm a bad business person and they will never listen to my ideas again. That just can't happen." So I asked myself, "If I had all the money in the world, how would I solve the problems they've thrown at us?" I took action by dedicating several full-time people to act as the customer's ombudsmen. My investors and key executives all said, "That's going backwards! We can't afford to do that. We'll go out of business fast if that's our new business model." I thought that it was better to go out of business fast rather than immediately, and I also thought that if things went smoothly with the one-year experiment, we could then withdraw the extra people we needed. The solution placated our customer (who understood our offer was a great deal, because to perform our experiment we were basically subsidizing their business), and we stayed in business, although that client didn't make us any money until a couple of years later.

The next time I was advised to call it quits came about a year later. We were about to sign a contract to install our systems at the largest division of one of the biggest and most respected electronics companies in the world. They had been thinking along similar lines themselves, and when we showed them what we had up and running, they realized that we were well ahead of them. They knew many members of the senior team I had assembled, and they believed we could deliver them major savings, fast. We needed only the CEO's signature on the contract. She had been very supportive of our deal until then, and we expected to get the green light any day. Instead, we got shocking news on a phone call from a company representative:

The CEO had decided this would be a great business for them to get into, and she had decided to create a new division to copy what we were doing and compete with us. To top it off, we soon heard that she had personally called several of our potential clients and offered them joint venture partnerships, potentially giving her company a huge lead in creating a more efficient global supply chain.

It was as if a bomb had gone off at iSuppli. We felt dazed, injured, and afraid. Several of my investors said, "Game over." Re-examining our business definitely might have been the logical thing to do at the moment. But my experience at IR in dealing with large companies told me they couldn't analyze situations as fast as a nimble special ist outfit like iSuppli could, nor could they implement solutions as quickly. Admittedly, I was afraid. But the CEO's actions just made me even more committed to show the world that nobody could manage the most complex supply chains in the world better than iSuppli. No retreat, no surrender. The shot across our bow just made us even more determined to do a great job building out our capabilities.

Fast forward another twelve months, when iSuppli was starting to find its groove, even though the dot-com bubble had burst and much of the electronics industry was in survival mode. At the time, we had 175 employees and a couple of experimental "demonstration" engagements going with a handful of clients in a few locations around the world. We were moving millions of parts a week. We were a 24/7 global operation. And our sophisticated supply chain management and information gathering processes, which we had exclusively developed, were reducing the volatility of the supply chains we managed.

Our largest, most sophisticated, and highest-profile client declared that they were ready to commit to our platform globally if we would commit to investing in a global buildout. We needed about fifteen million dollars to implement a global infrastructure. But at the end of 2002, after the dot-com debacle, nobody was investing in tech companies. Our investors said they'd figure out how to get us the money we needed, but they would need our client to sign a multi-year contract for our services, with a minimum guaranteed payment that would at least cover our extra costs—our VCs couldn't raise money for us to lose money. But the client, whose business was under considerable stress just like everyone else's in the tech world, refused to even consider guarantees. I went back and forth between investors and this client—and our other clients as well—looking for a solution that could secure the money we needed. After three months of this, our client said, "Enough; you're too financially insecure." They were going to go with our less sophisticated but better financed competitors. Unable to raise the money to go global, and with the defection of our highest-profile customer, we found our other supply chain management customers abandoning us.

The three months I spent trying to negotiate a solution to the problem of a guarantee also gave me time to think of alternatives. Because Plan A rarely works out as expected, entrepreneurs are strongly encouraged to have Plans B, C, and D at the ready. My Plan B was to focus on all the ways we helped our clients improve their supply chains that did not require the deployment of major global infrastructure. iSuppli had created world-class data collection and information analysis teams who had in turn created unique and valuable data subscription services that our clients did not want to see go away. It was exactly the information I had wanted at IR, information that nobody could yet provide about inventories, capacities, and how many products of which type were being used by which customer. Such information, when combined with iSuppli's supply chain management software and processes, helped us mange supply chains better than any customer could. This information was something everyone up and down the supply chain wanted. We had worked hard to crack the code on how to get that information legally, without using anybody's proprietary or confidential information. We had already started selling our data and information independently of our supply chain services while we proved out the other aspects of our business model. Those data and information services represented about one-third of the revenue we were earning at the time of this calamity.

So when I couldn't find funding, I had a back-up plan ready to shift iSuppli into being a "market intelligence provider" to the electronics world. But it required laying off three-quarters of iSuppli's employees. I had been up front with all employees throughout the crisis, providing weekly updates on the search for funding and talking candidly with employees who came by my office seeking the latest news. When all was said and done, nobody was surprised by the layoffs. More importantly, not a single person critical to maintaining our data collection and information business lost confidence in iSuppli and left the company—I kept the one-quarter of the team that was critical to the survival of the business.

At that point, the VCs saw iSuppli as a failure. We were allowed to stay in business because we still had money in the bank, but they wanted my head. A considerable fraction of my wealth was tied up in iSuppli, so I was fine with the VCs looking for any CEO who could make the company more valuable than I could. But in the meantime, I wasn't going to let that search divert me from making our market intelligence business as valuable as possible. I could have stomped off or decided to show the Board who was boss, but choosing someone to lead iSuppli to become more valuable was ultimately in everyone's best interests. About six months after the layoffs, the VCs officially called off the search for another CEO. They said that my vision to grow iSuppli's value as a market intelligence company was more compelling than the vision of any other CEO candidate. Even though my partners didn't realize it at the time, the third crisis in iSuppli's life had been averted because I had a solid backup plan.

A fourth existential crisis came as our clients continued downsizing and shrinking budgets for several years after the dot-com bubble burst. Despite the cutbacks, clients wanted us to provide them with ever more data and information. I believed that making our customers happy while growing our business was a great opportunity we couldn't pass up, lest our customers encourage competitors to deliver to them what we didn't. The challenge was that about a year was required to develop a new data or information service, and then another six to twelve months for enough customers to check that the accuracy of the data was to their satisfaction, and then to embed the information into their own systems. Only then did our data actually pay off for them. Although our investments in new services started to pay back in eighteen to twenty-four months—a relatively short time to get to cash flow breakeven—our VCs wanted none of it. They had written down their investments in iSuppli after we shut down our supply chain management business, and they were not going to give us any money to expand, even if it offered rapid payback.

During that time, I kept the company growing by loaning iSuppli money from my own savings and forgoing my salary to make it clear to everyone that these loans were entirely for the good of iSuppli. Everyone was happy, at least for a few months, about all the new data we had collected and the services our customers were eager to evaluate. But then my cash reserves dried up suddenly. My old company, IR, started to struggle with their profitability and the price of their stock plummeted, rendering the stock options I still owned worthless. With no ready way to fund the company I found myself in a position I had promised myself to avoid at all costs—needing to find new funds within ninety days to meet payroll. Failing to make payroll totally screws employees—the best of them leave immediately—and causes companies to collapse. If iSuppli collapsed because I ran out of money and missed payroll, I would be considered an incompetent entrepreneur; nobody would ever listen to me again. People outside of IR might even question my past accomplishments there. I couldn't bear such thoughts. To keep iSuppli running, I was willing to do anything legal that wouldn't bankrupt my family.

I took out a second mortgage on our house, which bought me some more time, but ultimately I had no alternative but to convince our VCs to invest more money. Getting someone new to invest wouldn't work because any new investor would want to go to the head of the line in recovering their investment. The existing professional investors would never agree to give anyone else more favorable terms than they had. Fortunately, iSuppli had continued to grow right through the dot-com bubble and the ensuing tech chaos, so the company still had value. It didn't make sense to let it collapse, although logic does not always drive decisions relating to money, power, and status. The negotiation with the VCs was painful and humiliating. I had to agree to my previous loans and investments being wiped out in order for iSuppli to be given three loans with extremely high interest rates that increased with time. We could pay back the loans only if we kept growing as fast as we were, and with no further investment. Paying back the loans in a timely fashion was practically impossible, but accepting the terms was the only viable alternative I had—and the VCs knew it.

iSuppli did continue to grow quickly, and we used much of the loans to finish building out several valuable new data services that further accelerated our growth. The loan package not only saved the company and everyone's jobs, but also worked out for me personally. By previously agreed-upon rights as the largest investor, I had to be given the opportunity to be part of the loan syndicate. I didn't have the money to participate at first, but IR's stock price soon recovered, making my options valuable again, so I was able to participate in the last two loans. Those loans carried the highest interest rates, which yielded me some decent returns when iSuppli was sold a few years later for $100 million.

I didn't let iSuppli fail because I couldn't face my perception of the consequences of defeat, while I could in the case of Table of Contents. Nobody realizes that the answer to "when to throw in the towel" is actually already made for you when you decide to commit to founding your company. I founded Table of Contents to validate myself as a "businessman" who knew how to create new business opportunities. I could not therefore let my startup drain my wealth if I wanted to continue to consider myself a good businessperson. By the time I started iSuppli, a decade after starting Table of Contents, my core motivations had shifted. I had proven to my satisfaction that I was very good at leading large global and complex businesses through difficult times while still capturing major opportunities along the way. IR was doing better than it ever had in its history despite intense global competition and very turbulent markets. By the time I started iSuppli, I wanted to prove I could create significant value on my own, free of family legacies. I could therefore not quit, no matter the financial impact, until the question of my ability to create value was resolved one way or another. I certainly wasn't going to let the existential crises I just described take me down—they were merely challenges I had to figure out how to overcome.

When entrepreneurs ask me the "when to quit" question, what they are really asking for is reassurance from a higher authority of sorts that their personal quest remains valid. The challenge most entrepreneurs face is that they do not understand their real motivations for having embarked on their quests—otherwise, they would already know what to do next.

The real question is therefore not when, but whether.

CHAPTER 11

WHETHER

The question of whether you should become an entrepreneur, or whether you should invest in your nephew's startup, is an existential one: Do you want to take a journey that you can never be totally ready for? We've discussed how you can best prepare:

- Make sure you will actually feel happy in making other people happy and asking for their money in return.
- Make sure you've accumulated "enough" of the essential assets to start.
- Make sure you're "good enough" to compete in an entrepreneurial league you will feel satisfied playing in.

Of course most entrepreneurs have never considered these prerequisites, and most entrepreneurs have failed. This book cannot offer anyone a magic formula, just essential facts and good examples. Unfortunately, meeting the criteria outlined here still does not guarantee success. It merely increases your odds of success—or, put another way, it reduces your risk of failure. Checking off all the boxes of motivations—a happy-making idea, adequate skills, and adequate assets—does not necessarily mean you should try starting your own company. Conversely, not having everything lined up doesn't preclude entrepreneurship from being the best move for you. Not even a crystal ball can adequately answer the question of *whether*. The more pertinent question is how the entrepreneurial journey will make you feel—and make the people you love feel—irrespective of how it ends. And since the journeys of high-risk and bedrock entrepreneurs are so different, the question of whether is also a question of which mode of entrepreneurship is best for you.

The first decade of Jordan's entrepreneurial career was glorious for him. In that relatively short time, the Sausage Kingdom had grown to providing sausages at dozens of airports, all southern California sports stadiums, at two of the most popular tourist destinations in the world, and to many fast-growing national food retailers like Trader Joe's and Costco. Along the way Jordan encountered plenty of challenges and crises (many, as we've seen, avoidable), but he was making more money than he had ever dreamed. At this point some entrepreneurs think about cashing out while they're ahead, but for Jordan, his Sausage Kingdom was now his life and nothing could make him give it up. What was impossible for Jordan to realize at the time was that the magnitude of his mistakes would grow with time because his skills and those of his team where not keeping up with his opportunities.

Jordan's eleventh year of business started with a call from the president of the Portland Trailblazers. The Trailblazers' president and Paul Allen, the owner of the basketball team and the retired co-founder of Microsoft, were such huge fans of Jody Maroni sausages that they offered him a prominent space in the shopping mall Allen was building next to Portland's basketball arena. Jordan's space was to be a fancy restaurant that served interesting sausages and featured a full bar. The thought tantalized Jordan. He could go upscale and become a major restaurateur—this would open up even more avenues for people to love him.

Jordan spent well over a million dollars of his own money to create a beautiful upscale beer and sausage restaurant. But people came to the mall only during basketball season—for over half of the year, Jordan's restaurant was empty. The entire mall was a financial disaster. Paul Allen could afford his losses, but almost all of Jordan's savings were wiped out. Still, profits were coming in from Jordan's other businesses, and he had successfully outfitted a larger factory and warehouse for all the business that Costco was bringing to him. With positive cash flow, Jordan felt growing the Sausage Kingdom as fast as possible was still top priority. He opened up more sausage stands in some smaller airports on his own, and he started to franchise Jody Maroni's Sausage Kingdom to several dozen individuals who had been soliciting him for the opportunity. When 9/11 hit, however, the airports and tourist venues where many of his storefronts were located emptied out and a large fraction of his franchises were put out of business, leaving him with big bills and no cash flow.

To make family matters even worse, his wife's stepbrother, who was upset because Jordan had never given him a job or listened to his ideas, started a rival sausage company. Jordan sued the brother-in-law, sending the family into further chaos. Within a month his wife left him. Ever sensitive to the people he loved, Jordan rented a house near his wife and kids, taking on additional expense to make it feel as if their family still worked.

And then Costco, Jordan's largest customer by far, started pressuring him for major price reductions. Jordan had bought and outfitted his new factory in order to accommodate the Costco business, and he still had big bills to pay for it. He felt insulted. After a year of haggling, Costco cancelled all their orders and went with a new vendor of specialty sausages who had copied Jody Maroni's flavors but used less expensive ingredients. Without Costco, the new factory was a financial disaster.

On top of all this, some of Jordan's franchisees were doing poorly, and without proper supervision or support, they began playing around with the franchise formula and skimping on quality. For the first time, Jordan received letters from customers upset about their experiences eating at Jody Maroni's Sausage Kingdoms.

For the next four years, Jordan was forced to lay off employees, close the new factory he outfitted to serve Costco, and close the new stands he had opened that were losing money. Because Jordan was afraid people would stop loving him for making the cutbacks, he procrastinated with his cost cutting, requiring him to borrow money to stay afloat.

At the end of the four years of cost cutting, the Sausage Kingdom finally started to make money again, and Jordan felt he could rebuild. But he sensed he should get professional help for his second attempt at growing his company. He wasn't confident anymore about his ability to put together franchising agreements or to pick franchisees, so he hired a headhunter to find him somebody who could reinvigorate growth through franchising. Recruiting proved to be more difficult than Jordan expected. Most experienced franchise executives weren't interested in working with him. One executive who was interested had food service experience but only limited franchising experience. Jordan still agreed to make him president of the company. The new president proceeded to borrow money to create logistics infrastructure, and he sold franchises to bar owners he knew who thought that good-tasting sausages would enhance their liquor sales. But the new president's inexperience at overseeing logistics infrastructure resulted in systems and software that didn't work properly, leading to additional losses. Some of the new franchisees began to default on their payments because their bar business did not increase as expected. Watching the losses mount up quickly, Jordan realized that his president had no idea how to fix the problems his decisions had caused. Jordan fired him. But the damage had already been done. With significant debts to pay, Jordan had to shut down the franchising operation a second time. He is still paying off those debts. He runs his original Venice Beach location and lives above the stand. He's revered by the other merchants of Venice, and referred to as "The Bard of the Boardwalk."

Jordan Monkarsh thinks a lot about whether he should have started his Sausage Kingdom. He broods about what he could have done differently: selling the Sausage Kingdom at its peak, hiring more experienced people to help him, or just asking for advice. But while those closest to Jordan no longer view him as a successful entrepreneur—he didn't hold his sausage empire or his family together—he feels good about most of what he's done: he made millions of people happy with the best sausages they'd ever tasted, he employed thousands of people, and many people loved him for what he did. He remains a hero to the small team that still works for him, and he revels in the attention and respect he receives from his loyal fans that still come to the Venice Beach Boardwalk just to satisfy their sausage habit.

Sure, asking for advice and mastering business and leadership skills early on rather than after the fact would have served Jordan well. But Jordan still did a stupendous job of taking an idea and growing it relentlessly into a big, profitable business, even though it doesn't feel like that to him now.

Every entrepreneur is challenged to question their motives and methods at points along their journey. Building a business, whether it's enormous like Walmart, or small like 1-800-AUTOPSY, is always, always stressful. And it is always hard work to create a business that makes large numbers of customers happy. All entrepreneurs, no matter how successful they ultimately become, get irritable and even depressed sometimes. Many entrepreneurs reach the point where they wonder whether they've made the right decisions in getting to where they are. That's when they should remember what they do to make others happy, and ask themselves how there might be more happiness to give. Jordan asked himself that question repeatedly, and it served to drive him forward. If the answer to this question loses its interest and excitement—if there seems to be no more happiness to give—then it's time to stop the journey and sell or close the business.

Today Jordan spends most of his spare time reading books on anthropology. For Jordan, reading about other cultures is as captivating as reading a thriller is to the rest of us. And Jordan looks forward to the hours he spends with his kids and grandkids. He's a happy guy, he's created lots of happy people, and sausages are much more interesting to eat because of Jordan. No one can justify thinking that Jordan should have ever quit while he was ahead.

Rags-to-riches-to-rags is a common story among entrepreneurs. Like Jordan, most entrepreneurs who do very well at some point are unable to sustain their peak value creation. Competition, business conditions, and customer desires are constantly changing. Staying focused for long periods of time is extremely difficult. About two-thirds of the businesses on *Inc. Magazine*'s annual list of the top 5,000 fastest-growing private companies in America either shrink or are sold disadvantageously after making the list. Success must be constantly won and re-won.

Jordan's story provides a cautionary tale about fundamental mistakes initially successful entrepreneurs can make. But it's also a meditation on whether the risks of entrepreneurship are worth taking and about what really constitutes entrepreneurial success. Is it starting an innovative company? Is it creating a profitable company that supports the entrepreneur and lots of employees while making customers very happy? Is it creating a company that lasts forever—or at least longer than a generation? Is it proving to your dad that you're good at something after all? Is it doing something that makes you happy, regardless of what a parent or others might think? The answers, as the stories of Sam, Walt, Estée, Ray, Jordan, Stephanie, Vidal, and Ken demonstrate, depend upon why you started the company in the first place—what you needed to prove to yourself by embarking on such a journey.

Because the journey is unpredictable, the key is preparation. Preparation, the subject of this book, minimizes entrepreneurial mistakes. You prepare yourself for your journey by:

- Focusing on your motivations (Why)
- Accumulating needed assets (How Much)
- Mastering essential skills (How To)
- Choosing where and against whom you'll compete (How Good)

Everyone profiled in this book prepared to some extent, and in every case the extent of the preparation largely determined how the business wound up. So the question of "whether?" starts with a direct question to every entrepreneur about whether they have prepared. No? Then don't do it!

Assuming you have prepared, then the question of *whether* becomes the question of whether to go high-risk or bedrock. Consider the starkly different characteristics of bedrock and high-risk entrepreneurs.

Bedrock	High-Risk
• I want to reduce risk of personal loss (money, status, relationships).	• I want to maximize personal gain (money, status, networks).
• Slow and steady wins the race.	• Shoot for the moon and fail fast.
• I can't afford failure nor can I justify it to those who are hurt by it.	• Failure is a learning experience.
• I will build my business with profits.	• Use as much of other people's money as you can get.
• I measure my success based on achieving my personal goals.	• I will build a valuable business by growing my stock price.
• Partnering with strangers is risky and should be avoided.	• Partnering with strangers is less risky than not having enough money to invest.

These are contrasting mindsets that lead to two dramatically different entrepreneurial journeys. Bedrock entrepreneurs come to understand that they succeed because of their personal ability to make their customers very happy—and to ask for money in return— and their ability to rally other people to help them do that. Because their journey is personal, failure is personal. Bedrock entrepreneurs therefore avoid unnecessary risks and invest time and effort to minimize risks associated with the steps they must take.

Many high-risk entrepreneurs feel the same way and only choose that path because they believe they cannot otherwise compete in the business they've chosen. Certain types of businesses are by their very nature high-risk and entrepreneurs that feel comfortable with risks do have an advantage when starting these companies. Businesses whose competitive advantages come from creating network effects or being first to develop the economies of scale to bring costs down to massively affordable levels require high-risk entrepreneurs and savvy venture capitalists. Businesses that are highly regulated and require years of testing, such as pharmaceuticals and medical devices, require large amounts of capital to support, and may also require a high-risk approach to be feasible.

But some high-risk entrepreneurs choose their path not because of need, but because of mindset. To some entrepreneurs, high risk connotes high return, perhaps because they think risk is related to return. But the economic theories of risks versus returns only apply in the aggregate across perfect markets with large numbers of buyers and sellers of well-defined units of risks, as with a specific stock or bond. High risk does not mean high return for an individual entrepreneur. The link does not even apply across the portfolio of most venture capitalists, since most VCs return to their investors much less money than would be expected for the added risk. Further, as we have seen with Sam Walton and Estée Lauder, *high returns can ensue from taking small risks, particularly when the small risks yield information directly related to how to improve returns with almost no risks.*

In order to align their objectives to those of their venture capital partners, high-risk entrepreneurs must set as their primary objective increasing the value of their company's stock, regardless of whether it aligns with their core motivations. Entrepreneurs with such a mindset have shifted their end objective from making customers happy to pleasing investors. These high-risk entrepreneurs greatly increase their personal risks that in time either customers or investors will rebel against them. Growing fast and potentially failing fast makes complete sense if it's all about making massive amounts of money quickly.

Many VCs claim to offer expertise and contacts that are valuable and that lower risk. However, relatively few entrepreneurs acknowledge that VC expertise and contacts were critical to their success.

Using VC expertise and contacts is a bit of a catch-22: an entrepreneur who needs the help of a VC to succeed is not someone VCs will feel comfortable letting lead a company of any value.

The point of this book is that all entrepreneurs are responsible for preparing for their journeys and navigating their journeys responsibly. Do *not* try it just because it sounds fun or even to prove something to yourself and your parents. There is too much at stake from a human perspective, even if you might not have much at stake financially. Vidal Herrera had little money at stake when he started 1-800-AUTOPSY, but he and his family had a great deal at stake personally. But Vidal was prepared for the entrepreneurial opportunity when he spotted it. If he had not thought about how he could lessen the pain he would feel while performing autopsies, and if he hadn't been prepared by being a highly skilled and efficient coroner's assistant, he would have failed at making the VA happy, and the failure would have literally killed him and destroyed his family.

Whether you should try to become an entrepreneur has nothing to do with any special traits, or charisma, or whether you love to take risks, or are great at computer programming. Those are myths. Ignore them.

The question is whether you have taken the time and invested the energy and thought in preparing, and whether you understand which entrepreneurial path is the best path for you. Anything short of responsibly preparing is a clear sign that you are not serious about your commitment to make other people happy.

CHAPTER 12

SO WHAT

Except for emergencies, the president of the United States does not travel on short notice. There are thousands of people involved in planning the travel of the president outside of the Washington, DC area. An exception, however, was made in March of 1992. Sam Walton had been awarded America's highest civilian honor, the Presidential Medal of Freedom, and George H. W. Bush directed his staff to arrange for him to fly down to Bentonville, Arkansas in just a few days' time to personally bestow the honor. Even though Sam was confined to a wheelchair by that time, he couldn't help but beam at the event in front of a crowd of more than a thousand friends, family, and associates. The president spent almost fifteen minutes talking about Sam and Helen. When it came time to receive the medal, Sam, always determined to do the right thing, rose from his wheelchair and stood while the president tied the medal around his neck.

Sam always wanted to do the right thing, which to him meant making things better and better. Not just for Walmart's customers and its employees, but also for his family and community. Unlike many other entrepreneurs, Sam never let his success come at the expense of those around him, and he never pretended he did it all by himself; he always credited Helen as being his full partner, and he was quick to give credit to others. What made Sam happy was making others happy, and that's why he is such an enduring and all-encompassing role model—he is what entrepreneurship is all about.

Sam may never have used a personal computer, but he made sure Wal-Mart used computers early on to stay at the vanguard of retailing. He never used a mobile phone either, but he made sure Wal-Mart had access to its own satellite communication links almost as soon as they were available so that he and his team could monitor the performance of his stores in real time. If Sam were still alive, he would surely be using the latest technology to help him supervise his stores and better serve his customers. Today's increasingly sophisticated technologies and tools may change the techniques entrepreneurs use to make customers happy, and ask for money, but nothing has changed the who, what, when, where, how, and why of entrepreneurship—the things you have to do and think about *before* you decide on the specific tools and techniques that may help you.

Nor has the pace of entrepreneurship changed, even though a great deal more information is instantly available today. There might be much more data for the CEO of a fast-growing company to review, but the pace of entrepreneurship is limited by the ability of the people affected to accept and implement that change, not by how fast software can do A/B testing on websites. No entrepreneur has ever achieved a faster pace of continuous improvement on such a large scale for as many years as did Sam and his team. The entire management team discussed and outlined proposed improvements every Saturday morning, and Sam expected the improvements they approved to be implemented the following week. Sam inspired his management team to want to change, and he spent his time making sure there were no impediments. Sam Walton is a timeless role model.

Stephanie DiMarco and Ken Marlin are contemporary role models who also exemplify timeless aspects of entrepreneurship. They are savvy about the latest ways of extracting money from their happy customers (i.e. business models) and what tools are available for doing that extraction most productively (i.e. technology). But, as we've seen, Jordan Monkarsh, Vidal Hererra, Estée Lauder, Walt Disney, Ray Kroc, and Sam Walton all shared strong implicit motivations for succeeding as entrepreneurs and all developed the skills and deliberately accumulated the assets their businesses would require to grow and prosper. The lessons of entrepreneurship are timeless.

Pioneering the Future

These lessons are more pressing today than ever because our future is shaped by how we think entrepreneurship works. The fundamental principle of entrepreneurship makes entrepreneurship a core component of the well-being of our society. Entrepreneurs must challenge the status quo to get any attention and to get any business. By improving the customer experience they set new standards and expectations in both big and small ways in almost all fields. And large corporations copy the techniques and methods that entrepreneurs prove work—where entrepreneurs go, many soon follow. *Successful entrepreneurs change what we do and what we want.* Because entrepreneurs create and get us to accept change by offering us products and services that make us happy, they bear a large responsibility for the direction of our society.

Entrepreneurs get us to change by offering us a choice and then convincing us that it's the better one. Our diversity of choice, today and in the future, is contingent on the different backgrounds and ambitions of large numbers of nascent entrepreneurs, each undertaking a different journey to get what they want, as well as to deliver to us what we want. We need large numbers of entrepreneurs, but the number of entrepreneurs we're getting is actually shrinking.

Successful entrepreneurs also need to convince us that the choice they offer is enough of an improvement on what was previously available. They can convince us with facts and demonstrations, or they can convince us by manipulating our desires. "Mmmm, that looks good." Jordan Monkarsh made me think that when he waved his Jody

Maroni sausages at me thirty years ago—I could not resist trying one. It was pure manipulation by someone with great marketing instincts. Fortunately for me Jordan is a very ethical guy, and there was nothing unsavory about his savory sausage.

Entrepreneurial Responsibilities

We must nonetheless realize that *the fundamental principle of entrepreneurship necessarily places our society on a trajectory toward more and more hedonism,* with more and more focus on satisfying short-term and fleeting desires, many of which we are being manipulated into wanting in the first place. Why? Because it's far easier, less costly, and faster to manipulate us into having a fleeting desire than it is to offer products and services that create the type of happiness that comes from a sense of well-being. It's very profitable business to push the limits of desire.

Entrepreneurs and corporations alike have gotten so good at understanding the science of manipulation, the science of creating desires, the science of trust, and the science of habit formation that they can get many people to feel fleeting happiness with temporary goods and services and still want to give money in return. And with good marketing people and great lobbyists, the entrepreneurs and corporations that make money off this hedonism can make sure society doesn't think too much about the waste and the by-products of all this fleeting happiness.

There will always be some entrepreneurs willing to exploit our hedonistic tendencies as long as there are many of us willing to hand over our money to feel fleeting, superficial, manipulated happiness. And when the laws remain silent on these actions, the large corporations who feel their priority is to appease shareholders irrespective of their products' overall impact on society will soon follow.

Some entrepreneurs succeed by appealing to our baser instincts. We outlaw prostitution and gambling in many places and drug-dealing in most places, but immoral entrepreneurs still offer these services and use their cunning to evade the law. Although the insights we've discussed could serve equally well as a guide for someone starting an enterprise that distributes illicit drugs, we all have to hope this book will not be used to do so. While not illegal, recently, entrepreneurs have learned how to make large numbers of mostly men happy by making pornography available for free so that a small percentage of users will give money to see more. Many parents worry about the effect all this free pornography is having on their children and on our society. Now families with children must invest time and resources to monitor what their children are watching on the Internet at home or even at a friend's home. Entrepreneurs have repeatedly shown that it's good business to make food more appealing by making it sweeter and sweeter—consider the enticing smells of Cinnabon and hence our society's problem with obesity. Whatever it is that we can be made to want is what some entrepreneurs will help us get. Because of the impact of entrepreneurship on our society, we have an obligation to help our entrepreneurs succeed, but also to be our society's moral compasses.

The media hype surrounding high-risk entrepreneurs who are suddenly worth a billion dollars distorts the perspective of large numbers of would-be entrepreneurs. The implication that becoming rich, fast, is the objective of all "real" entrepreneurs has driven some aspiring entrepreneurs to do whatever it takes to succeed, which sometimes includes circumventing or breaking laws. Why not cut corners, use unethical suppliers, falsify records, or rush products to markets before they're fully tested? Why not exploit the naiveté of users seeking bliss? Why not capture the personal information and profiles of children and sell them to other companies? The misguided hype about entrepreneurship encourages entrepreneurs to justify socially questionable behaviors in the name of innovation and disruption.

Entrepreneurs can help us find our better self and help us help others. Entrepreneurs have brought us better medicines and medical treatments and amazing prosthetics. They have made education more accessible to those without it. They have made us safer in our cars. And entrepreneurs have made food that's good for us and tastes good too. But these are not the entrepreneurs we read about because they didn't become wealthy quickly.

Entrepreneurs don't have to be driven by profit when they ask for money in return for their services. They can ask for money from donors or foundations in return for providing happiness in the form of food, education, or medical services to those without it.

We need to understand that whenever we discuss entrepreneurship, we are also discussing morals and values—what makes us happy by making our lives and our society better.

Ensuring Ethical Entrepreneurs

Nearly all of our educators, policy makers, media pundits, and even politicians say that we must become more entrepreneurial in our lives and at our jobs. The problem is that we all use the word "entrepreneurial" differently, each of us having some, perhaps unconscious, motive for wanting entrepreneurship to be what we want it to be. Nobody in our society can force entrepreneurs to accept the expectations that others set for them. But in glorifying entrepreneurship or disdaining it, we are nonetheless attempting to manipulate entrepreneurs into doing what we want. This is true whether you are a parent arguing for or against your grown child considering entrepreneurship, or you're a billionaire wanting to look cool to loads of aspiring entrepreneurs so you can get first pick at investing in future billionaires.

But our entrepreneurial fantasies will lead to fewer benefits and more adverse consequences for all of us. Our society's future well-being depends upon inspiring a large percentage of the population to be moral entrepreneurs who create long-term good without needless waste.

Laws won't make that happen. There will always be plenty of entrepreneurs cunning enough to circumvent any law. We must understand and accept the magnitude of the impact of entrepreneurship on our society and make it a priority to educate our children about how entrepreneurship really works, and the imperative of moral entrepreneurship. This education should be integrated into the high school curriculum, perhaps with existing civics or modern history courses. Teaching the basics of entrepreneurship in high school will help ensure that we educate students not only about the skills but also about the ethics of entrepreneurship. The morals of our society are ensured only when we pass down our beliefs to the next generation. Only if we teach the basic tenets of entrepreneurship in high school will entrepreneurship be perceived as a powerfully moral act of helping others by making them truly happy.

The focus of our entrepreneurial education should rest on three tenets:

1. Entrepreneurs make other people happy and ask for money in return. By doing so, entrepreneurs play an essential role in shaping the future of our society.
2. Entrepreneurship may or may not be right for everyone, but it is a critical choice we all have to make. If you do want to be an entrepreneur, then choose thoughtfully between the two possible paths: bedrock and high risk.
3. Chances of being a successful entrepreneur are greatly enhanced by understanding the Who, What, When, Where, How, and Why of entrepreneurship.

These tenets summarize the cause and effect of entrepreneurship. Teaching these tenets to older teenagers as they begin to visualize and experiment with their place in the world will be highly relevant to them and therefore memorable. By studying the cause and effect of entrepreneurship along with history, social studies, and literature, students will appreciate how entrepreneurship has helped make the world "better." The ethical dimensions of history, literature, and social studies encompass the morals we want to pass along to our children—teaching the tenets of entrepreneurship at the same time would be teaching our children how to shape a more moral future.

Undermining Our Bedrock

There's another extremely worrisome problem with the direction of entrepreneurship. The hype around entrepreneurship is making our society less entrepreneurial, not more. Entrepreneurship as measured by how many new companies are created each year and also by the number of people considering starting a company is in long-term decline. Entrepreneurship is still big: more than 600,000 new companies a year are born in the United States, and more than ten million people are considering starting a company. But twenty years ago there used to be 800,000 new companies a year. And at times there have been thirteen million people aspiring to launch their own businesses.

Bedrock entrepreneurship is declining, and so is the success rate for aspiring high-risk entrepreneurs. The hyper-charged interest in our current herd of billion-dollar unicorns will certainly fade with time, just as it did when we hyped railroad entrepreneurs, or automotive entrepreneurs, or entertainment entrepreneurs, or even savings and loan entrepreneurs. But this time the hype, buttressed by an active and wealthy venture capital industry focused on high-risk entrepreneurs who aspire to make it big, fast, has seduced aspiring entrepreneurs to pursue more risky ventures in the few business domains where big numbers can accumulate quickly.

And hundreds of thousands of ambitious and energetic young people are out to prove that they are special and that they deserve to be billionaires after a couple of years of showing their ideas around. They fill hundreds of new incubators and accelerators with thousands of teams, and they make up the tens of thousands of startup teams applying to join. But as we saw in the "What If" chapter, venture capital is funding no more new high-risk entrepreneurs than it had before, so virtually all of the growing numbers of aspiring high-risk entrepreneurs fail or are going to fail.

Why are these aspiring entrepreneurs being led on? Because it is in the best interest of venture capitalists to have as large a flow of ideas and as large a number of ambitious people as possible coming to them so that the VC firm can choose the best. And if the aspiring entrepreneur doesn't understand the "How To" of scaling up an idea, then the VC can always replace the entrepreneur with someone who does.

By luring more and more aspiring entrepreneurs to take the high-risk route, we are doubly undermining the essential bedrock foundations of our society. First, many of the high-risk entrepreneurs we're leading on to failure could have been successful bedrock entrepreneurs and contributed to our society's well-being in a more desirable way than by wasting their time and somebody else's money. Second, the current hype is based on very narrow definitions of entrepreneurship and a glorification of failure that dissuades many potentially capable entrepreneurs from even trying: "I am not a coding savant and I need eight hours of sleep and I don't want to lose money my family may need." None of the entrepreneurial role models profiled in this book who changed society for the better were coding savants, walked around sleep-deprived for long periods of time (although they all did work long hours), or risked losing any money their families needed.

Dangerous Myths

As we've seen, many myths about entrepreneurship hurt us as individuals and hurt our society. To recap:

- **Myth:** *It just takes a great idea.* We've learned from William Shockley that ideas aren't enough. Entrepreneurial success requires not just an idea but also all of the things discussed in the How To, How Good, and How Much chapters.
- **Myth:** *All entrepreneurs innovate.* Sam Walton was proud that he borrowed ideas from wherever and whomever he could.
- **Myth:** *Entrepreneurs share certain essential traits.* Entrepreneurs differ more than they resemble each other because entrepreneurial success requires leveraging

your differences to distinguish your product or service from others.

- **Myth:** *Entrepreneurs are risk-tolerant.* Bedrock entrepreneurs work to minimize potential losses.
- **Myth:** *Disrupting markets is the best entrepreneurial strategy.* Significant happiness can be created by making existing things work better.
- **Myth:** *Market forces always drive entrepreneurs to improve our society.* Entrepreneurs look to deliver happiness, often where no market yet exists, and they sometimes deliver happiness that is fleeting that can cause long-term harm to society.
- **Myth:** *Only one in ten entrepreneurs succeeds.* This myth implies that we measure every entrepreneur's success using the same metric regardless of what the entrepreneur really wants or cares about.
- **Myth:** *Failure is always good because it always makes you better.* Failing by taking unnecessary risk is just stupid. Savvy entrepreneurs never risk more than they can afford and they experiment with what they don't know.
- **Myth:** *The beginner's mindset is essential for innovating as an entrepreneur.* To succeed as an entrepreneur you need to have mastered the specific skills required to deliver your product or service more reliably and cost-effectively than others already in the business.
- **Myth:** *Successful entrepreneurs are tech-savvy.* Successful entrepreneurs deliver happiness. Technology can never be more than a tool to help an entrepreneur be more effective at delivering happiness or collecting the money received in return.

Instead, we need to understand these truths about entrepreneurship:

- Entrepreneurs leverage their differences to make their products and services more valuable.

- Entrepreneurs make people happy and ask for money in return.
- Leadership and strong teams turn mundane ideas into entrepreneurial successes.
- Almost all of us can learn the essential skills of entrepreneurship.
- Risk-taking is a choice.
- Experiments avert failures.
- Most successful entrepreneurs start small and grow as they gain skills and confidence.
- Bedrock entrepreneurs fail much less often than high-risk entrepreneurs, yet have the same potential for impact and wealth creation in most markets.
- Making large numbers of people happy is exhausting and costs money, so unless you really love asking for money in return for making someone or some business happy, entrepreneurship is probably not for you.

The Dividends of Ethical Entrepreneurship

It's time we told the truth about entrepreneurship. Entrepreneurship is a big deal; it involves big numbers, and it likely involves each of us directly or indirectly. About half of us will have attempted being an entrepreneur in our working careers. Most people know an entrepreneur, and many of us have been asked to invest in the business of someone we know. But the fantasies we have about entrepreneurship have discouraged many capable people with great things to offer from becoming entrepreneurs, and encouraged many of our aspiring entrepreneurs to choose paths that unnecessarily lead to failure.

An estimated $530 billion—yes, *billion*—is spent on launching startups every year. Most of that money comes directly out of the entrepreneurs' pockets, or from the equity in their houses, or from debt. Much of it also comes from gifts, loans, or investments from friends and family. Only 10 to 20 percent of this money, depending upon the year and the state of frenzy in venture investing, comes from complete strangers and professional investors. Spending on startups is an exceedingly measurable part of our economy. This is money that goes to buy equipment, pay contractors, hire help, and pay rent to landlords. And most of this money is wasted needlessly by ill-prepared entrepreneurs with virtually no chance of success. But many of these startups could have succeeded if their founders had realized the straightforward steps they could have taken to turn things around. Telling the truth about entrepreneurship will help many more entrepreneurs succeed, waste less money, time, and effort, and destroy fewer families, while at the same time increasing entrepreneurship overall.

Furthermore, telling the truth about entrepreneurship to everyone as they begin to think about their careers will help focus entrepreneurship on increasing overall well-being while reducing the temptation for aspiring entrepreneurs to make their money from manipulating the lonely, weak, impressionable, and most of the rest of us into indulging fleeting pleasures.

A great deal can be gained from refocusing our conversation about entrepreneurship, learning from great entrepreneurial role models, and exposing the myths that lead entrepreneurs to take on needless risks, waste large amounts of money and resources, and fail when they could have succeeded. We will be more competitive in more types of businesses. Our products and services will improve at a faster rate. More jobs will be created. Most importantly, living the truth about entrepreneurship will make us all happier in more meaningful ways.

NOTES

Since this is not an academic treatise, I list only the most relevant sources rather than complete lists of references pertaining to a particular point.

Chapter 1: Truth Matters

By opening day . . . My version of the opening adds detail and differs in tone and perspective compared to the version cited in Sam Walton's autobiography (page 58), *Made in America,* Bantam (New York), 1992. In his book, Sam quotes David Glass' telling of his story about attending the opening. My depiction of the opening of Wal-Mart number 2 in Harrison, Arkansas was derived from my interview with Clarence Leis on December 16, 2016. Clarence was the manager of Wal-Mart number 1 at the time and helped personally with the planning and execution of the opening of store 2. I also added details based upon archival photographs of the event from the Walmart Archives. Additional details came from an interview with Grace

McCutcheon, who participated on the team preparing store 2. She is quoted in Vance Trimble's book (page 105), *Sam Walton: The Inside Story of America's Richest Man*, Dutton Adult (New York), 1990.

Over 60 percent of working men and women . . . This datum comes from a Gallup survey conducted March 18–20, 2005. The results of the survey can be found at: http://www.gallup.com/poll/15832/majority-americans-want-start-own-business.aspx.

. . . if you're male, the chances are about 50/50 . . . See page 13 of Paul D. Reynolds' essential book, *Entrepreneurship in the United States: The Future is Now*, Springer (New York), 2007. Women attempt to be entrepreneurs at about half the rate of men—the reason for this disparity is hotly debated and remains an open question.

More than 30 percent of the population at any point in time is either engaged in entrepreneurship or directly related to someone that is. . . . This estimate comes from an extrapolation of data from the ongoing Global Entrepreneurship Monitor (GEM) program. In his forthcoming book, *Business Creation: Ten Factors for Entrepreneurial Success*, Edward Elgar (Gloucestershire, UK), to be published, Paul Reynolds extrapolates from GEM data that there 17.8 million nascent entrepreneurs—entrepreneurs actively trying to create a profitable business—in the United States as of 2016. I then use data from the sister study of GEM, the PSED (Panel Survey of Entrepreneurial Dynamics) II, as found in Reynolds, Paul D., and Richard T. Curtin. "Business creation in the United States: Panel study of entrepreneurial dynamics II initial assessment." *Foundations and Trends® in Entrepreneurship* 4.3 (2008): 155–307. Using data on page 206, Table 5.3 we find that approximately 21 percent of these nascent entrepreneurs are teamed up with their spouse and another 7 percent with another direct relative. From the numbers we can estimate 74.9 million adults are directly related to a nascent entrepreneur. That represents 30.5 percent of population eighteen and above in 2016.

. . . **Since funding from friends and family constitutes an important source of funds for many startups you stand a great chance of
being asked to invest in a startup sometime** . . . For an overview,
see   http://www.kauffman.org/what-we-do/resources/entrepreneur-
ship-policy-digest/how-entrepreneurs-access-capital-and-get-funded.
These data on funding come from the *Inc. Magazine* lists of the 5,000
fastest growing companies in the United States. A more comprehensive analysis of where entrepreneurs raise their money can be found
at: Robb, Alicia M., and David T. Robinson. "The capital structure
decisions of new firms." *The Review of Financial Studies* 27.1 (2014):
153–179.

. . . *bedrock entrepreneurs.* **That term describes 99.5 percent of
all entrepreneurs who create more than 90 percent of all the new
wealth generated by entrepreneurs** . . . To estimate this number I
equate high-risk entrepreneurs to entrepreneurs who seek early-stage
funding from venture capital firms. Only 0.31 percent of the companies founded in 2012 received early-stage venture backing according
to Gornall, Will, and Ilya A. Strebulaev. "The Economic Impact of
Venture Capital: Evidence from Public Companies." (2015), which
you can download here: https://papers.ssrn.com/sol3/papers.cfm?ab-
stract_id=2681841. My 0.5 percent estimate takes into account the
fact that entrepreneurs with very high aspirations start businesses
with larger teams on average than entrepreneurs with lesser aspirations, with this data coming from Reynolds, Paul D., and Richard T.
Curtin. "Business creation in the United States: Panel study of entrepreneurial dynamics II initial assessment." *Foundations and Trends® in
Entrepreneurship* 4.3 (2008): pages 204 & 248. This difference implies
a high-end estimate of 0.44 percent of all entrepreneurs being high-
risk that add any wealth (it excludes aspiring high-risk entrepreneurs
that fail to get venture capital backing). The wealth creation percentage depends greatly upon both the definition of wealth creation and
how it is estimated for the large number of private companies that
exist. While stock market and venture capital valuations get all the
publicity, stock valuations only represent the wealth created for inves-

tors and not for employees. Job creation is a better rough estimate of wealth creation for society as a whole. Puri, Manju, and Rebecca Zarutskie estimate in their article, "On the life cycle dynamics of venture-capital- and non-venture-capital-financed firms," *The Journal of Finance* 67.6 (2012): 2247–2293 that VC-backed companies are responsible for creating between 5.3 and 7.3 percent of all the jobs in the United States during 2001–2005. Pundits often just focus on public company stock valuations and therefore can quote much larger numbers for the impact on VC-backed companies on wealth creation. Gornall and Strebulaev estimate that VC-backed companies account for 18 percent of the stock market capitalization, as of 2015, of all companies that have gone public. Public companies represent just 4,300 of the 5.8 million companies in the United States.

Chapter 2: Who

Collectively known as the Austrian School . . . This is the most all-encompassing definition of an entrepreneur I have come across: "In any real and living economy every actor is always an entrepreneur;" from Lugwig Von Mises, *Human Action*, Yale University Press (New Haven), 1949, p. 253. For an overview article of why the Austrian School thinks what they think you can read, Kirzner, Israel M. "Entrepreneurial discovery and the competitive market process: An Austrian approach." *Journal of economic Literature* 35.1 (1997): 60–85.

Meet Jordan Monkarsh . . . The information about Jordan Monkarsh comes from a series of interviews and email exchanges held from July 2015 through August 2017.

. . . fifteen million full-time entrepreneurs in the U.S. today . . . See this summary of the latest information from the Bureau of Labor Statistics: https://www.bls.gov/spotlight/2016/self-employment-in-the-united-states/pdf/self-employment-in-the-united-states.pdf.

. . . **almost six million businesses that they started** . . . See the tables listed at https://www.census.gov/data/tables/2014/econ/sus-b/2014-susb-annual.html. It should be noted that the latest count of businesses is from 2014 while the latest count of self-employed people quoted above is from 2016. Anyone wanting to develop theories or calculate statistical relationships based upon the available data concerning entrepreneurs has to pay close attention to the definitions used and the time ranges associated with when the data were accumulated. For our purposes the numbers of established firms in the United States changes only slowly with time so these comparisons are legitimate for the purposes of the arguments I make in this book.

. . . **Right now nearly 18 million people are actively trying to start about 9.5 million businesses** . . . These data come from Reynolds, Paul. *Business Creation: Ten Factors for Entrepreneurial Success*, Edward Elgar (Gloucestershire, UK), to be published, based upon information from Reynolds & Hechavarria, [2016] Global Entrepreneurship Monitor: Adult Population Survey Data Set, 1998–2012. ICPSR20320-v4. Ann Arbor, MI: Inter-university Consortium for Political and Social Research [distributor], 2016-12-14. http://doi.org/10.3886/ICPSR20320.v4.

. . . **and millions more are thinking about it** . . . See Reynolds, Paul. "When is a Firm Born? Alternative Criteria and Consequences," *Business Economics*, to be published, 2017. He discusses in this article that the GEM and PSED surveys define "nascent entrepreneurs" as people who are *actively* engaged in starting a company and exclude people in their statistics that have not accomplished a minimum set of tasks within prescribed time frames. This criteria resulted in 9.8 percent of the survey respondents that said they were involved in starting a company not being counted, implying that close to two million people are thinking about it but may not be doing enough to be officially counted using the PSED or GEM criteria and then many others that are only thinking and not yet taking any action.

On average an entrepreneur is no smarter, stronger, more extroverted, or insomniac than the rest of us. . . . There is a rich and extensive set of data that describes entrepreneurs. The best place to get a summary of this research is from chapter 3: Who Becomes an Entrepreneur in Scott Shane's, "The Illusions of Entrepreneurship: The Costly Myths That Entrepreneurs, Investors, and Policy Makers Live By," Yale (New Haven), 2007. I want to emphasize that this statement applies to all entrepreneurs as a group and may not apply to any group of specific entrepreneurs. We do not know and cannot say whether launching a successful cybersecurity startup may require some minimum level of IQ or whether starting a successful graphic design firm would preclude someone who is color blind. This broad statement is meant to be a strong statement that traits—psychological or physiological characteristics we are born with or that develop early in life—do not preclude anyone from being some type of entrepreneur. As we'll discuss later, motivations are a far more important determinant of entrepreneurial success.

. . . less than 10% of all entrepreneurs who are far richer than the rest of the working population . . . ibid. See Figure 6.4 on page 108. Scott Shane's figure is derived from Quadrini, Vincenzo. "The importance of entrepreneurship for wealth concentration and mobility." *Review of income and Wealth* 45.1 (1999): 1–19. For an overview of the macroeconomics of how entrepreneurship concentrates wealth see: Quadrini, Vincenzo. "Entrepreneurship in macroeconomics." *Annals of Finance* 5.3 (2009): 295–311.

The wealth represented in the *Forbes* magazine list of 400 wealthiest Americans has been almost entirely created by entrepreneurial endeavors. . . . This derives from a report of an undergraduate research associate of mine, Yash Huilgol: "Tracking Wealth From Entrepreneurship Using the Forbes 400 List of Wealthiest Americans," dated 19 June 2015, unpublished. The report showed that of the 396 people on the Forbes 400 list 124 inherited their wealth from an entrepreneur, 263 made their wealth directly from entrepreneurship, and only 9 had no direct connection to entrepreneurship—although those 9 include Steve Balmer, Meg Whitman, Eric Schmidt and others who helped grow entrepreneurial ventures.

. . . the number of rich entrepreneurs is in the millions . . . This statement derives from the fact that here are fifteen million people who report their primary activity as being self-employed and as previously cited about 10 percent of them are far richer than the rest of the population. Retired wealthy entrepreneurs would add to these numbers.

Ninety percent of entrepreneurs . . . make less than they could by offering the same sets of skills and experiences to an established employer. . . . See Figure 6.3 on page 107 the previously cited "The Illusions of Entrepreneurship: The Costly Myths That Entrepreneurs, Investors, and Policy Makers Live By." Shane's figure is derived from Quadrini, Vincenzo. "The importance of entrepreneurship for wealth concentration and mobility." *Review of income and Wealth* 45.1 (1999): 1–19.

Stephanie DiMarco is a classic example. . . . The information about Stephanie DiMarco comes from a series of interviews and email exchanges held from July 2015 through May 2017.

. . . research to date shows that the correlation between success and any characteristic or even any group of characteristics is so small as to be irrelevant to anyone's decision to become an entrepreneur. . . . See Zhao, Hao, Scott E. Seibert, and G. Thomas Lumpkin. "The relationship of personality to entrepreneurial intentions and performance: A meta-analytic review." *Journal of management* 36.2 (2010): 381–404. While the authors find some relatively small correlations between certain characteristics and broadly defined entrepreneurial performance, they state, "It is also appropriate for educators to advise students that personality explains 'only' about 10 percent of the variance in firm performance, and they should not place undue weight on this one set of factors." In Frank, Hermann, Manfred Lueger, and Christian Korunka. "The significance of personality in business start-up intentions, start-up realization and business success." *Entrepreneurship & Regional Development* 19.3 (2007): 227–251 the authors conclude that the correlation of personality to business success "practically drops to zero." Finally, Paul Reynolds in his "Start-up Actions and Outcomes: What Entrepreneurs Do to Reach Profitability." *Foundations and Trends® in Entrepreneurship* 12.6 (2016): states emphatically on page 528, "<u>What you do is more important than who you are</u>." (Underlining is from the article.)

Over half of the entrepreneurs in the United States work on their own . . . See Reynolds, Paul D., and Richard T. Curtin. "Business creation in the United States: Panel study of entrepreneurial dynamics II initial assessment." *Foundations and Trends® in Entrepreneurship* 4.3 (2008): page 204.

Founding a company with a spouse or other direct relative as a partner is also common, occurring in over a quarter of the cases. . . . ibid. page 206.

Among high-risk entrepreneurs, however, founding companies with relative strangers is common. . . . ibid. page 248 finds 53 percent of entrepreneurs aspiring to build a "substantial" company team up with strangers. Noam Wasserman, in his classic book on entrepreneurship, *Founder's Dilemmas*, Princeton (Princeton), 2012, finds only 16.1 percent of the large number of VC-backed founding entrepreneurs he has tracked founded their companies alone (see pages 73–74).

. . . **many high-risk entrepreneurial ventures fail at least in part because of a break-up among key members of the founding team.** . . . The tricky aspects of picking and working with founding team members is a major focus of Noam Wasserman's *Founder's Dilemmas*.

. . . it *does* increase familial stress . . . See Parasuraman, Saroj, and Claire A. Simmers. "Type of employment, work–family conflict and well-being: a comparative study." *Journal of Organizational Behavior* 22.5 (2001): 551–568.

Chapter 3: What

Entrepreneurial opportunities are everywhere. . . . I do not mean to imply that "everything" is an entrepreneurial opportunity nor that "all" entrepreneurial opportunities are easy to spot and easy to exploit. Additionally, this statement is not meant to imply that anyone is able to exploit any given opportunity (which opportunities any given person can realistically pursue is the subject of chapter 7: How Good). A more specific statement would be, "every field and market holds entrepreneurial opportunities for those that take the time and expend the effort to understand where the market incumbents are failing to make their customers happy with their products and services."

The United States collects a great deal of data about its businesses and has a well-established system for organizing them into over 1,000 different industries. . . . See https://www.census.gov/eos/www/naics/ for a description of the North American Industry Classification System. The exact number of NAICS codes (1,057) is quoted in the 2017 NAICS Manual (https://www.census.gov/eos/www/naics/2017NAICS/2017_NAICS_Manual.pdf) on page 14.

Currently, high-risk entrepreneurial activity *is* concentrated in software related businesses . . . The National Venture Capital Association, Yearbook 2016, gives a breakdown of all venture capital investments in dollars in 2015 on page 13, Figure 7.0, as follows: Software 40 percent, Biotechnology 13 percent, Consumer Products and Services 8 percent, Media and Entertainment 8 percent, IT Services 7 percent, Financial Services 5 percent, Industrial/Energy

5 percent, Medical Devices and Equipment 5 percent, and Other 9 percent.

Vidal Herrera's entrepreneurial journey . . . The information about Vidal Herrera comes from a series of interviews and email exchanges held from July 2015 through May 2017.

Sam Walton grew up with just enough. . . . The information on Sam Walton comes from a large number of sources. His autobiography, *Made in America*, has been a prime source, as were many of the oral histories compiled by the Walmart Museum. Of particular importance were:

- Interview with Loretta Boss Parker, conducted by Kenneth Durr, October 4, 2011 at Bentonville, Arkansas.
- Interview with Gary Reinboth, conducted by Fritz Steiger, May 2, 2012, WMTV Studio, Bentonville, Arkansas.
- Interview with Jim Dismore, conducted by Fritz Steiger, July 1, 2012, Denver, Colorado.
- Interview with Claude Harris, conducted by Fritz Steiger, October 8, 2013, WMTV Studio, Bentonville, Arkansas.
- Interview with Clarence Leis, conducted by Fritz Steiger and Derek Lidow, December 16, 2016, WMTV Studio, Bentonville, Arkansas.

I have also had access to historical documents archived at the Walmart Museum. When I quote an archival document or oral history I will cite it specifically in the notes. Vance Trimble's book, *Sam Walton: The Inside Story of America's Richest Man* has occasionally provided an additional perspective.

. . . she [Helen Robson] had been valedictorian and a varsity athlete at her high school . . . Helen's brother Frank recounts Helen being her class valedictorian in an oral history. Evidence of Helen's lettering in fencing comes from artifacts held by the Walmart Museum.

. . . **backed by a $20,000 loan from Helen's dad** . . . I quote here Sam's recollection from his *Made in America* (page 28). Vance Trimble and others quote a $25,000 figure but do not take into account that $5,000 of that amount came from Sam and Helen's personal savings.

The transistor was co-invented by William Shockley . . . Joel Shurkin's biography of William Shockley, *Broken Genius: The Rise and Fall of William Shockley,* is the most comprehensive descriptions of the man, based upon his personal papers and also extensive interviews with family and those that worked with him. The point of view of Robert Noyce, a pivotal employee of Shockley Semiconductor and later founder of Fairchild Semiconductor and Intel is told in Leslie Berlin's book, *The Man Behind the Microchip: Robert Noyce and the Invention of Silicon Valley.* The best descriptions of William Shockley's leadership lapses are contained in the book *Crystal Fire: The Invention of the Transistor and the Birth of the Information Age*, by Michael Riordan and Lillian Hoddeson (see pages 247–248).

Steve Jobs and Steve Wozniak initially tried to sell PC boards to hobbyists . . . see page 66 of Walter Isaacson's book *Steve Jobs,* Simon and Schuster (New York), 2011.

They make their customers so happy that the customers gladly give them money in return. . . . This is my summation of entrepreneurship. I along with my research associate Yash Huilgol spent much of a summer of 2015 looking for precedents and/or research relating to customer happiness and well-being and startups—to no avail (we found plenty of research relating entrepreneurship to the happiness of the entrepreneur).

. . . **most aspiring entrepreneurs, consciously and subconsciously, attach a social status to the entrepreneurial opportunities they decide to pursue or reject.** . . . See for example, Anderson, Cameron, et al. "The local-ladder effect: Social status and subjective well-being." *Psychological Science* 23.7 (2012): 764–771.

Chapter 4: Why

Over a million aspiring entrepreneurs every year in the United States do succeed in starting profitable enterprises. . . . This is derived from an estimate of the annual number of total new entrepreneurs derived from the "Rate of New Entrepreneurs" found in the *Kauffman Index of Startup Activity*, accessible at: http://www.kauffman.org/kauffman-index/reporting/startup-activity. I estimate that 30 percent of these 4 million annual new entrepreneurs reach profitability. The 30 percent number comes from page 463 of Reynolds, Paul D. "Start-up Actions and Outcomes: What Entrepreneurs Do to Reach Profitability." *Foundations and Trends® in Entrepreneurship* 12.6 (2016): 443–559. The data summarized in Table 5.1 for the United States in the PSED I and PSED II studies indicates that less than three out of ten nascent entrepreneurs—those entrepreneurs that have diligently started to found a business—have reached "profitability" after six years. Profitability is defined in these studies as making enough money to cover expenses and pay salaries.

About 70 percent of the people who actually become full-time entrepreneurs in a typical year abandon their efforts or do not make any money back whatsoever . . . ibid. These data also show that after seventy-two months almost half have abandoned their efforts, with less than 25 percent still trying to make a go.

. . . thousands of studies, led by many brilliant researchers, have yielded valuable insights on why we do what we do and also why we do some things with more determination, passion, and intensity than others. . . . For an in-depth overview of this research see: Elliot, Andrew J., and Carol S. Dweck, eds. *Handbook of competence and motivation*. Guilford Publications, 2013.

. . . making our own trade-offs between immediate pleasure and long-term feelings of well-being and purpose. . . . See for example: Ryan, Richard M., and Edward L. Deci. "On happiness and human potentials: A review of research on hedonic and eudaimonic well-being." *Annual review of psychology* 52.1 (2001): 141–166.

. . . the difference between implicit and explicit motivations . . . This refers to a great body of work by the famous psychologist David McClelland. You can read the book, McClelland, D.C., *Assessing Human Motivation*, General Learning Press (New York), 1971, but you can get a strong sense of the work in the review article: McClelland, David C., Richard Koestner, and Joel Weinberger. "How do self attributed and implicit motives differ?" *Psychological review* 96.4 (1989): 690–702.

Implicit and explicit motivations are different than intrinsic and extrinsic motivations and often get confused. . . . They are nonetheless related as intrinsic motivations often, particularly in childhood, align with implicit motivations. How extrinsic motivations can become internalized as implicit motivations is described in Ryan, Richard M., and Edward L. Deci. "Self-determination theory and the facilitation of intrinsic motivation, social development, and well-being." *American psychologist* 55.1 (2000): 68.

Most of us are pretty bad at fulfilling our explicit motivations if we can't do it quickly. . . . See the previously cited article, "How do self-attributed and implicit motives differ?"

. . . our brain protects us from feeling too badly about failing to achieve all our explicit motivations. . . . See for example, Bénabou, Roland, and Jean Tirole. "Mindful economics: The production, consumption, and value of beliefs." *The Journal of Economic Perspectives* 30.3 (2016): 141–164.

Academics have spent a great deal of time studying the explicit reasons aspiring and successful entrepreneurs cite for having taken on the burden of starting an enterprise. . . . To understand the state of the research into entrepreneurial motivation see: Collins,

Christopher J., Paul J. Hanges, and Edwin A. Locke. "The relationship of achievement motivation to entrepreneurial behavior: A meta-analysis." *Human performance* 17.1 (2004): 95–117 and Shane, Scott, Edwin A. Locke, and Christopher J. Collins. "Entrepreneurial motivation." *Human resource management review* 13.2 (2003): 257–279 and Carsrud, Alan, and Malin Brännback. "Entrepreneurial motivations: what do we still need to know?" *Journal of Small Business Management* 49.1 (2011): 9–26.

Entrepreneurs often cite making money as their motivation. . . . See page 246 of the previously cited Reynolds, Paul D., and Richard T. Curtin. "Business creation in the United States: Panel study of entrepreneurial dynamics II initial assessment." Wealth and financial security is overall the second most important motivational dimension of entrepreneurs in the U.S. after autonomy and independence. See also, Wasserman, Noam. "RICH VERSUS KING: THE ENTREPRENEUR'S DILEMMA." *Academy of Management Proceedings*. Vol. 2006. No. 1. Academy of Management, 2006.

Josephine Esther Mentzer's [Estée Lauder] life was transformed by an insult. . . . This vignette is from Estée Lauder's autobiography, *A Success Story*, Random House (New York), 1985. The more complete and factual biography is Lee Israel's, *Estee Lauder: Beyond the Magic*, Macmillan (New York), 1985.

Chapter 5: What If

Jeff Bezos is spending hundreds of millions of dollars to build the rockets and the support organizations to enable him to travel to Mars . . . See for example Nick Stockon's *Wired* article, "Jeff Bezos' New Rocket Could Send the First People to Mars," 9.13.16; https://www.wired.com/2016/09/blue-orgins-new-glenn-rocket/.

High-risk entrepreneurs play a disproportionately important role in job and wealth creation . . . see my notes from chapter 1 on how 99.5 percent of all entrepreneurs create over 90 percent of all the wealth created by startups.

. . . less than a fraction of a percent of all startups create around 10 percent of all the wealth created by startups . . . ibid.

The entire field of venture capital works in almost perfect synchronization, , . . . author's discussions with a multitude of venture capitalists. I do know of one VC who refuses to hold his partner's meeting on a Monday.

. . . most venture capital firms do not actually invest in startups. About a third do, but most don't. . . . See Yearbook 2016, National Venture Capital Association, figure 1.05 on page 20.

Two-thirds of all venture investment dollars go into more mature startups. . . . ibid., figure 3.10 on page 33.

Research has shown that the more successful a venture backed startup, the more likely the venture capital firm is to try to replace the founder. . . . See Wasserman, Noam. "Founder-CEO succession and the paradox of entrepreneurial success." *Organization Science* 14.2 (2003): 149–172.

VC partners are usually allowed to spend 2 percent each year on their own salaries and expenses, sometimes reduced to 1.5 percent after five years. . . . Every firm negotiates their fees with their largest "anchor" limited partners but 2 percent is the basis around which they start their negotiations. See Robinson, David T., and Berk A. Sensoy, "Do private equity fund managers earn their fees? Compensation, ownership, and cash flow performance," *Review of Financial Studies* 26.11 (2013): 2760–2797 for a statistical review that shows the median VC fund charges 21.4 percent in management fees over the lifetime of the fund.

A few [startup investments] will do better than expected but the overwhelming majority stumble or hit some unanticipated constraint. . . . See Da Rin, Marco, Thomas F. Hellmann, and Manju Puri. *A survey of venture capital research*. No. w17523. National Bureau of Economic Research, 2011, pages 78–90.

. . . the majority of venture capital funds fail to return to their investors a lot more money than was originally invested . . . ibid.

. . . most venture capital firms return less than a compounded 13 percent ROI. . . . ibid.

As of 2015, there were 718 active venture capital firms in the U.S. Only 238 of these firms invest in early stage startups . . . See the note above, "most venture capital firms do not invest in startups . . ."

There are an estimated 300,000 angel investors in the U.S. . . . The Angel Capital Association and The Angel Resource Institute are both good resources for information about angel investing. See https://www.angelcapitalassociation.org/faqs/#How%20many%20angel%20investors%20are%20there%20in%20the%20U.S.?

In aggregate angel investors invest just as much money as VCs in startups . . . The Center for Venture Research at the University of New Hampshire estimated angel investors invested $24.6 billion in 71,110 startups in 2015 (https://paulcollege.unh.edu/sites/paulcollege.unh.edu/files/webform/Full%20Year%202015%20Analysis%20Report.pdf). According to the North American Venture Capital Association 2016 Yearbook VCs invested a total of $59 billion in 2015 but only $21 billion of that amount was invested in seed or early-stage rounds.

Angel investors want their money back . . . See https://www.

angelcapitalassociation.org/faqs/#How_do_I_know_my_business_
is_right_for_an_angel_investment_.

**Accelerators take a small ownership in companies started by
teams** . . . A summary of the investment offers of Global Accelerator
Network members can be found at http://gan.co. Y Combinator
offers $120,000 for a 7 percent stake in companies they accept into
their program.

In the United States there are about 300 accelerators . . . The number
quoted can vary widely depending upon the exact definition of what
is an accelerator. Brookings (https://www.brookings.edu/research/
accelerating-growth-startup-accelerator-programs-in-the-unit-
ed-states/) found nearly 700 companies in the United States that
claimed to be an accelerator but found only 172 that fit their definition. That definition comes from Susan Cohen, a professor at
University of Richmond, who authored the most widely used definition: offers seed capital, working space, networking, and mentorship
for a limited duration, culminating in a "demo day." Susan Cohen
has counted 300 US accelerators as of early 2015 (https://www.
quora.com/How-many-accelerators-incubators-are-there-around-
the-globe). By her definition most university based, government
funded (most prominently I-Corps), or non-profit accelerators do
not meet these criteria.

**Accelerators mentor and train over 4,000 teams each year in
their programs, including more than 12,000 aspiring entrepreneurs.** . . . This number is my estimate based upon thirteen startups
accelerated at each of Susan Cohen's 300 accelerators, each startup
with at least three team members.

**A small number of accelerated companies from the top dozen most
highly regarded programs (i.e., the top 2.5 percent accelerators)
receive funding by VCs** . . . See Hallen, Benjamin L., Christopher B.
Bingham, and Susan Cohen. "Do Accelerators Accelerate? A Study of

Venture Accelerators as a Path to Success?" *Academy of Management Proceedings*. Vol. 2014. No. 1. Academy of Management, 12955.

By the time Wal-Mart went public, Walton was personally responsible for millions of dollars of personal debt. . . . See page 130 of Vance Trimble, *Sam Walton: The Inside Story of America's Richest Man*, Dutton Adult (New York), 1990.

Sam offered small percentages of ownership of each store that he opened to . . . the store managers he wanted to run his stores. He also offered to let a store manager buy a larger ownership if he . . . was willing to pay for some of the store opening costs. . . . "All the stores were opened under different arrangements. It was a collection of partnerships and individual ownerships . . . including all the store managers who could raise money to invest." Sam Walton, quoted in *Walmart World*, October 1987, page 2.

By the time Sam started thinking about taking Wal-Mart public he had opened twenty Wal-Marts along with the thirteen Ben Franklin franchises he owned that remained very profitable and he had eight more Wal-Marts being planned and constructed. . . . Wal-Mart Stores, Inc., Preliminary Prospectus Dated September 4, 1970 as accessed at the archives of the Walmart Museum.

In order to go public Walton had to reconcile how, with unanimous consent, several dozen part owners of individual stores would each own some percentage of the original Wal-Mart shares. . . . I am referring here to a document titled, "Wal-mart Stores, Inc. Adjusting Entries, 1970," The Walmart Museum.

After the IPO Sam Walton and his family owned 61 percent of the company shares, the public owned 20 percent, with the remaining 19 percent owned by store managers and executives (of which about 4 percent belonged to his brother). . . . see the Wal-Mart Stores, Inc., Preliminary Prospectus cited above.

Chapter 6: How To

Hearing the stories while holding in my hands the documents Sam had on-hand when he made the decisions being described illuminates how he came to do what he did. . . . A small fraction of the documents made available to me are cited in the Bibliography.

Virtually all entrepreneurs learn on the job. . . . There is little agreement among entrepreneurship researchers or entrepreneurs about what should be taught or the efficacy of what has been taught. The largest global program teaching business skills to young people was shown ineffective relative to the student's feeling they had acquired entrepreneurial skills. See Oosterbeek, Hessel, Mirjam Van Praag, and Auke Ijsselstein. "The impact of entrepreneurship education on entrepreneurship skills and motivation." *European economic review* 54.3 (2010): 442–454. It should be noted however that education achievement, as simply measured by how many years of schooling, has a significant impact on entrepreneurial success.

Within a year his sales doubled and within three years he was outselling both of his competitors. . . . *Made in America*, page 35.

Sam had enough money socked away to buy another Ben Franklin store . . . Vance Trimble quotes on page 61 Sam having $55,000 saved up by the time he left Newport.

. . . owning 15 Ben Franklin franchises. . . . This number is a best estimate as Walton did close some of the Ben Franklin franchises while opening others, even after opening the first Wal-Mart in 1962. This estimate is based upon a review of store openings and closings through the end of 1969 prepared by Nicholas Graves, senior archivist at the Walmart Museum, but questions remain as to whether all non-Wal-Mart stores were Ben Franklin franchises.

. . . his notes from a store visit read, "Getting a request here from

our older customers in this store. **Why don't we have our aisles signed by departments, like in grocery stores?** . . . The quotes in this section are from a transcript of Sam Walton's packet tape recorder transcribed on February 1, 1990.

He even bought the local Bentonville bank . . . This is best documented by Vance Trimble, see pages 93–96.

Entrepreneurial success boils down to understanding how to put together productive, competitive, and self-sustaining enterprises. . . . A more in-depth analysis of the 5 core skills shared by most successful entrepreneurs can be found in my book *Startup Leadership*, Wiley (Hoboken), 2014.

Sam mastered his change leadership skills by doing what is now referred to as *deliberate practice*. . . . See for example, Anders Ericsson and Robert Pool, *Peak: Secrets From the New Science of Expertise*, Hougthon Mifflin Harncourt (New York), 2016.

Virtually no one learns these entrepreneurial leadership skills in the classroom. . . . See the above note "Virtually all entrepreneurs learn on the job."

. . . **pictures of Sam at work in his office is to see great piles of paper** . . . The most illustrative photograph of Sam at work in his office comes from the *Wal-Mart World* 1987 interview of Sam on the twenty-fifth anniversary of Wal-Mart.

A high percentage of founding partners cannot agree on what to do next once their company becomes established. . . . See for example: Ensley, Michael D., Allison W. Pearson, and Allen C. Amason. "Understanding the dynamics of new venture top management teams: cohesion, conflict, and new venture performance." *Journal of business venturing* 17.4 (2002): 365–386.

Chapter 7: How Good

Walt Disney barely made it as an animator and as a head of an animation studio. . . . The definitive biography of Walt Disney is Neal Gabler's, *Walt Disney: The Triumph of the American Imagination*, Vintage Books (New York), 2006. Additional information about Roy Disney's part in building Disney can be found in Bob Thomas', *Building a Company: Roy O. Disney and the Creation of an Entertainment Empire*, Hyperion (New York), 1998.

Barry, who founded and runs a successful self-funded firm . . . Barry is an alias used in respect for the privacy of the real person.

As of 2013 the Census Bureau reported 249 different "Automobile and Light Duty Motor Vehicle Manufacturing" companies in the United States . . . See the data table of "U.S. & states, 6 digit NAICS" found at https://www.census.gov/data/datasets/2014/econ/susb/2014-susb.html.

Chapter 8: How Much

The most popular scale in use right now is the "Grit Scale." . . . See Duckworth, Angela L., et al. "Grit: perseverance and passion for long-term goals." *Journal of personality and social psychology* 92.6 (2007): 1087.

. . . the Grit Scale really measures how well our *explicit* motivations align with our *implicit* ones. . . . See the conclusions of the previously cited McClelland, David C., Richard Koestner, and Joel Weinberger. "How do self-attributed and implicit motives differ?" *Psychological review* 96.4 (1989): page 700.

. . . through self-awareness our motivations can become more

focused and have more impact. . . . See the same conclusions to the same article cited above.

. . . **we can use techniques such as cognitive reappraisal to miti-gate our irrational fears, or phobias, that interfere with achieving our core implicit motivation**. . . . See for example: Silvers JA, Buhle JT, Ochsner KN. Ochsner KN, Kosslyn SM. "The neuroscience of emotion regulation: basic mechanisms and their role in development, aging and psychopathology," *The handbook of cognitive neuroscience*, Oxford University Press (New York), 2013.

. . . **the success of the enterprise hinges on** *evolving* **the team with increasingly sophisticated skills** . . . See chapter 4, Enterprises Are Also Needy, in *Startup Leadership*.

Money does matter in entrepreneurship, but not as much as you might think. . . . See Robb, Alicia M., and David T. Robinson. "The capital structure decisions of new firms." *The Review of Financial Studies* 27.1 (2014): 153–179. See Table 5 to see that the average owners equity invested in a firm that survived three years ($31,784) was similar to the amount of equity invested by owners of firms that did not survive ($31,609).

Jason Fried, the founder of 37signals . . . This information comes from several Skype meetings with Jason from 2011 till 2015 that he had with students from my Princeton *Entrepreneurial Leadership* class.

Ben Chestnut and Dan Kurzius took a similar route . . . see https://www.nytimes.com/2016/10/06/technology/mailchimp-and-the-un-silicon-valley-way-to-make-it-as-a-start-up.html?_r=1.

Chapter 9: Where

Uganda and Peru are far more entrepreneurial . . . See page 155, figures 9.4 and 9.5 of the previously cited Reynolds, *Entrepreneurship in the United States: The Future is Now.*

Even in the United States, Silicon Valley is still not close to being the most entrepreneurial place. . . . See the rate of business owners as quoted on page 12 in: Morelix et. al., The 2016 Kauffman Index, main street entrepreneurship, Metropolitan Area and City Trends, http://www.kauffman.org/kauffman-index/reporting/-/media/60c4bff5bb-c74a2181db7fd7d0dd6e64.ashx.

Silicon Valley is not even the top place in the world to start a fast-growing company. . . . See Table 5, page 13, in: Mtoyama and Arbesman, *The Ascent of America's High-Growth Companies,* Kauffman Foundation Report; http://www.kauffman.org/-/media/kauffman_org/research%20reports%20and%20covers/2012/09/inc_geography.pdf.

Silicon Valley is the best place in the world to start high-risk venture capital-backed companies. . . . Silicon Valley based companies received $25 billion in 2016 according to the PwC and CB Insights MoneyTree Report, dated January, 2017. That's 36 percent of all the venture capital invested in 2016.

Ken Marlin broke the news . . . The information about Ken Marlin comes from a series of interviews and email exchanges held from June 2015 through May 2017.

Not all large organizations breed future entrepreneurs. . . . There are no studies I know of that show certain businesses or types of businesses are better or worse at breeding future entrepreneurs or successful entrepreneurs. I base this statement on anecdotal evidence from talking to high-level executives in a broad range of firms and industries. Executives in risk adverse industries (e.g. insurance), highly regulated industries (e.g. utilities), and industries where innovation is considered risky (e.g. mining) often describe a reticence to experiment. Anecdotally the number of industries that breed this reticence appears to be shrinking with time.

My grandmother . . . invented the backless bra. . . . See United States Patent 1,794,785, issued to Shirley Maxwell of Los Angeles, California, titled "Brassiere and Harness," filed on September 26, 1928.

The cells that my father developed were the best available in the U.S. at that time . . . See for example, United States Patent 2,414,233, issued to Eric Lidow of Los Angeles, Calif., titled "Photoelectric Cell," filed August 3, 1942.

Silicon Valley culture also erects higher hurdles for success. . . . For an article about how Silicon Valley makes non-tech businesses uncompetitive see: https://www.nytimes.com/2016/09/19/technology/how-tech-companies-disrupted-silicon-valleys-restaurant-scene.html?_r=0. Silicon Valley housing prices (see http://www.mercurynews.com/2017/01/16/a-silicon-valley-down-payment-could-buy-you-an-entire-house-in-much-of-the-u-s/) make even STEM savvy employees look for work outside the area; see for example: http://blog.indeed.com/2016/03/02/why-tech-workers-leaving-silicon-valley/.

. . . *vibrant entrepreneurial ecosystem* **(VEE)**. . . . Entrepreneurial ecosystem is a common term in the entrepreneurial research literature. It is well described in two Kauffman Foundation reports: Bell-Masterson, Jordan, and Dane Stangler. "Measuring an entrepreneurial ecosystem," (2015), available at: http://www.kauffman.org/what-we-do/research/2015/03/measuring-an-entrepreneurial-ecosystem and Motoyama, Yasuyuki, et al. "Think locally, act locally: Building a robust entrepreneurial ecosystem." (2014), available at: http://www.kauffman.org/what-we-do/research/2014/04/think-locally-act-locally-building-a-robust-entrepreneurial-ecosystem. Both these reports use the term "vibrant entrepreneurial ecosystem." The term entrepreneurial ecosystem is an established term that is more typically associated with clusters of high-growth companies (note: remember that high-growth does not necessarily mean companies founded by high-risk entrepreneurs). Research on entrepreneurial ecosystems is becoming extensive and though it focuses on high growth enterprises it applies just as well to the clusters of successful shops and restaurants or car dealerships that are found in many metropolitan areas. For a good review of the research see, Mason, Colin, and Ross Brown, "Entrepreneurial ecosystems and growth oriented entrepreneurship." *Final Report to OECD, Paris* (2014): 1–38.

. . . it still took [Sam] seventeen years of opening and running fifteen other Ben Franklin stores before he felt confident that he could open, run, supply, and merchandise a discount store of his own. . . . Sam only had thirteen Ben Franklins when the company went public eight years after opening the first Wal-Mart because he did not renew some franchise agreements and he closed some stores as he began to concentrate on building the Wal-Mart brand. The Walmart Museum spreadsheet prepared by Nickolas Graves shows that there were eighteen different Ben Franklin franchise stores Sam operated at one time or another between 1945 and 1970.

Chapter 10: When

Ray Kroc never asked "when?" . . . Ray Kroc wrote an autobiography, *Grinding It Out: The Making of McDonald's,* St. Martin's Press (New York), 1977, but it is very self-aggrandizing. John Love's book, *McDonald's: Behind the Arches,* Bantam (New York), 1986 is very trustworthy. Lisa Napoli's book, *Ray & Joan: The Man Who Made the McDonald's Fortune and the Woman Who Gave It All Away,* Dutton (New York), 2016 fills in interesting and relevant details relative to Ray Kroc's alcoholism and obsessiveness.

Chapter 11: Whether

The first dozen years of Jordan's entrepreneurial career . . . The information about Jordan Monkarsh comes from a series of interviews and email exchanges held from July 2015 through August 2017.

. . . relatively few entrepreneurs acknowledge that VC expertise and contacts were critical to their success. . . . See Figure 19 of the Kauffman Foundation report: Wadhwa, Vivek, et al. "Anatomy of an entrepreneur: Family background and motivation." (2009), available at: http://www.kauffman.org/what-we-do/research/2010/05/the-anatomy-of-an-entrepreneur. This figure states that 26 percent of founders receiving venture capital backing feel the advice/assistance provided to them by their investors was "extremely important" or "very important" while 45 percent felt it was "slightly important" or "not at all important."

Chapter 12: So What

The president spent almost fifteen minutes talking about Walton and Helen. . . . See https://www.walmartmuseum.com/explore/#/search/query/medal%20of%20freed/artifact/27917294261.

Entrepreneurs and corporations alike have gotten so good at understanding the science of manipulation, the science of creating desires, the science of trust, and the science of habit formation that they can get many people to feel fleeting happiness . . . For a good overview on the understanding of how to generate trust see David DeSteno, *The Truth About Trust: how it determines success in life, love, learning, and more*, Hudson Street (New York), 2014.

Entrepreneurs have brought us better medicines and medical treatments and amazing prosthetics. . . . I profile Dean Kamen in my book *Startup Leadership*.

They have made education more accessible to those without it. . . . I profile Wendy Kopp in my book *Startup Leadership*.

They have made us safer in our cars. . . . You can read about the design of airbags and how they never resulted in any significant entrepreneurial gain at https://en.wikipedia.org/wiki/Airbag#Origins.

Entrepreneurship as measured by how many new companies are created each year and also by the number of people considering starting a company is in long-term decline. . . . See Hathaway, Ian, and Robert E. Litan. "Declining business dynamism in the United States: A look at states and metros." *Brookings Institution* (2014). This decline has impacted even the high-tech sector; see the Kauffman Foundation report: Haltiwanger, John, Ian Hathaway, and Javier Miranda. "Declining business dynamism in the US high-technology sector." (2014), available at: http://www.kauffman.org/what-we-do/research/2014/02/declining-business-dynamism-in-the-us-high-technology-sector. Finally, see Clifton, Jim. "American entrepreneurship: Dead or alive." *Gallup Business Journal* (2015), available at: http://www.gallup.com/businessjournal/180431/american-entrepreneurship-dead-alive.aspx?g_source=american+entrepreneurship%3a+dead+or+alive&g_medium=search&g_campaign=tiles.

Bedrock entrepreneurship is declining, and so is the success rate for aspiring high-risk entrepreneurs. . . . The long-term decline in the number of new businesses started each year noted above is a direct measurement of the decline in bedrock entrepreneurship, since bedrock entrepreneurs dominate entrepreneurship metrics. The success rate of high-risk entrepreneurs is hard to measure directly but can be indirectly estimated by the increase in number of companies being accelerated, the increase in the number of companies receiving angel funding over the past fifteen years, versus the lack of increase in the number of companies receiving first time seed or early stage funding from VC firms—so more high-risk entrepreneurs must be failing.

An estimated $531 billion . . . is spent on launching startups every year. . . . This estimate comes from Laura Entis, "Where Startup Funding Really Comes From," *Entrepreneur Magazine*, November 20, 2013 (https://www.entrepreneur.com/article/230011). These types of estimates can depend heavily upon the definition of a "startup" and what is considered spending on the startup and what would be "normal" spending. This *Entrepreneur Magazine* estimate equates to 3.18 percent of the US GDP in 2013.

ACKNOWLEDGMENTS

I have benefitted from extensive support and significant encouragement in making this project possible. First and foremost, I want to acknowledge the wonderful entrepreneurs that let me pry into their lives over the past several years: Jordan Monkarsh, Stephanie DiMarco, Vidal Herrera, and Ken Marlin. The book would not have been possible without them, and without their having put up with all my questions, follow-ups and emails. Jordan, Stephanie, Vidal, and Ken have become role models for me and I hope they will become role models for all those that read the book.

I also have benefitted enormously from the support I have received from the team at the Walmart Museum. Alan Dranow, the Executive Director of the Walmart Heritage Group, has granted me access, enabled multiple visits, and facilitated many valuable discussions and meetings with people who had personally worked with Sam Walton during his earliest entrepreneurial days. Nicholas Graves, the senior archivist of the Walmart Museum, worked hard preparing materials for my visits and answering my incessant follow-up questions. Shane Buxman, the archivist intern, also helped to prepare for my visits and find documents to answer my questions. I would also like to thank Fritz Steiger for letting me sit in on several of his oral history recording sessions. I am particularly appreciative to Clarence Leis for coming by the Walmart Museum to let me pepper him with additional questions about the early days of Wal-Mart. Peggy Hamilton shared some great anecdotes about how Sam ran his meetings, which enabled me to add some color to my description of events. I would also like to acknowledge the specific memories Alice Walton shared with me about her father.

While there is an extensive body of research in entrepreneurship, Paul Reynolds stands out as having led or advised all four long-term studies of randomly selected entrepreneurs in the United States (The Kauffman Foundation Survey, PSED I and II, and Global Entrepreneurship Monitor—GEM being the global version of PSED). Paul has thankfully put up with countless questions about this data. I also appreciate the effort Paul put into finding answers to questions where data had not yet been published. I would like to acknowledge Noam Wasserman and Howard Aldrich for their supportive advice and counsel as I have become more deeply involved with entrepreneurial research. The various sessions I have had with Princeton Anthropology faculty, Carolyn Rouse and Rena Lederman, on ethnographic methods have helped me be a better and more empathic observer.

I could not have written this book without the significant support that I receive from Princeton University, specifically the Keller Center for Innovation in Engineering Education. The Executive Director of the Center, Cornelia Huellstrunk, has unconditionally supported my various extra-curricular activities, for which I am greatly appreciative. The entire staff of the Keller Center: Beth Jarvie, Lillian Tsang, J.D. Jasper, and Stephanie Landers, have enabled me to stay focused on pushing the envelope of entrepreneurial education and entrepreneurial questioning. The Deans of Princeton's School of Engineering and Applied Science, Vince Poor and more recently Emily Carter, have also been very supportive, as have been the former Directors of the Keller Center, Sanj Kulkarni, and Mung

Chiang, as well as the new Director, Margaret Martonosi. My fellow entrepreneurship and design thinking faculty members at the Keller Center, Sheila Pontis, Chris Kuenne, Marty Johnson, Kef Kasdin, Ed Zschau, John Danner, and Shahram Hejazi, always stimulate thought provoking conversations that have helped shape my understanding. I also acknowledge Yash Huilgol's extremely productive summer of research assistance.

I have a wonderful team that helps me specifically with my writing and my books. Jud Laghi has been a great and savvy agent and Carolyn Monaco has taught me more about publishing business books than I ever realized that I needed know. Jill Totenberg has introduced me to more great editors of all types than I could have ever met on my own. Bruce Tucker is one great editor and also a wonderful person to work with. It has been a pleasure indeed to work with Lia Ottaviano, Scott Waxman, Sarah Masterson Hally, and Christine Saunders at Diversion Books.

Finally, as with entrepreneurship, writing a book is a family affair. My two sons, Arel and Teel, provide me insightful and unvarnished conversations, inputs, and appraisals. And my wife Diana is my muse, my great supporter, and one very savvy confidant.

I am a very lucky person!

Derek Lidow

INDEX

DEREK LIDOW is one of the few New York Stock Exchange CEOs who left to start new companies from scratch—with unequivocal success. Lidow was CEO of International Rectifier, a $2 billion publicly held semiconductor company, before leaving to found iSuppli, a leading market research firm, which he sold for $100 million in 2010 to the global information leader IHS. Today, Lidow is giving back by teaching at Princeton University where he launched its campus-wide "design thinking" curriculum. He also works with Princeton's aspiring entrepreneurs and their young companies.

Lidow has long demonstrated a rare ability to operate successfully in corporate, entrepreneurial, and academic environments. His novel contributions to research and analysis have forever improved companies as diverse as Sony, Samsung, Philips, Goldman Sachs and IBM. He has advised many of the world's governments and largest companies. And he continues to drive innovation in research through ongoing projects with a number of partners.

Lidow is a frequent contributor to publications such as *The Wall Street Journal, Harvard Business Review, Inc. Magazine,* and *Entrepreneur.* He is also a media commentator whose coverage includes *The New York Times, Bloomberg BusinessWeek, Forbes, The Economist, Nikkei, Reuters,* and *Taipei Times.*

Lidow's degrees come from Princeton and Stanford where he earned a PhD in applied physics as a Hertz Foundation Fellow. He is based in New York City and Princeton, NJ. For more, visit **DerekLidow.com.**

FREE RESOURCES
FOR ENTREPRENEURS

VISIT **DEREKLIDOW.COM:**

STARTUP LEADERSHIP MAP

How do you beat the long odds of building a
successful enterprise? Derek Lidow's Startup
Leadership Map helps by laying out the critical
concepts you and your team must manage as
your startup matures through its four classic stages.

CREATE YOUR
OWN PERSONAL
LEADERSHIP STRATEGY

Derek Lidow shares the very same assessment he
uses when coaching entrepreneurs to define their
personal leadership strategy.

This assessment helps you explore your startup motivations and traits
so you can leverage your strengths and mitigate your weaknesses. You'll
create a customized strategy. You'll also get a tool to help you develop
a stronger bond with your mentors and others who can help you find
success.